The
Jack the Ripper
Whitechapel
Murders

"And where might he be? Where shall we hope to uncover the faded traces of that far distant crime?"

Sophocles
Oedipus Rex

The
Jack the Ripper
Whitechapel
Murders

by

Kevin O'Donnell

based on the researches of
Andy and Sue Parlour

TEN BELLS PUBLISHING

Published 1997 by Ten Bells Publishing
Registered Office
Springbank House
20, Spring Road
St. Osyth
Essex CO16 8RP

Copyright © 1997 Ten Bells Publishing

ISBN No. 0 9531269 00 (cased)
ISBN No. 0 9531269 19 (limp)

Designed, typeset and printed in the UK by
The Lavenham Press Ltd,
Lavenham, Suffolk CO10 9RN

Contents

Acknowledgements

We would like to thank all those connected with N+N Films for their help and encouragement, especially Nick Pocock, John Canavan, Phil Day and Denis Somerville Baddeley. Without their combined, intuitive sense of a good story, and marketing know-how, this project might never have seen the light of day. Thanks also are due to Kevin Riordan for computer know-how, and also to Peter Veal and Rowena Turner for advice on legal details and the profession of barrister.

Thanks are due to David Melville Hayes and Elsie Hayes, David Brown and his mother, Sister Winefride of the Providence Row Refuge, 'Charles', Pearl Lonsdale, Frank Gardiner, Steve Unger, Sven Evander of the Swedish Church and his daughter, Ann, Jane Whittle, Brian Essam, for his history of the Whitechapel unfortunates, Bruce Ryall of Arcade Photographics, Clacton-on-Sea, Stewart Evans, Donald Rumbelow, Mark Reeve of New World Promotional Clothing and Mike Fuller of Financial and Secretarial Services for his technical advice. Also thanks to Paul Begg, Martin Fido and Keith Skinner, authors of 'Jack The Ripper A–Z', for the use of their illustrations. Our special thanks to Maggie for always keeping the 'blue room' available.

The following libraries for their invaluable assistance: Cambridge, Clacton-on-Sea, Colchester, Felixstowe, Ipswich, Oxford, Tower Hamlets, Westminster and The Hulton Deutch Picture Library. The record offices at Kew, Chancery Lane, St. Catherine's House and Somerset House. The county record offices of Cambridgeshire, Essex, Oxfordshire and Suffolk; The Felixstowe Family History & Museum Society, The British Railway Museum, York, and Robin Gillis and Roger Appleby of the Met. and City Police Museums.

A special thanks is also due to Keith Skinner for helping with details of research and generally keeping us on our toes. Thanks also to Paul Begg for lengthy discussions over copious pints, and to John Ross of the Black Museum.

Our appreciation to Lavenham Press for their professional advice, especially David Munson for his help and enthusiasm.

Finally, to our families and many friends, who have patiently listened to our Ripper ramblings over the past five years, our heartfelt thanks.

K.O'Donnell, Andy & Sue Parlour

Foreword

When I was first invited to write the Foreword to this book, I instinctively declined. I have never considered myself to be an author, in spite of my two colleagues, Paul Begg and Martin Fido, generously allowing my name to be alongside theirs, on the cover of *The Jack The Ripper A To Z.*

What brought about this Damascus like conversion was a recognition of the painstaking commitment which Andy and Sue Parlour have given to their research. Andy's conversation invariably commences with disarming opening gambits, such as – "did you know that James Kenneth Stephen's 47th cousin, 5 times removed, went to the same school as the nephew of Sir William Gull's brother-in-law, by his sister's first marriage?" (How had I missed that!) Although I write this, tongue in cheek, it is, nevertheless, representative of the extraordinary lengths to which Andy and Sue were prepared to go, in their untiring quest for that elusive 'connection'.

I identified with this passion.

When I was working on *The Ripper Legacy* with Martin Howells, I was anxious that Martin, who was structuring the narrative, should include every fact and snippet of background detail that I had come across during the research. Even the material which led nowhere I insisted should go in! I felt, for the sake of our credibility, we must let readers know that we had traced back Montague John Druitt's ancestry through four generations and had established contact with present day collateral descendants of his family. The fact that they couldn't tell us anything didn't matter! If readers weren't aware of all our abortive research, then they would reject the book as shallow and lightweight. Fortunately, Martin saw the danger I was leading us into and tactfully jettisoned all of the irrelevant material. In a similar fashion, the Parlours have been equally well served by Kevin O'Donnell's skilful crafting of their industry and research.

I've already mentioned (intentionally) James Kenneth Stephen and Sir William Gull, which is where this book anchors itself. With Gull, I believe they are very close to something – although I'm not quite sure what that something is! But all credit to them for ferreting out and preserving the 'long-standing' oral tradition, associating Gull with the Whitechapel Murders, which has existed for over a century amongst the small community of Thorpe-le-Soken. It's also worth noting that one of our most senior and revered Ripper authorities, Don Rumbelow, had as far back as 1975 (probably earlier) observed – "the other name which frequently crops up in these theories is that of Sir William Gull . . ."

There is an honesty and openness about this book which I find very engaging. I may not agree with their central idea of a conspiracy theory, but I'm quite sure others will endorse their belief. Perhaps this conflict of opinion will encourage further research and generate new discoveries.

Whatever the outcome, the compilers of this book bring with their contribution a cheerful and good natured attitude. In the present climate of Ripper studies, this is truly welcome.

Keith Skinner
London
June 30th 1997

Introduction

Until about 18 months ago, I had no interest in the Ripper or any real knowledge to speak of beyond having watched the Michael Caine TV thriller in the late eighties. I was approached by a company based at Pinewood Studios to write up the researches of Andy and Sue Parlour. I have been writing screenplays for Nick Pocock at 'N+N' for some time, and I must admit that I did not immediately relish the prospect of working on the Ripper. This was a gory story about a mad killer and whores.

Nick had travelled to Clacton to interview Andy and Sue Parlour, in their hotel. Hours later, after seeing stacks of documents and files full of photographs, Nick returned, intrigued, convinced that they had a good story.

Andy's fascination with the Whitechapel murders was rekindled when he and Sue began to research the Parlour family tree. Andy is related to Mary Ann Nichols, the Ripper's first victim in 1888. Memories of family traditions and gossip began to focus. Andy's maternal and paternal forebears originated from the Whitechapel area. Andy had been brought up in the East End, and moved to Essex in the 1960s, where there exists quite a community of former East End folk. Their stories are often hilarious, a real life 'Del Boy and Rodney' collection of characters and scams that could have come from the TV series, 'Only Fools and Horses'. I have listened to various tales of scurrilous deeds, such as burning a mountain of tyres and covering Clacton in smoke for days, and plucking a nearby farmer's chickens and then hiding them in a suitcase as the police searched the premises. Whatever Andy had to do with adventures such as these stopped when he met Sue. She put her foot down! Andy has used this network of familiar contacts to find work of one sort or another over the years, from running a timberyard to running a hotel. His cheek and gift of the gab have opened many doors for them in their Ripper research. Various ideas, stories and artefacts have emerged from this community and their friendly connections, for their grandparents would have been alive at the time of the murders. The year 1888 is not all that long ago. Andy and Sue have been a pair of workhorses, trekking around the sites, raiding libraries and record offices, as well as interviewing people. I can also compare them to a couple of ferrets, seeking out information that has eluded others. They have had a natural interest, time and patience, to unearth new material surrounding the Ripper murders which is presented here for the first time. This book is designed as a concise and clear account of the characters, events and theories. If you only ever read one book on Jack the Ripper, then this one will give you as much as you need to know. My background in writing educational textbooks has shaped the product – clear, concise, and highly visual.

The Parlours have their own theories, and these are presented at the end. They speculate upon the identity of the killers, but they have unearthed new evidence that should suggest that there was a cover-up at work, a conspiracy that might have involved people in government circles. These are almost secondary to the peculiar cluster of folk traditions that have shaped their viewpoint and enriched their material, with Andy as a living link with one of the victims!

I found the Ripper story a fascinating and frustrating detective story that centres on five poor women of the Victorian underclass. They were roughly treated in life, and cruelly murdered. They have never known justice, and I felt an empathy with them as I looked into their stories. I would like to dedicate this book to their memory, for peace for their souls, and to the ongoing work of the Providence Row Refuge in the heart of Whitechapel, at 50, Crispin Street, as well as its other houses, where one of the victims, Mary Kelly, is thought to have stayed when she first came to the area.

The story of Jack the Ripper still fascinates a century on from the Whitechapel murders. The sinister events took place from 31 August to 8-9 November 1888. It is generally accepted that five murders are to be laid at the hands of the Ripper –

(1) Mary ('Polly') Ann Nichols – 31 August in Bucks Row.

(2) Annie Chapman – 8 September in Hanbury Street.

(3) Elizabeth Stride – 30 September in Berner Street.

(4) Catharine Eddowes – 30 September in Mitre Square.

(5) Mary Jane Kelly – 9 November in Miller's Court.

Each of these women had her throat cut, from left to right. Each one, except for Stride, had bad stomach mutilations. The savagery seemed to increase as the killings went on. Kelly's body was almost unrecognisable – it was butchered like an animal!

These five women were all in the same, small area of Whitechapel, yet why were these five chosen from the thousands of prostitutes in the East End?

There are two schools of thought about the killer:

(a) He was a disturbed, serial killer, picking his victims at random.

(b) There was a conspiracy involving government and royalty – possibly the Prince of Wales, or his son, Prince Albert Victor.

The serial killer view compares the Whitechapel murderer with men such as the Yorkshire Ripper, Peter Sutcliffe. They seek revenge and/or express lust and guilt with their violence against prostitutes. The actual Ripper would have been an insignificant, disturbed man. The Preface to Colin Wilson and Robin Odell's 'Jack the Ripper, Summing Up and Verdict', makes this telling remark:

> "I have always had the feeling that on the Day of Judgement, when all things shall be known, when I and other generations of "Ripperologists" ask for Jack the Ripper to step forward and call out his true name, then we shall turn and look with blank astonishment at one another when he announces his name and say, "Who?"..."

The conspiracy theory tells a grander story and makes a more compelling read though it has been based on hearsay and slender evidence. Two main versions of it have been largely discredited, with the rambling memories of an old man, and fake diaries in evidence. Hopefully the Parlours will gently open the case once more.

Kevin O'Donnell

The Year 1888

The five murders usually attributed to Jack the Ripper took place in the Autumn of 1888, between August and November. Before reading on any further about the incidents or the society of the day, we thought it would be helpful to set the year 1888 in the context of the history of the time.

In the USA: George Eastman perfected the first Kodak camera.

In Britain: James Kier Hardie decided to stand as the first Labour candidate, after separating from the Liberals.

In Germany: electromagnetic waves were discovered by Heinrich Hertz.

In France: Vincent Van Gogh moved to Arles, in Provence, where he painted Sunflowers, The Drawbridge, Yellow Chair and Pipe, and The Cafe Terrace.

In Russia: Tchaikovsky completed his fifth symphony.

Listed below are various key dates from just before the time of the Whitechapel murders –

The American Civil War was fought from 1861-1865.

Florence Nightingale was active in the Crimea from 1854–1856.

The first motorcar ran in Germany in 1885.

General Gordon was killed in Khartoum in 1885.

God save the Queen?

"God will never allow such a wicked man to come to the throne.

(A Royal footman, commenting about the Prince of Wales)

Protests and Civil Unrest

13 November, 1887 became known as 'Bloody Sunday'. Nearly 100,000 unemployed people marched to Trafalgar Square in defiance of the government, who had outlawed such gatherings the year before. In October, the Prime Minister, Lord Salisbury, had ordered that the Square should be railed off, for it was a common meeting place for agitators of varying persuasions. The rally was banned under an Act that allowed the police the power to 'regulate' processions. Most did not bother to read the Act; George Bernard Shaw did. He argued that the Act gave no power to prohibit and thus he urged people to ignore the ban. Other socialists and Marxists were present, encouraging the crowds. Eleanor Marx, daughter of Karl Marx, urged the workers to lose their chains, while the artist William Morris declared himself a radical. The Fabians were present, too, along with George Bernard Shaw and Annie Besant (a founder of the Theosophical Society). They thronged with the masses who brandished any weapon they could find – pokers, knives, sticks, and iron bars. Morris took up a position at the head of the march from the north. All went well until they reached Bloomsbury. There, in the space at the west of High Holborn, they encountered the forward section of the march being chased by a handful of police. Some looked to Shaw, "Shaw: give us a lead. What are we to do? "Nothing," said Shaw. "let every man get to the Square as best he can." At this point, he saw the last violence before they reached Trafalgar Square. An elderly middle-class Jew took on a police officer with his fists up. The policeman knocked him out with his baton. The southern part of the march fought more furiously over Westminster Bridge into Whitehall, with the sound of the barrack bugles sounding . When Shaw arrived in the Square, the cavalry were already there, riding around in threes. Police walked four abreast in between the cavalry and the marchers.

Four thousand police faced them, and behind them, 300

George Bernard Shaw, c1890.

Opposite page: *H.M. Queen Victoria. Born May 24, 1819. Came to the throne June 20, 1837. Daughter of the Duke of Kent, second brother of King George IV.*

1

The 'Bloody Sunday' riot, Trafalgar Square, November 1887.

Lifeguards and the same number of Grenadier Guards. The military were armed with muskets and bayonets, and were not afraid to use them. The government had warned that any riots would be met by brutal force. The crowd surged on and pressed against the wall of police. Scuffling broke out, and two men tried to break through, Cunningham Graham and John

Burns. Graham, tall and stocky, was knocked to the ground and had to spend six months in a prison infirmary. Shots were fired, and by midnight, the crowd had dispersed and all was quiet. One person had been killed and about 150 were injured in the struggle. Shaw challenged the Act in the case against Graham and Burns, and the government tried them by another statute, claiming that gatherings in the Square were illegal as it was the property of the Commissioner of Woods and Forests!

The Chief Commissioner of Police was General Sir Charles Warren. He had replaced Sir Edmund Henderson the year before. Warren had been sent on the second expedition to Khartoum to relieve General Gordon. He subsequently went to Bechuanaland to restore order, being awarded the GCMG. He then commanded troops at Suakim before being recalled to Britain. He brought his military experience to bear. His swift and ruthless actions brought press condemnation and he had given the police a public relations disaster.

Lord Salisbury.

A riot had been brewing for months since 'Black Monday' on 8 February, 1886. Then, a large group of the unemployed had assembled in Trafalgar Square. About ten percent of the workforce could be reckoned as out of work then, and socialist feeling ran high in the country. Ever since Marx had settled in London in 1849, Britain had become the centre of socialist thinking. His daughter carried on the cause after his death in 1883, along with Frederick Engels, and it was only in 1888 that the second volume of his influential 'Capital' was published.

Sir Charles Warren, Metropolitan Police Commissioner.

The crowds gathered that Monday to hear the socialists John Burns and Henry Campion, and the Marxist, H. M. Hyndman. The crowd were roused to a fever pitch, and a faction broke away, marching along Pall Mall, St James Street and Piccadilly, along to Mayfair and Hyde Park. The windows of various Gentlemen's Clubs were broken, and the 2,000 strong crowd carried red flags and cudgels. About £50,000 worth of damage was done that night. The police mistakenly sent their reserve force to the Mall, rather than Pall Mall, and two days later, as London was in the grip of a heavy fog, there was rumour of another riot. Many West End shopkeepers barricaded themselves in, expecting the worst.

This riot did not materialise, but the Home Secretary chaired a special committee whose report blamed the police of "grave mistakes", resulting in Henderson's resignation and Warren's appointment. Tensions ran high in the months that followed until the Bloody Sunday riot burst forth.

The riots showed the worsening divide between rich and poor in late Victorian England. Social conditions at the bottom of the ladder were appalling. The average middle or upper class Victorian had no contact or appreciation of the plight of the working class. They were like the distant and exotic tribes heard about in Africa. Conditions in the slums of the East End were none the more noticeable for being so near to the metropolis. It has been estimated that there were 900,000 slum dwellers in the East End. One writer summed up the place as, "an evil plexus of slums that hide human creeping things; where filthy men and women live on penn'orths of gin, where collars and clean shirts are decencies unknown, where every citizen wears a black eye, and none ever combs his hair." Another contemporary description asserts, "Every room in these rotten and reeking tenements houses a family, often two. In one cellar a sanitary inspector reports finding a father, mother, three children and four pigs! In another room a missionary found a man ill with small pox, his wife just recovering from her eighth confinement, and the children running about half naked and covered in dirt..."

The 'poor' officially were reckoned at about 75,000. These were men who could not find regular work. This included seasonal workers, such as builders or dockers, or the victims of market forces such as smaller artisans and craftsmen. Casual labourers might earn a good wage of 15 to 20 shillings a week for heavy lifting, but they were left exhausted, and ate and drank heavily. The women often found work in sweat-shop tailoring. Trouser finishing might bring tuppence ha'penny a pair, and children as young as seven could be found sewing sacks, or shelling peas, or match selling. It was a hand to mouth existence. Fifty five percent of children died before they were five years old!

The Fenian Troubles

Matters were made worse for the government by the Irish troubles which resulted in murders and dynamite explosions in London and the Provinces. Gladstone's Liberals were returned to power in 1886, and tried to send a Bill through Parliament granting Home Rule for the Irish. This was defeated, and Gladstone dissolved Parliament and fought the election on this single issue. The result was a resounding defeat for the Liberals and a victory for the Conservatives, under Lord Salisbury, gaining 316 seats.

Damage to Scotland Yard by fenian bomb.

There had been trouble with the Irish for years, and this came to a head with the murder of the new Irish Chief Secretary in Dublin, Lord Cavendish, along with his Undersecretary, Thomas Burke. The Fenians spearheaded the opposition to English rule, and orchestrated dynamite campaigns in London. On one occassion, in 1884 they attempted to blow up Scotland Yard. The Special Irish Branch was established in 1884 to investigate their activities. (This was the forerunner of the Special Branch).

Lord Salisbury headed a government that was stemming back a tide of ill feeling and mistrust in the country. It might not have been so bad had the monarchy formed a potent symbol of national pride and identity, as in the Second World War. However, nothing could have been further from the truth. The Royals were immensely unpopular and many feared that the throne would topple and England would become a Republic.

The Queen

Victoria came to the throne on 20 June 1837 at the young age of 18. She ascended the throne amidst a flow of romance and hope after the elderly and distant monarchs of the House of Hanover. Even so, there were five attempts on her life early in her reign, by madmen, attention seekers or political radicals. The first was on 10 June 1840, exactly four months after her marriage to Prince Albert of Saxe-Coburg-Gotha, when Edward Oxford fired two shots at the royal carriage as the Queen went to visit her mother, the Duchess of Kent. He was overpowered and declared insane, being committed to an asylum. There was some suspicion that the Duke of Cumberland was involved, hoping to unseat the monarch and take her place, but this could never be proved.

The second attempt was in 1842 while riding in the Mall. A man, John Francis, shot at the carriage and ran into the crowd. Victoria insisted on riding out the next day, and the man fired again. This time, a passing soldier overpowered him and he was sentenced to death. Victoria intervened and this was commuted to transportation for life.

The third attempt was on 3 July 1842, while driving to the Chapel Royal in St James. A "deformed lad", John William Bean, fired at the party, but the first Victoria knew of it was when she returned. Victoria felt that the crime of high treason sounded too daring and romantic, and this was changed by a Bill to 'high misdemeanours' for attempts on her life. Bean was sentenced to 18 months imprisonment.

The fourth attempt took place on 19 May 1849, only months before Victoria was due to visit Ireland. An Irishman, William Hamilton, just tried to frighten her with an empty pistol. He was given 7 years transportation.

The fifth attempt was on 27 June 1850 when she was leaving Cambridge House. Robert Pate, a retired lieutenant of the 10th Hussars, approached her and struck her with a cane. He was sentenced to 7 years transportation.

The Queen became a recluse after the death of her beloved Prince Albert. She mourned him obsessively after his death in 1861. She had Albert's bed made up every day, and his chamber pot scoured. She held a treasured object of her dead husband when contemplating important decisions, hoping to receive a supernatural communication. She even took the Prince of Wales and his new wife, Alexandra, eldest daughter of King Christian IX of Denmark, into Albert's mausoleum so he could bless their union. When her grandson was born, it was she who named him, without consulting the parents. He was to be Albert Victor, and every King of England was to be called Albert forevermore!

She refused to be present at public events and two more attempts were made upon her life during her reign. On 27 February 1872 she was returning from a drive in Regents Park when Arthur O'Connor, a Fenian sympathiser, leapt out at her in the grounds of the Palace and waved a pistol in her face, demanding that Fenian prisoners should be released. He was sentenced to one year's hard labour and 20 strokes of the birch.

The seventh and final attempt on her life was on 2 March 1882 when her train had arrived at Windsor station amidst cheering crowds of Eton boys. Roderick Maclean, a starving Scottish poet, fired at her with a six chamber, rapid fire revolver. He missed, and the boys overpowered him. He was protesting about the low poor relief that he was expected to live on. He was declared insane and committed to an asylum. At this, Victoria flew into a rage and declared, "If this is the law, the law must be altered."

Her reclusiveness made her a miser. She hoarded £200,000 of her allowance from the country each year, and a scurrilous pamphlet was circulated in 1871, called, 'What Does She Do With It?'. Gladstone commented, "The Queen is invisible and the Prince of Wales is not respected."

Rumours appeared that she was to abdicate, and, on 6 November 1871, the radical MP, Sir Charles Dilke, attacked her for dereliction of duty and urged her deposition.

The Prince of Wales

Albert Edward ('Bertie'), the Prince of Wales was even more unpopular. He developed an odious reputation as a womaniser and as a gambler. He was brought up in his father's shadow. Victoria, shortly after his birth, wrote to her uncle, "You will understand how fervent my prayers to see him resemble his angelic father in every, every respect, both in body and mind. I delight in the fact that I possess such a perfect husband. I cannot say what a comfort and support my beloved Angel is to me."

Prince and Princess of Wales.

Bertie was starved of familiar affection, and was pushed through his youth with a heavy regime of academic studies and stern tutors. Once he arrived at University, he was a freer spirit and yearned to throw restraint to the winds. Rumours of his

7

youthful lusts prompted his parents to send him on military training in Curragh Camp, in a remote part of Ireland. Here, it was thought, he would be well out of the way of any trouble with women. His fellow officers, however, had other plans. A black haired young actress, Nellie Clifton, was the guest of an officer and she was sneaked past the Commander into Bertie's bed. He seemed no stranger to things carnal, and she went on to boast about her Royal conquest. News reached the Palace, and Albert was mortified. He ordered a full enquiry and rushed Bertie back to Cambridge. Albert wrote to his son, "You have caused me the greatest pain I have yet felt in this life. You must not, you dare not be lost. The consequences for this country and for the world would be too dreadful."

Albert travelled to see Bertie and castigated him. Travelling through bad weather, Albert became feverish. He had contracted typhoid fever, in fact, and he died on 14 December 1861. Victoria always held Bertie partly to blame for his death. She once said, "I shall never look at him without a shudder.." and she steadfastly refused to allow Bertie any role in State affairs, keeping full hold of the reigns of power herself. This spiteful stubborness resulted in Bertie having too much time and money on his hands. After his marriage on 10th March 1863, he moved to Marlborough House in central London and fell in with a group of high class rakes such as Henry Chaplin and Sir Frederick Johnstone. He travelled with the Marquis of Hastings, who introduced him to the brothel scene, and once, in Paris, it was said that a naked courtesan was served up on a silver platter, in jest, at an orgy.

Another notorious rake, Frank Harris, claimed in his self-published autobiography, that he used to tell Bertie the filthiest of jokes, and relates the various sexual adventures that the Prince was involved in. He would frequently take a ride in a hansom cab with a woman, and have intercourse while travelling about the City. He would woo and charm the wives of various gentlemen, dallying in their rooms, and telling the footmen not to disturb them. Once, on a shooting party in Scotland, he was so overcome with lust for a young woman, that he pulled her down in the heather in full view!

Bertie was no stranger to scandal throughout his career. Lady Susan Pelham-Clinton's child was rumoured to be his. One of her advisors kept him regularly informed of her progress throughout the pregnancy. Though he denied the child was his, High Society gossiped that it was.

Bertie was taken to court over an affair in 1869-70, in the

Mordaunt divorce case. Lady Mordaunt had declared that the father of her new born son was Lord Cole, and when divorce proceedings were brought by Lord Mordaunt, Bertie was named by her as she listed many lovers. At this juncture, Bertie was treated courteously when in court, and was cheered by the crowd when he left. Bertie was able to deny the affair as Lady Mordaunt's father, Sir Thomas Moncrieff, had her declared insane, and found doctors who would confirm this. She was institutionalised and her testimony invalidated.

Prince Albert Edward 'Bertie'.

The publicity surrounding the case began to take its toll. Rumours spread about Bertie, and Alix was taken to the nation's heart as the virtuous and long-suffering Princess. On one occasion, when she appeared in the Royal Box at the Theatre, the crowd cheered. They began to hiss when Bertie appeared beside her, shortly afterwards. The radical press were eager to spread rumours, and Henry Labouchere edited the journal, 'The Truth' which loved to 'out' the Royals with any titbit of scandal. A crude satirical collection of tales about Bertie's adventures also circulated under the punning title of 'The Coming K___.'

A divorce scandal nearly dragged Bertie into court again in 1876 when Lady Ayelsford had an affair with Lord Blanchford, the elder brother of Randolph Churchill. Apparently, Bertie had written several very compromising letters to Lady Ayelsford. The letters did not come to light in court, to the relief of the Royals. Bertie's unpopularity grew worse within the nation and abroad. In 1885, Bertie toured Cork and was hissed and booed by the crowds, who threw onions at him. In 1888, the Kaiser, Bertie's nephew, refused to visit Austria while Bertie was staying in Vienna, such was the mistrust between them.

A final scandal brought the Prince to court, and his treatment this time was very different from the Lady Mordaunt case. The Tranby Croft affair of 1891 involved Bertie's other well known vice – gambling. Bertie received an allowance of £100,000 per annum from the country, and he spent it all on reckless living. There were frequent claims that financiers in France were in pursuit of debts. The Tranby Croft affair started when Bertie was a guest at the Yorkshire home of Arthur Wilson, a wealthy shipowner. The illegal game of baccarat was being played, and Sir William Gordon-Cumming was discovered to be cheating. Bertie foolishly made him sign an undertaking that he would never gamble again. Sir William agreed on condition that the matter was kept quiet, but such a matter could not be kept from the social circles. He responded by suing the Wilsons for slander. Bertie was summoned to court to give evidence. He was treated dismissively and, this time, was jeered at by the crowds. The Prince was accused of encouraging baccarat and was said to accuse Sir William on the flimsiest of evidence. He was reprimanded for not reporting the matter to Sir William's commanding officer. The weakness of the monarchy was attested in the courtroom by Sir Edward Clarke, Sir William's counsel. He referred to the sacrifices made by some to support "a tottering throne or prop a falling dynasty."

Bertie loved fires and firefighting. He volunteered his services, along with other gentry of the time, in helping the London fire services. The services began as local bands of men commanded by the gentry at their mansion houses. By the late nineteenth century, the National Firebrigades Union tried to maintain national standards in training and equipment, having their annual summer camps with drill competitions. Bertie kept his personal uniform and equipment at Chandos Street Fire Station, near Charing Cross. He was rumoured to have a flat in nearby Watling Street, above a butcher's shop, that he would use when on these sorties. There was also a fire station in Watling Street that kept engines, and thus the story is highly likely. He would make a night of fighting a fire, spending time socialising in the station afterwards. One report exists from a

Fire Brigade Review July 1891. Before the Kaiser, Wilhelm II, Edward, Prince of Wales, Captain Eyre M. Shaw, Chief Officer M.F.B.

fireman who witnessed Bertie at work on the King and Queen Granaries fire; "Through the height of the fire, his Royal Highness shared the smoke and the water with us all, and gave a hand here and there just like one of ourselves.....Through it all the Prince, who seemed to bear a charmed life, worked with a zeal and knowledge that would have done credit to any trained fireman, unrecognised by the onlookers, and un-noticed by the rank and file of the Brigade."

Bertie worked as an ordinary fireman and 'mucked in' with the others. He was also very generous with his cigars afterwards, and thus increased his popularity with the men. Sometimes he would go and play billiards at the fire station with the Duke of Sutherland and other companions hoping that a fire call would come in. On other occasions, Captain Shaw, President of the Metropolitan Fire Brigade Union, would send a brigade trap for the Prince. Bertie was the obvious royal to be approached to review the Union demonstration at Crystal Palace in 1891, although the Prince deferred to his nephew the Kaiser, as he was visiting London at the time. Bertie had some narrow escapes, such as the time when the horses tumbled into a hole in the road and the carriage almost turned over! The Queen seems to have tolerated Bertie's adventures in the Brigade for this kept him from less savoury pursuits. Captain Shaw was certainly rewarded by her, being made Knight of the Bath.

A more sinister note is struck by the Watling Street connection, though, for his flat was rumoured to be a venue for wild orgies and liaisons with prostitutes. Given all that is known about his character, this is eminently likely.

Prince Albert Victor

Bertie's son. Albert Victor Christian Edward, known as 'Eddy' could have been a beacon of hope. Unfortunately, he was no stranger to scandal, himself. Eddy was widely believed to be bisexual. He was tutored at Cambridge between 1883 and 1885 by James Kenneth Stephen, whose uncle was Sir Leslie Stephen, the editor of the Dictionary of National Biography, and whose younger cousin was Virginia Woolf. J. K., or 'Jem', Stephen was a member of the select group, the Cambridge Apostles. Both Stephen and Eddy had rooms in Neville's Court, the "Cambridge attics". The Apostles were founded in 1820 as a debating group to discuss, privately , doubts and controversial points about the Christian faith. It became gradually more

Prince Albert Victor (Eddy).

elitist and was based at Trinity when J. K. Stephen was a member. Their maxim was, "the love of man for man is greater than that of man for women." This was known as "the higher sodomy". It is suspected that there was a homosexual undercurrent to their fellowship, though this cannot be proved. Their talk of 'higher sodomy' might be merely Platonic in intent. It is pointed out, though, that the successors of this group formed the homosexual spy ring of the 1930s!

Eddy had his friends and his cultural interests suggested by J. K. Stephen. A photograph of a gathering of these associates includes seven members of the Apostles. Some, such as Michael Harrison, in his 'Clarence', have wondered if there was a homosexual relationship between the two men, but Stephen is a complex character. From the evidence of some of his poems, it is assumed that he was a mysogynist, but other writings suggest otherwise. An obscene Cambridge song at this time might refer to a relationship between J. K. Stephen and Eddy, speaking of "the bastard Stephen". Herbert Stephen, J. K.'s brother, remarked that a firm relationship had developed between them. It is possible that there was a sexual bond between two men so friendly and close from public school circles, in an all male environment. One of Stephen's poems might allude to such a relationship under the euphemism of 'sucking peppermints'. It is obscure, though, and speaks of an enigmatic 'K.;

Prince Eddy (seated centre in bowler hat) with J. K. Stephen standing behind him in soft white hat. To Eddy's left is Harry Lushington Stephen (JK's younger brother); most of the others in the group are also Apostles.

THE WEST-END SCANDALS.

COMMITTAL OF THE EDITOR OF THE "PRESS" FOR TRIAL

A DEFENCE FUND OPENED.

Lord Euston emphatically denies the libellous statement, and explains the circumstances under which he once visited the house in Cleveland-street.

The editor of this paper has been committed to take his trial at the sessions of the Central Criminal Court, which open on Monday, 16 December. The proceedings were initiated last Saturday morning, when on the application of Mr. Lionel Hart, instructed by Messrs. Lewis & Lewis, Justice Field granted his fiat for the commencement of criminal proceedings against Mr. Ernest Parke, whose solicitor, Mr. Minton Slater, offered no opposition. At Bow-street Police Court the same afternoon, Mr. George Lewis obtained from Mr. Vaughan a warrant for

LORD EUSTON.

Mr. Parke's arrest, the Earl of Euston supporting the application by testifying to the truth of the affidavit he had made denying the libellous statements complained of. Sergeant Partridge was sent with the warrant to the *Star* office, but being by inadvertence informed that Mr. Parke had left, went to his place of residence at Clapham. Meanwhile, however, Mr. Parke heard of the issue of the warrant, and at once went to Bow-street

"See where the K., in sturdy self-reliance,
Thoughtful and placid as a brooding dove,
Stands, firmly sucking, in the cause of science,
Just such a peppermint as schoolboys love..."

Whatever we deduce from his Cambridge days, Eddy was reputed to have relationships with both sexes. He was in and out of relationships, and seemed to lack emotional maturity. He was insecure in his own identity from youth, and seemed to develop a love of hunting to bolster his image, and his time in the Hussars was a bore to him, apart from the wearing of the uniform. He was writing passionate letters to the young and pretty Lady Sybil St Claire Erskine while seemingly committed to Princess Helene d'Orleans in 1890.

The scandal that could have toppled him was in 1889. Number 19 Cleveland Street was a homosexual brothel, run by Charles Hammond. This came to the police's attention when a young delivery boy, Swanson, was questioned for having too much spending money in July of that year. Apparently, another boy, Newlove, a Post Office clerk, had taken him to 19 Cleveland Street. Newlove was questioned and broke down. Another Post Office clerk, Veck, who often posed as a clergyman, had introduced him there. Veck was overheard offering Newlove money to defend himself on 9 July. Though the house was constantly watched by police, Veck was not actually arrested until 20 August. Detective Frederick Abberline was in charge – the same Abberline who was in charge of forces on the ground in the Whitechapel murder inquiry. The delay seems most odd, unless the police actually wanted the chief offenders to make good their escape. On 10 July, Hammond's furniture was removed and sent to France. He followed soon afterwards. Lord Arthur Somerset, the Extra Equerry and Superintendent of the Stables to the Prince of Wales, was a regular client, and he, too, travelled to France. A letter from Bertie, contained in the DPP file on the case states that he was pleased that Somerset had been allowed to escape. When pressed by the Home Secretary, Lord Salisbury refused to have Hammond extradited from France to answer charges. Eventually, only Veck and Newlove were charged. Veck was given four months imprisonment, and Newlove nine months. The press pointed out the injustice of the sentences, for Veck had introduced the boy to the brothel. Also, these were staggeringly lenient sentences for the time as sodomy could carry a heavy prison sentence and life imprisonment was not uncommon!

14

The reason for the delay might become apparent when it is clear that Eddy was suspected of being a regular client. The DPP refers to him simply as 'P.A.V.' – 'Prince Albert Victor'.

The ruthlessness of the government in covering this affair up can be seen in the treatment of Ernest Parke, the young editor of 'The North London Press'. He attacked the mishandling of the scandal and asked difficult questions. He hinted at Royal involvement by referring to "more highly placed and distinguished personages." He also named Lord Euston as a regular client of the brothel. He claimed to have six witnesses who had seen Euston enter the brothel. The DPP file names Euston, too, in the evidence of one John Saul, a male prostitute, "he went to Hammond's with me on one occasion. He is not an actual sodomite. He likes to play with you and then 'spend' on your belly." Saul's statement is dated 10 August, and Parke did not become aware of the scandal until a month later. Saul was not perjuring himself for Parke's benefit. However, Euston brought criminal proceedings against Parke for libel. Saul's evidence was dismissed by the judge as unworthy as he was a self-confessed homosexual! Parke was found guilty and sentenced to one year in jail. He had been effectively silenced.

Hammond.

Catholic Suspicions

Eddy caused consternation when he declared that he wished to marry Princess Helene d'Orleans. She was a Roman Catholic, and both Crown and Parliament could not agree to that. Victoria wrote that such a marriage would have "the very worst possible effect". Indeed, the Act of Settlement excluded the heir to the throne from marrying a Catholic. The royal inheritance would then be forfeited. Lord Salisbury consulted the Lord Chancellor, and Salisbury seems to have been convinced that revolution would have been the result if the marriage had gone ahead. Anti-Catholic feeling still ran high in Britain, with stories of the persecution of Protestants under Queen Mary taught to children from such fiery sources as Foxe's Book of Martyrs – the tortures of the Inquistion, hangings and burnings. The Martyrs' Memorial to the likes of Cranmer, Latimer and Ridley was only erected in Oxford in the late 19th century, partly as a reaction to the rise of the Oxford Movement. Anglican clergy who sought to introduce more Catholic ritual and vestments faced pillory and prosecution. One London vicar was pelted with bread pudding for daring to place candles on the altar and put his choirboys in surplices. The Public

Lord Arthur Somerset.

15

Worship regulation Act came into being in 1874 as the Archbishop was worried about the rising popularity of ritualism. The Church Association, an extreme Protestant group, was a prime mover behind this, seeking to keep the Church of England more on the Reformation side. They even secured a prosecution against the saintly Bishop of Lincoln, Edward King, in 1888. During 1877-1882, four priests were sent to prison, one for as long as 545 days for such seemingly harmless matters today as using a chalice of wine mixed with water (the Roman custom) and having altar candles. There were mob tactics, too, such as those organised by John Kensit, who became Secretary of the Protestant Truth Society in 1890. He rented mobs who would harass High Church clergy and disrupt their services. Actual Roman Catholic clergy were troubled, also. In 1850, a mob burned an effigy of Cardinal Wiseman in Bethnal Green and smashed the windows of Catholic Churches. When King Edward VII attended a Roman Catholic mass at St James Church in Spanish Place, West London, in 1910, he was severely criticised. His earlier desire to visit the Pope in 1903 was warned off. Balfour lamented the sectarianism that prevented it, declaring, "This is absurd. But the people we have to deal with are absurd, too!"

It was ironic that the Churchmen who had shown the most interest in the slum parishes were the Anglo-Catholics. They felt a passion for the poor and illiterate, for the incarnation of God in Jesus of Nazareth was at the centre of their faith. He had been born in a lowly stable and embraced the reality of ordinary mortals. Their sense of mission led them to the poor. Also, ritualistic worship offered something colourful and visual. It was aptly suited for a non-book people who could touch, taste, see and do things that were a glorious breather from their daily grime. There were colourful robes, flickering candles, golden crosses, clouds of incense and pools of holy water. Churches such as St Peter's, London Docks under Fr Lowder, became shrines for the Catholic movement, and ministered faithfully to the local workers.

To return to the theme of royalty, a Catholic wife was thus an impossibility. Eddy was made the Duke of Clarence and Avondale in 1891, and engaged to Princess Mary of Teck in December of that year. He died the following January of pneumonia which complicated an earlier influenza. Some suggested it was the dreaded syphillis, but there is no evidence to warrant this, though this would be believeable. Other rumours circulated that he had been murdered to clear the throne for someone more suitable. Reports circulated that his finger nails had blackened before he died, indicating poisoning. Another, curious legend stems from Osborne House on the Isle of Wight. This suggests that a story has been passed down by staff that Eddy did not die in 1892, but was hopelessly insane. He was then hidden away at the House where he died in 1930 and his grave is marked by a plain, marble tablet. Interesting tales, and while not inconceivable, they are without any evidence to seriously back them up. It seems that Eddy truly died in 1892 and the monarchy's future thus rested with Bertie, for better or for worse.

Sin City

"... London, that great cesspool into which all
the loungers and idlers of the Empire
are irresistibly drained."

(Dr Watson, in Arthur Conan Doyle's 'A Study in Scarlet')

In 1878, the British Medical Journal was still debating whether menstruating women might turn a joint of ham rancid by merely touching it. Victorian prudery held back discoveries about gynaecology, diseases and sexuality. An internal examination would only be offered to a woman in an emergency, and then, usually, under a dark sheet in a blacked out room. This timerity also stretched to the social attitude to women. The middle class mother was an aspiring lady. Her household was populated with domestics which freed her to do good works, or to while away the time in some frippary. While upper class ladies were free to move about with their powerful husbands because of their established wealth and connections, the middle class wife was tied to the house, for her husband was tied to the place of work. The home became a sacred retreat from the nasty, masculine workplace, and women were to be protected at all costs. They were mothers, and thus elevated to the status of near goddess, but it was all image and tinsel; there was no emotional or physical freedom.

For a man to have sexual intercourse with his wife was like doing it with a guardian angel. Men were often exhorted to have sexual relations once a month, or only once a week if they really had to. The Victorians had taken to heart older ideas that sex should only be for procreation, and that reason was higher than emotion. It is not surprising, then, that prostitution flourished for men to release their baser urges. Sex with a prostitute demanded no emotion, it was quick and fleeting. Some even argued that this was a favour to their wives as it expiated their urges and stopped the good ladies being pestered.

Whatever excuse might be used, there were numerous prostitutes, and numerous reasons why they had turned to this ancient profession. The Chief of the Metropolitan Police in 1839 said there were 7,000 prostitutes in the City. Others put the figure much higher, near 80,000, which is probably closer

Opposite page:
Commercial Street, Whitechapel showing 'The Britannia' public house (left) on the corner of Dorset Street.

19

to the truth. There were three broad categories of reason for becoming a prostitute in Victorian England.

A few respectable women wanted to break free from social convention and the home, and took to the stage coupled with prostitution among a high class clientele. Such women in England were discreet, and thus tolerated, like Lilly Langtry, one of Bertie's mistresses. On the continent, in the big cities, they were celebrities, entertaining the rich and famous, bathing in champagne and dancing naked for their entertainment, such as Cora Pearl in Paris. She could earn up to 5,000 francs a night, when a skilled craftsman at the time would have earned 1 or 2 francs a day! There were fashionable prostitutes in England who moved secretly in high circles, such as Mabel Gray or Nellie Rousby. Another was Catharine Walters, known as 'Skittles' who earned her nickname by playing skittles with young men of the British diplomatic service in Paris, where she had retreated after being bought off by a ducal family to break off her affair with their elder son. She married Wilfred Scawen Blunt, a poet and traveller, and returned to London where she hosted lavish parties in Park Lane, attended by the Prince of Wales.

The majority of women were in low paid employment, minor domestics, shopgirls, milliners and so forth, who sought to supplement their meagre wages. Perhaps a seduction or the enticement of more money had led them along this track. The poorer women were desperate, leading a hand to mouth existence, and some were afraid to apply for parish relief in case their children were taken off them.

William Acton wrote, in 1862:

"Unable to obtain by their labour the means of procuring the bare necessaries of life, they gain, by surrendering their bodies to evil uses, food to sustain and clothes to cover them. Many thousand young women in the metropolis are unable by drudgery that lasts from early morning till late at night to earn more than from 3s. to 5s. weekly...."

Henry Mayhew.

A fascinating, contemporary account can be found in Henry Mayhew's works, one of the founders of 'Punch' magazine. His accounts of the Victorian underclass in 'London Labour and the London Poor' (1851) are devastating reading. He proceeds to outline the major classes of prostitute who one might find around the Haymarket or Regent Street area. The highest class were the middle class girls with good connections, associating with gentlemen to earn their keep after having their characters ruined by seducers and rogues in the homes or in their place of work. Some girls had come from the Provinces, to escape from an unhappy relationship with a stepfather, or they had run off with a lover to be deserted by him. These women rented 'houses of accommodation' which were clean and tasteful rather than take them to their own lodgings. There were some French, Belgian and German girls among this class.

The second class of women were the plainer domestic servants or the daughters of labourers, perhaps as young as 13. They were more poorly dressed, with "ill suited crinoline". They were out to supplement their meagre income, or had fallen on hard times, perhaps having escaped from the home. They would seek to be taken to a lodging house for their services. Some were members of Dress Houses where they were kept in fine clothes to attract the men, but were charged high rent and kept in such chronic debt that they were virtual prisoners.

The third, and lowliest class, were the "worn out prostitutes and degraded women". They would go with almost anyone for a few pence, shop boys, errand boys, labourers or thieves. They would disappear into a sordid alley and not bother with any sort of lodging house.

Mayhew goes on to describe other categories of prostitute, such as the 'Sailors' Women' such as one might find in Shadwell, Spitafields, or parts of Whitechapel. Here, public houses would offer music and a venue for sailing men to pick up local women. Some of these houses were run as brothels. He mentions one, 'Paddy's Goose' that was popular with the navy, when he was writing, for the landlord had sailed along the Thames with banners, recruiting labourers for the navy during the Crimean War!

Mayhew also mentions the amateur women, the Dollymops, who picked up men, usually soldiers, for a few pence, and used this to supplement their wages. They had neither the class nor the experience to be regular professionals! Some prostitutes were 'Soldiers' Women' and might move about from barracks to barracks within the country. He spoke to one such in Knightsbridge. She had started as a shop girl in a bakers in Chatham until a young soldier had caught her fancy and she followed the camps around. He had even given her a little money to follow him to Ireland, which she did. Then there were 'Thieves' Women' who were seduced as young girls and put to service in a cheap brothel or used by the seducer until he tired of her.

Two different lodging houses are described. One was

clean but populated with many prostitutes. The landlord charged threepence per night and asked no questions about anyone who stayed there so long as they had the money. This was on two floors. The first floor had cubicles separated by sheets of deal board for married couples, and the second floor was for the singles with rows of beds. There were clean sheets only once a week, and they became filthy very quickly! The second lodging house charged the same price but the owner was more discriminating about whom he let in. The clientel was mainly made up of labouring men, and they sat, smoked and chatted amicably. A smaller lodging house proved to be very different. This was a two storey house with the upper floor divided into four rooms. The owner lived downstairs with her daughter and four prostitutes were upstairs. The owner paid five shillings per week rent, while she charged the four women four shillings a week. Conditions were basic and pitiful. One room reeked of opium and one woman was described as an "animated bundle of rags".

Mayhew interviewed several women in his investigations. One Haymarket woman said:

"I sometimes go to the Haymarket, either early in the evening, or early in the morning, when I can get away from the printing; and sometimes I do a little in the day-time. This is not a frequent practice of mine; I only do it when I want money to pay anything. I am out now with the avowed intention of picking up a man......I always dress well..... I have good feet, too, and as I find they attract attention, I always parade them. And I've hooked many a man by showing my ankle on a wet day...."

Mayhew also spoke to a young girl of about 23 who was a virtual prisoner in a house off Langham Place. There were fine decorations and they dressed her in quality clothes, but she was not free to leave of her own accord. She had been given into the care of a woman by her labouring parents and had been broken in gradually for a few months in a different house and then brought here. They had made her drunk and she had signed some papers and she thought these gave them legal power over her. She expected to be there until she died unless something turned up.

A more disturbing trend in Victorian England was the quest for the virgin prostitute. This was largely as a result of the spread of sexually transmitted diseases such as syphilis and gonorrhea. In 1869, of the 9,000 prostitutes in the seaports, about 1,500 were under the age of 15. Demand soon overran supply, for obvious reasons, and all sorts of tricks were employed to fake virginity. The most common ones involved a piece of sponge, soaked in blood, being inserted into the vagina prior to intercourse, and the use of astringents to tighten the walls of the vaginal passage. Certain doctors could be relied upon to produce certificates authenticating virginity. The squalid areas around the docklands abounded in brothels specialising in virgins, such as Maxwell's in Betty Street and Keeley's in Dock Street. One man, William Sheen, was famed for being able to supply both boys and girls. There were cases of seven year old girls being raped in fashionable brothels, and one incident where a four year old girl was lured into a brothel and raped twelve times. Under age children were often gagged, strapped down and drugged, even chloroformed, in sound-proofed rooms, where flagellation and sodomy might also occur. The better class of house kept a resident doctor who repaired any damage afterwards.

William Stead was a typical Victorian eccentric. He was deeply religious, having had a stern upbringing full of the fear of Hell, but he had various moral lapses and affairs throughout his life. He was a radical, pioneering journalist, working as editor of the Pall Mall Gazette.

He ran a series of articles about prostitution amonst young girls, especially virgins, in 1885. He set out on the precarious attempt to prove that he could buy a virgin. He used the pseudonym 'Charles' and frequented Theatres and fashionable restaurants. His contact with the Underworld was one Rebecca Jarrett, a fortysomething ex-brothel owner who had repented of her sins and turned to the Church. She visited the brothels that she knew of and found Eliza Armstrong. She met Stead and they took tea before going to a house of accommodation. Stead related the sorry tale in the Pall Mall Gazette of July 6, 1885, under the title, 'A CHILD OF THIRTEEN BOUGHT FOR £5'. He changed some facts and exaggerated the account. He revealed that the girl was acquired by the brothel owner for a sovereign. The mother was drunk, and the father was indifferent, being told that she was going to a 'situation'. The girl was sold on for £5, £3 down and £2 to follow when her virginity was certified. The little girl was told that she must go with this strange woman to a situation. A local midwife provided a certificate of virginity after a brief examination. A small vial of chloroform was also provided to dull the girl's inevitable pain. The girl was taken to a house of accommodation and drugged and put to bed. The man entered and she was heard to scream "There's a man in my room; oh, take me home...!"

William Stead.

This fanciful account shocked the readers, and was unfortunately based upon many true incidents happening in the capital. Eliza's parents were indignant, though, for they felt it had completely misrepresented both them and their daughter, Eliza, and they complained to Scotland Yard. A rival newspaper, Lloyd's Newspaper, took up their cause with gusto.

Eliza had been examined, meanwhile, by a doctor, to prove that Stead had not touched her, and then he sent her briefly to Paris to recover. She was later found in Stead's own garden. He had not sought her parents' permission to send her abroad, which made matters worse. The midwife and Rebecca Jarrett were both sentenced to six months, and Stead to three months. He actually relished his time in jail, having his own armchair, a comfortable bed and a desk. Every November 10th, he would walk across Waterloo bridge dressed in his prison clothes to celebrate his sacrifice for the cause of truth and justice! Stead eventually perished on the Titanic – perhaps a fitting way to end such an unconventional life!

The spread of sexually transmitted diseases, and moral campaigning by Church groups led to a change in the law. The Contagious Diseases Acts of 1864, 1866 and 1869 allowed prostitutes, or those suspected of that profession, to be given compulsory examinations to test their state of health. This was particularly apposite for syphilis cases in women, where the initial symptoms would clear up without much discomfort and the disease would still be carried without the woman realising it. The initial symptoms in men were far more obvious and painful with inflammation and pain in the penis. Unfortunately, the moral campaigners were so offended by the thought of any woman being so indecently treated, that they pressed for the repeal of these laws. They were successful in 1886, having stopped the examinations a year earlier. Their real campaign was to stop prostitution altogether, and they were partly successful in 1885 when brothel keeping was made illegal. Organised prostitution was now a crime, and went underground. A blind eye was often turned to individual soliciting , though. Much of the soliciting clientele at the Haymarket as described by Mayhew would still have gone on openly, though women did risk arrest and sometimes were.

The area of Whitechapel where the Ripper found his victims was known as "the wicked quarter mile". Here, poor women struggled to live hand to mouth, and met their men in the alleyways or at the many public houses. They were cheap, going out for a 'threepenny knee-trembler' or two a night.

They would earn their doss money and either drink the rest or live off the proceeds for basic essentials. Most of the women were haggard and worn out by their way of life, ill and tired in their forties. They were unattractive and missing teeth, often drunk at night. The five Ripper victims were of this underclass, though one was about 24. She was the odd one out of the pack, still young and attractive with much spirit left in her. These women, some living on and off with men in various digs and lodging houses, were classed as 'unfortunates' a euphemism for the lowest level of prostitute.

The Haymarket – midnight.

POLICE THE ILLUSTRATED NEWS

LAW COURTS AND WEEKLY RECORD

INQUEST ON FIFTH VICTIM AT ST GEORGES IN THE EAST

FIFTH VICTIM

MORTUARY

INSPECTOR REID

THE BERNER ST VICTIM.

TWO MORE WHITECHAPEL HORRORS. WHEN WILL THE MURDERER BE CAPTURED ?

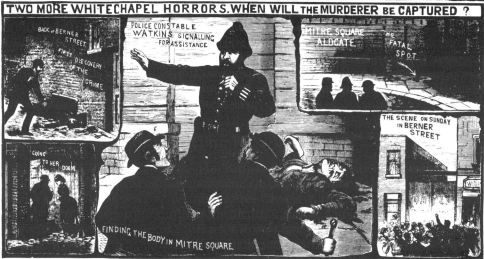

BACK OF BERNER STREET FIRST DISCOVERY OF THE CRIME

POLICE CONSTABLE WATKINS SIGNALLING FOR ASSISTANCE

MITRE SQUARE ALDGATE

THE FATAL SPOT

THE SCENE ON SUNDAY IN BERNER STREET

GOING TO HER DOOM

FINDING THE BODY IN MITRE SQUARE.

THE FIFTH VICTIM OF THE WHITECHAPEL FIEND.

FINDING THE MUTILATED BODY IN MITRE SQARE.

"Ghastly Crimes by a Maniac"

"There was nothing the Victorians enjoyed
more than a horror that did not touch
them personally"

(Raey Tannahill)

Despite its poverty, crime and violence, Whitechapel had
known few murders before the Ripper. In the previous year,
1887, there were 71 cases of violent death reported, but these
were not actual murders. Accidents accounted for 69 of these,
and the remaining two were suicides. The highest number of
non-violent deaths reported were due to disease such as tuber-
culosis and meningitis. The brutal murders of 1888 were thus
shocking and frightening. They were a 'media sensation' of
their day.

The First Murder

The Ripper murders are now generally believed to have begun
with the discovery of a body at about 3.40am on Friday August
31st 1888. Charles Cross, a carman, and Robert Paul found the
body at the gates to a stableyard in Buck's Row, adjacent to 2
Buck's Row. They thought the body was an old tarpaulin at first,
but saw it was a woman with her skirts pulled up. They could
not see clearly whether she was alive or dead without a lamp,
and it was common to find drunks in this state. Cross felt one
of her hands and realised that she was stone cold. He listened
for breathing and pulled her skirt down. The two went off to
find a policeman, not wanting to be late for work. They found
PC Jonas Mizen and he walked off to the murder site. PC John
Neil was already there, as it was his beat. He saw that the throat
was cut by the light of his lantern. He had noticed blood oozing
from a wound in the throat just prior to seeing this, when examining the body.

Dr Llewellyn was sent for and he made a basic examination
of the body, confirming that she was dead. He guessed that she
had been dead for no more than thirty minutes. The body was

then taken to the mortuary at the Old Montague Street Work-house Infirmary. As it was lifted, the back appeared to be covered with blood, and a mass of congealed blood, about six inches in diameter was left where the body had been lying and this had run towards the gutter. Police Inspector John Spratling of J, or Bethnal Green Division, arrived at Buck's Row, after the body had been removed, to make notes for the coroner. He went on to the mortuary, and saw that the body had been more mutilated than they had realised. The abdomen had been savagely cut, exposing the intestines. Llewellyn was called back, and he examined the body more thoroughly. The next thing was to identify the body. A procession of East Enders trickled through the mortuary doors with no results. Her belongings were listed – a brown overcoat with seven large buttons showing a woman on a horse with a man standing by the side; a brown linsey frock; a white chest flannel; white chemise; two flannel petticoats; a pair of brown stays; black ribbed wollen stockings; a black straw bonnet with black velvet trimming; and a pair of men's boots. Her underwear was marked as belonging to the Lambeth Workhouse. Inquiries there led the police to William Nichols, her estranged husband. He was a printer from the Old Kent Road, and he identified the body on 1st September. He reportedly said, "I forgive you, as you are, for what you have

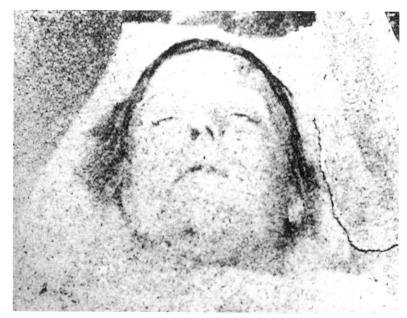

Mortuary photograph of Mary Ann Nichols.

Buck's Row in the 1960s (now named Durward Street). Mary Ann's body was found in the entrance to the garage.

been to me." as he stood over the body of Mary Ann Nichols, also known as 'Polly' Ann.

Llewellyn concluded that there was no sign of a struggle, or a bloody trail near where the body was found. The murder had presumably occurred in Buck's Row, a badly lit and narrow area, with houses only on the south side. Spratling's notes recorded the extent of her injuries:

".....her throat had been cut from left to right, two distinct cuts being on the left side. The windpipe, gullet, and spinal cord having been cut through, a bruise apparently of a thumb being on the right lower jaw, also one on the left cheek. The abdomen had been cut open from centre of bottom of ribs on right side under pelvis to left of stomach: there the wound was jagged. ...."

He goes on to point out that there were two small stabs to the genitalia, though no organs had been removed.

Detective Inspector Frederick Abberline of Scotland Yard, who was later to be placed in charge of investigations on the ground, was present at Buck's Row at 8.00am, reviewing the murder site and looking for clues. With him was Inspector Helson, J Division. There were no signs of stains apart from what was observed immediately near the body, and the two men felt that she could not have been murdered there. The inhabi-

Researcher Sue Parlour standing on the spot where Mary Ann's Body was found.
(Photo: Andy Parlour)

tants of Buck's Row had heard nothing out of the ordinary. Mrs Emma Green, of 2 Buck's Row, had been sleeping in a front room which almost overlooked the site of the murder. She had had a poor night's sleep, but had heard nothing. Walter Purkiss, the manager of Essex Wharf, opposite, had spent the night there and they had not been disturbed.

The motive was assumed to be the activity of a blackmailing gang who had sought vengeance on an unfortunate because she had not paid her dues. They saw an earlier street murder, that of Martha Tabram, on 6th August as the work of the same gang. She had been stabbed 39 times, mainly to the belly, breast and private parts by a combination of a small knife and what might have been a bayonet. Her throat had not been cut, though. The killer or killers of Nichols had fled, presumably disturbed by the arrival of Cross and Paul. They would have made their way to the Whitechapel Road and away into the night.

Nichols' last movements were recorded by the police. Apparently, she had last been seen about 11.00pm on the night of Thursday, 30 August when she was walking along Whitechapel Road. She left the Frying Pan public house at 12.30am in Brick Lane. At about 1.40am she was in the kitchen at 18 Thrawl Street. She told the deputy that she had no money yet for a bed, but to keep her one for she would soon return with the fee. "I'll soon get my doss money. See what a jolly bonnet I've got now." she quipped. She was drunk. She was last seen at 2.30am on the corner of Whitechapel Road and Osborn Street by one Ellen Holland, a lodger in the same house. She realised that Nichols was very drunk and asked her to return with her. She refused, saying that she would soon be back, and walked off in the direction of Buck's Row, crossing over the boundary into the police district of J Division. Ellen had heard the Whitechapel Church clock chime 2.30 so she was certain what time it was.

'Polly' Ann Nichols was about 43 years old when she died. Reaction to the death was one of shock and morbidity, for though life was rough and cheap in Whitechapel, people were not used to such savagery. The rumours of a blackmail gang gave way to the idea of a maniac at loose. As early as 31 August, the 'Star' ran the headline:

"A REVOLTING MURDER.
ANOTHER WOMAN FOUND HORRIBLY
MUTILATED IN WHITECHAPEL.
GHASTLY CRIMES BY A MANIAC."

By 8 September, this was the press concensus, with the East London Observer also connecting the Tabram and Nichols' murder. Morbid onlookers visited the green gates of the mortuary, or went to the spot in Buck's Row. An undercover newsreporter went with one crowd and listened as the women bent over what they thought might be bloodstained paving stones and heard them share their sympathy for the victim and their anger at the killer, as well as some fear for themselves. "No matter what she was, poor thing, 'taint for the likes of us to judge her now." Women screwed up their faces and clenched their fists, mimicking what they would do to the killer if they had him. A story ran in one paper about a gang of thieves being responsible, claiming that they had robbed a woman and laid a knife at her throat, threatening to do her like the others if she screamed. It was pure fiction, and most dismissed it as such. There was no motive for Nichols' death – she had no valuables to her name to rob.

She was buried in the City of London Cemetery, Ilford on Thursday afternoon, 6 September. A large crowd gathered to see the coffin, and the police had to surround the hearse to keep them away. Mary's father, two of her children and one of her nephews joined the procession as it made its way to Ilford, along the main road where uniformed police were stationed every few yards. The inquest had begun on 3 September, held by Wynne Baxter. This was resumed on 17 September and concluded on 22 September, with the verdict of murder against person or persons unknown. The only difficulty with this was over who was to blame for having the body washed before it was properly examined at the mortuary – James Hatfield, who had assisted with this, claimed the police instructed him to do so. The police denied it.

One man had been suggested as a suspect in these early investigations – John Pizer, known as 'Leather Apron', who was in the habit of ill treating prostitutes. He kicked and punched his victims but did not cut them. He did, however, carry a sharp knife, the sort used to trim leather, and he had threatened women with it. The 'Star' described him as "a Jewish slipper-maker who has abandoned his trade in favour of bullying prostitutes."

He was arrested on Monday 10 September (two days after the next Ripper murder) by Detective Sergeant William Thick. He had many long knives for his trade, but his claim that he had been hiding in his Mulberry Street house for days was backed up by several alibis. He also had a good alibi for the night of Polly's murder – he was in a lodging house in Holloway Road. There was not enough evidence to keep him, and he was set free. This was enough to start a dose of anti-semitism, as foreign Jews with their different customs became suspects. Whitechapel had a large Jewish, immigrant population with their own butchers, slaughterers, places of worship, and clubs. One writer, the lawyer Ingleby Oddie, described the East End of his day:

"Most of the married women wore black wigs, the idea being that they should conceal their charms from the eyes of all save their lawful husbands. Many of the women carried hens under their arms, on the way to have their throats cut by a priest according to ritual with a clean knife without a notch in the blade which was carefully shown to and inspected by all his patrons."

There was a sense of being swamped by foreignness, and when the Jewish communities moved out of the East End earlier this century, they were replaced by Asian families. The area is still one of a highly immigrant and ethnic population.

Mortuary photograph of Annie Chapman.

The Second Murder

Just before 6.00am on 8 September, 1888, John Davis, a carman employed at Leadenhall Market, went out into the backyard of 29 Hanbury Street, where his family had a room on the third floor. Seventeen people lived there at this time, with a family of five in the attic. What was once accommodation for the loom-weavers of Spitalfields had now become a lodging house frequented by local prostitutes, using the backyard or the first floor landing. Davis found Annie Chapman's body lying on her back, parallel to the fence to her left. Her dress was pulled up to her knees revealing her striped stockings. Her intestines were placed over the left shoulder. Davis raised the alarm by crossing over to Barclays, a packing case makers, and telling two workmen who ran off to Commercial Street Police Station and a small crowd gathered in the backpassage of Hanbury Street. Inspector Chandler took charge at 6.00am. A torn scrap of envelope lay beside the body, containing a screw of paper and two tablets. The scrap of envelope was marked with the crest of the Sussex Regiment, and bore the writing, 'M', 'Sp' presumably for 'Spitalfields' and the number began with '2'. The post mark was 'London, 28 August, 1888'. A folded and saturated leather apron lay nearby beside an outside tap (the apron added more fuel to the 'Leather Apron' fire but this turned out to belong to one John Richardson, who lived in the ground floor of the house. He had been into the backyard at 4.45 and seen no sign of the body then). There was also an empty nail box and a piece of flat steel – presumably unrelated to the murder.

Dr Bagster Phillips arrived at about 6.30am to inspect the body. He had this sent to the Whitechapel Infirmary Mortuary off Old Montague Street. He noted that Chapman's pocket had been sliced open, and its contents were laid out neatly by her feet. These included a piece of coarse muslin, two combs, and two polished farthings, with the Queen's head placed uppermost. The coins were mentioned in press reports of the same

The rear yard of 29,
Hanbury Street where
Annie Chapman's body
was found lying between
the steps and the fence.

34

day, though no mention was made of them in the later inquest. They reappeared in press accounts two weeks later, along with the mention of a pile of rings. Abbrasions on her finger suggest she had been wearing at least one ring, and these had been removed – but it is uncertain how many or whether they were at the murder scene.

Dr Phillips carried out his post-mortem examination and recorded the severity of the wounds she had received. Her left arm had been deliberately placed across her breast. The legs were drawn up and the face turned to the right. The tongue protruded slightly through the front teeth and was swollen, suggesting that the breathing had been interfered with before the throat was cut, though Phillips still felt that loss of blood was probably the cause of death. The neck had almost been severed by two jagged incisions from the left. A handkerchief that she had been wearing was still in place and had not been tied on afterwards. There was bruising to the upper eyelid and chest. Two bruises on the chest were the size of a man's thumb. The abdomen was ripped open and some internal organs were missing – the uterus, the upper portion of the vagina and the posterior two thirds of the bladder.

Phillips concluded that the killer had some anatomical knowledge and saw that the cuts were clean and precise, carried out with a long bladed knife of at least 6 inches, and probably like a post mortem knife or a slaughterman's knife. There was no sign of alcohol in the stomach, and she had been very ill, malnourished, and had disease of the lungs and the membranes of the brain.

Annie was identified at 11.30am on 8 September by Amelia Palmer. Amelia knew that she had been ill for Annie had complained that she would have to go to the Infirmary. John Evans, the nightwatchman of the lodging house, identified her on 9 September, as did her brother, Mr Fountain Smith of 44 Bartholomew Close, EC. Investigations revealed what was known of her last movements. She was in the kitchens of Crossingham's lodging house at 11.30pm, 7 September. She was seen in there at 12.12am by one William Stevens. She was tipsy, and she struggled with a box of pills which broke and they scattered over the floor. She picked up a torn envelope scrap and wrapped the pills in this.

By 1.35 am he had returned after going out for a drink. Timothy Donovan, the deputy at the house, saw her even more drunk, eating a baked potato. When asked for her doss money she replied, "I haven't got it. I am weak and ill and have been in the Infirmary. Don't let the bed. I'll be back soon." A watchman said that she had told him, "I won't be long Brummy. See that Tim keeps the bed for me." It is possible that she was not drunk, but ill, for the post mortem showed that she had not consumed any considerable amount of alcohol. At 5.30am she was seen outside 29, Hanbury Street talking to a man slightly taller than herself who looked foreign. He asked her, "Will you?" and she replied "Yes." Shortly afterwards, Albert Cadoche, of 27, Hanbury Street, went into his backyard and heard a voice say "No!" and then a thud. He thought nothing of it, but this had probably been the murder taking place. Dr Phillips had estimated that the death had occurred about two hours before his arrival at 6.30am but he admitted that the coldness of the night, and the large loss of blood, made it difficult to be precise.

Amelia Palmer said of the deceased, "Taking her altogether she was generally very respectable. I never heard her use bad language in my life, and I know no one who would injure her."

The inquest was held on 10 September, presided over by Dr Wynne Baxter, and continued on 12 September. John Pizer ('Leather Apron') also appeared to give evidence of his whereabouts at the time of the murder, for which he had an alibi. Abberline was present on 13 September. On 19 September Dr Phillips was called to give a more precise account of the wounds, as the room was cleared of women and boys. He expressed the opinion that the internal organs might have been removed for an illegal trade in parts of the uterus. He stated that some months earlier, an American had approached the sub-curator of a pathological museum and offered £20 for good uterus specimens.

The press began to speculate as to the killer's motive – possibly he was a religious maniac out to reap vengeance upon prostitutes, or he had some grievance against them for some ill that had befallen him. The 'Suffolk Chronicle' wrote:

"This person whoever he might be, is doubtless labouring under some terrible form of insanity, as each of the crimes has been of a most fiendish character...."

Annie Chapman was buried secretly on 14 September at Manor Park, with members of her family in attendance.

The Third Murder

At about 1.00am on Saturday 30 August, Louis Diemschutz returned with his horse and cart to Dutfield's Yard, Berner

Street. He was a salesman of cheap jewellery and the steward of
the nearby International Workingmen's Educational Club. He
had been out for the previous afternoon and evening, selling
his jewellery at Westow Hill Market, Sydenham. He was going
to leave the goods in the yard before stabling the horse at
George Yard, Gunthorpe Street. His horse hesitated at the
entrance to the yard. Diemschutz felt something soft behind
the gates with his long-handled whip. He struck a match and
saw the unconscious figure of Elizabeth Stride. He suspected
that she might be drunk, and he went to get help from the
nearby club, returning with a group of men. They found that
Stride's throat had been cut, and they tried to find a policeman. PC's Lamb and Collins finally arrived several minutes
later. Diemschutz told 'The Times' the following day that Stride
held a packet of cachous sweets in one hand. Mrs Diemschutz
later reported that she had been in the kitchen on the ground
floor of the club and she had heard no screams or sounds of
any kind.

George Dutfield, the owner of the yard, lived at nearby
Gower Walk. Ordnance Survey maps of the time suggest that
there was an alleyway between Gower Walk and the yard, and so
it presumably had a back entrance. The killer might have made
good his escape through this alley.

Attention has been brought to the report of the inquest in
the Times of 2 October 1888 by Paul Daniel (The Ripperologist
10, April 1997). This mentioned the testimony of Morris Eagle,
who returned to the club at about 12.35 am. He passed the
entrance to the yard, but saw no sign of Stride or a body. He
must have been back at the club for about 20 minutes when "a
club member named Gilleman came upstairs and said, 'There's
a dead woman lying in the yard.'..." Eagle, and a friend Isaac
Kozebrodski, rushed off and found the body, oozing blood.
They rushed off to find the police. Whether Gilleman had
found the body just prior to Diemschutz is a moot point, as it is
assumed that the latter's arrival surprised the Ripper and
stopped any further mutilations. Gilleman could have been
responding to Diemschutz's cry for help, of course, as the times
roughly match up in the testimonies. Clearly, the yard had not
attracted any onlookers when Diemschutz casually drove in.

Dr Phillips was summoned to Leman Street Police Station
and then he was sent on to Berner Street, arriving around
2.00am. Meanwhile, Dr Blackwell of Commercial Road arrived
with his assistant, Edward Johnston, after being contacted by
PC Collins. Stride was lying on her left side, as though that was

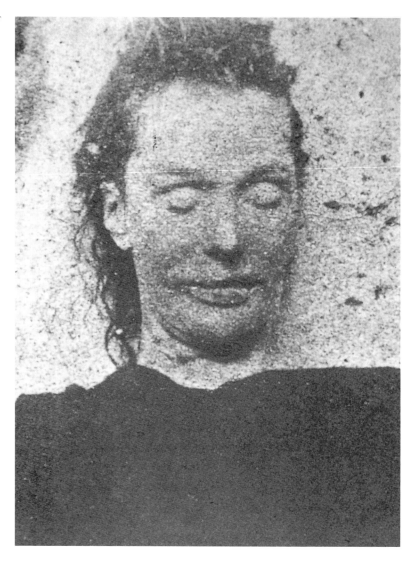

Mortuary photograph of Elizabeth Stride.

the way she had fallen. Her right hand was placed on her chest, and her legs were drawn up. The throat was deeply gashed in a single, clean cut, but Phillips saw that the knife was different – it was short, rounded and about one inch across. There was a bloodstain under the right brow where Phillips thought there was an abrasion, until this was washed and the skin was still present. There was clotted blood on the right hand, which Phillips could not explain. The throat had been cut in a few seconds, as the hand still holding the sweets might suggest. The cut was less deep than Chapman's, and there had been no attempt to sever the vertebral bone.

Dr Blackwell reckoned that she had not been dead for more than half an hour. If he arrived at Berner Street at about 1.16am, then the murder took place at about 12.46am. Though her hands were cold, there was some warmth still left in the rest of her body, including her face.

At 3.00pm, at St George's Mortuary, the post mortem was conducted with Dr Blackwell in attendance. The throat had been cut when she was lying on the ground, and some confusion reigned over how the murderer pushed her down. Her left side was extremely muddy and Phillips suggested that the killer pushed her down from her left side and stood on her left, cutting the throat and avoiding the flow of arterial blood. This would have meant that he was not bloodstained and he could have sneaked away undetected while Diemschutz was in the club getting help.

Stride's body was identified on Sunday morning, 30 September by John Arundell and Charles Preston, who also

Berner Street (now renamed Henriques Street). Elizabeth Stride's body was found just inside the entrance to Dutfield's Yard (marked by cartwheel).

resided at 32, Flower and Dean Street. The Parlours have made some new discoveries about Stride through talking with a former pastor of the Swedish Church, Sven Evander. He has recounted oral traditions about Stride and released material from the Parish Registers and the Church diary of the time. (See further in the chapter 'Five for Sorrow') The pastor, Johannis Palmer, had only been at the Church for about six months, and had caused a revolution in exactitude! He reorganised the filing and records which were somewhat slipshod prior to his arrival. The entry for 30 September is amazing. This reads:

"In the morning at 1 am Elisabeth Gustafsdotter Stride was murdered in Berner St. She had often received assistance from the Church. (Murdered by Jack the Ripper?)"

Extract from pastor's diary 30th September 1888 – In the morning at 1am Elizabeth Gustafusdotter Stride was murdered in Berner Street. She had often received assistance from the church. (Murdered by Jack the Ripper?) (Published for the first time.)

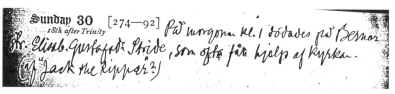

The point is that the name 'Jack the Ripper' is usually thought to have appeared with the first letters sent to the press, the 'Dear Boss' letter and the 'Saucy Jack' postcard. Extracts from these were published on 1 October, but the full reproduction only came on 4 October. The name 'Jack the Ripper' was mentioned in some newspapers on 1 October and 2 October along with extracts. We have a diary entry using the name a full day before anyone had printed it. It is likely that 'Jack the Ripper' was one of the names used for the killer on the streets of Whitechapel, along with 'Leather Apron', before the letters were ever sent! (See further on the letters in the chapter, 'From Hell'). We can also recognise a note of uncertainty as to whether Stride really was a Ripper victim in the diary extract. It is, of course, possible that the Ripper reference was written in the September 30th entry a day later, after reading the newspaper. Given that Pastor Johannis Palmer was noted for his pedantic efficiency on organisational issues and matters of record, it is unlikely. Also, the entry goes on after the reference to the Ripper. It was a long entry, and the name 'Jack the Ripper' was thus not entered later.

Investigations revealed that Stride had been seen by J. Best and John Gardner at 11.00pm, leaving the Bricklayer's Arms in Settles Street, with a young man of clerkly appearance and they headed in the direction of Commercial Road and Berner Street. The couple sheltered from the heavy rain and the men chided them saying, "That's Leather Apron getting round you!" The man was about 5'5" tall, with black moustache, sandy eyelashes, wearing a morning suit and a billycock hat. Gardner added that she had a flower pinned to her dress.

William Marshall, of 64 Berner Street saw her opposite his house at about 11.45pm with a stout man, middle aged, about 5'6" with a black cutaway cloak. He looked like a clerk as he wore no gloves, carried no stick and wore a round cap with a small peak. He heard the man say "You would say anything but your prayers" and then they walked past him, but the nearest gaslight was twenty feet away, so Marshall could not give a good description. They went off towards Dutfield's Yard.

At 12.30 am, PC William Smith saw a woman he thought was Stride talking to a man opposite the murder scene. The woman was wearing a red rose. The man was respectable in appearance, about 5'7", with overcoat, dark trousers, and a felt deerstalker on his head. He thought he was about twenty eight.The Police Gazette added that he had a dark complexion and a small dark moustache.

At 12.45, Israel Schwartz, a Hungarian Jew who had poor English, said that a man stopped and spoke to a woman in the gateway to the yard. The man tried to pull her into the street, and then threw her down on the footpath. Schwartz crossed over, and noticed a second man lighting his pipe in the shadows. The first man shouted "Lipski!" and Schwartz, panicked, ran away. The second man followed him as far as the railway arch at the end of the street. Schwartz described the first man as aged thirty, about 5'5" with dark hair and brown moustache, with dark jacket and trousers and a peaked cap. The second man was thirty five, 5'11", light brown hair, dark overcoat, old black, felt hat with a wide brim, and he held a clay pipe.

The term "Lipski" was a common term of abuse for a Jew after the death of Israel Lipski, a Jewish immigrant who had been tried for the murder of Miriam Angel on 28 June 1887, at 16 Batty Street, which ran parallel to Berner Street. Lipski lodged in the attic, and Mrs Angel on the second floor. Lipski poisoned her, and was found hiding under her bed. He was hanged on 22 August 1887. Oddly, the owners of the house were also called Lipski, though they were no relation, and they had moved away by the time of the Ripper murders. Abberline felt that Schwartz was shouted at as a warning to not get involved.

James Brown, a dock labourer, walked down Berner Street at 12.45am and noticed a couple standing by a wall, opposite the murder site. He heard her say, "Not tonight. Some other night." The man was wearing a long dark coat. Brown felt he was almost certain that the woman he saw was the same as the one lying in the mortuary.

A similar sighting was held by Mrs Fanny Mortimer of 36 Berner Street. She assumed it was of a young man and his sweetheart, standing at the corner. She also reported seeing a man walking along with a black bag. He turned out to be Leon Goldstein, for he went to Leman Street Police Station to identify himself. The bag had carried empty cigarette boxes.

Another, and more problematic witness was Matthew Packer, a fruiterer of 44 Berner Street. He was interviewed by Sergeant White at 9.00am on 30 September. Packer's statement said that he had closed his shop at 12.30am and that he had seen no one at that time nor had he heard anything suspicious. This was not what he told the 'Evening News' on October 4th. Here, he claimed to have seen Stride and to have sold some grapes to a man who was with her. The police reinterviewed him and took him to Scotland Yard for questioning. He also visited the mortuary and believed the body to be the same as the woman he had seen. Packer claimed to have sold half a pound of black grapes for 3d to a man between twenty five and thirty, about 5'7" tall with a long black coat, a soft felt hat and broad shoulders. Stride was playing with a flower which was red on the inside and white on the outside. They stood by the club for about half an hour and appeared to be listening to the music. He now said he closed about 11.30pm. Packer gave even more details to the 'Daily Telegraph' of 6 October, and they produced some sketches of the man from which Packer selected one of a man wearing an American type hat. It is impossible to know what to make of Packer's testimony, though the police said they found spat out grapes and a grape stalk in a grid at the murder site. Phillips found no grapes in Stride's stomach, but he confirmed that stains on her handkerchief were of fruitjuice.

The discrepancies in the sightings and the number of men seen have caused much debate. Swanson, at the time, felt that Schwartz was more likely to have seen the murderer, as the killing took place no more than fifteen minutes later. But, it was not certain, for she would have still had enough time to solicit again. It seems the police did not suspect the second man seen by Schwartz.

The inquest on Stride was held on October 1, 3, and 5th. Dr Phillips commented upon the dissimilarity between this and Chapman's death. Some have wondered if Stride was a Ripper victim after all, and might have been a victim of a domestic dispute. She had left Michael Kidney, a violent man she had lived with for the best part of three years, only on the Tuesday before the murder. He said that Stride often went missing, and was difficult when drunk. He had even tried to padlock her in. On October 1, he turned up drunk at Leman Street police station, claiming that he had heard something which might have prevented her death. When pressed for information, he was not forthcoming.

Most Ripperologists include Stride as a Ripper killing, because of the torn throat from the left and the similarity in appearance of the man seen at the scene with other reports. The senior police at the time also saw this as a Ripper murder – though they often counted Tabram as a Ripper victim, too . The 'saucy Jacky' postcard posted on 1 October 1888 (see 'From Hell' chapter) refers to a double event and claims the two victims for the Ripper. The lack of mutilations are explained as a result of the killer being disturbed, though why a smaller, short bladed knife should have been used remains a mystery, when, only a short time later, that same night, another murder took place that bore all the unmistakeable hallmarks of a Ripper killing.

The Fourth Murder

The night of 29 September was to become known as the night of the 'Double Event' for a second body was found soon after that of Elizabeth Stride. At 1.40am, PC James Harvey walked his beat along Duke's Place and Church Passage into Mitre Square. He saw no sign of anything out of the ordinary. At approximately 1.45am, PC Edward Watkins came into the square from the opposite side. He discovered the body of Catharine Eddowes in the south west corner. He immediately approached George Morris, the nightwatchman for Kearly and Tonge's, and sent him off to find help. Morris went out into Aldgate and found PC Harvey and PC Holland. Dr. Sequeira was brought from Jewry Street – he claimed that he had arrived at 1.45am. The incident was reported to Bishopsgate Police Station at 1.55am, and the police surgeon, F. Gordon Brown was sent for. Inspector Collard reached the square at 2.03am. Three boot

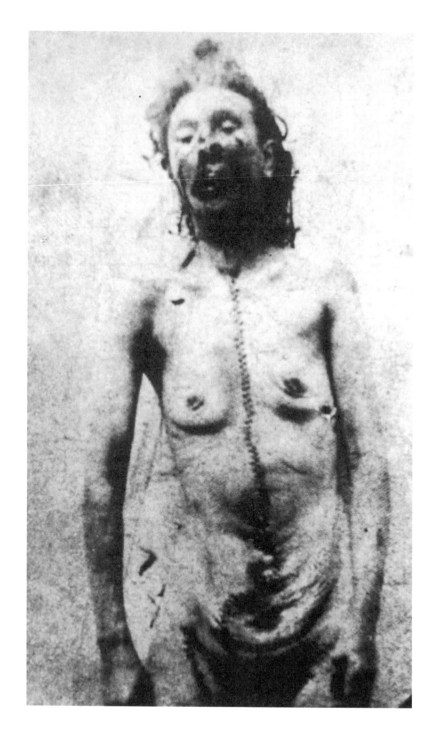

*Mortuary photograph of
Catharine Eddowes.*

buttons, a thimble and a mustard tin containing pawn tickets were found near the body. The tickets were for an Emily Birrell's man's shirt, and for John Kelly's boots. These helped to identify the body. The body was on its back, the head turned to the left. The right leg was bent at the knee, and the palms were open and upwards as though that is how she had fallen. The abdomen was exposed and the intestines were drawn out and placed over the right shoulder. A piece was cut out and placed between the body and the left arm, apparently on purpose. The throat had been cut, and clotted blood was on the pavement by the side of the head. Her various possessions were still about her person, including trinkets such as a small tooth comb, a tin match box, a red leather cigarette case and two short clay pipes. There was still warmth in the body, and Brown reckoned that she had died within the half hour.

The body was taken to Golden Lane Mortuary, and a piece of her ear dropped out of her clothing when it was removed. The face was mutilated. A cut went through the lower left eyelid of about a 1/4". The upper eyelid was scratched, and the right eyelid was cut by 1/2". There was a deep cut from the bridge of the nose down to the jaw on the right side. The tip of the nose was loose, and the upper lip was split. Two triangular flaps of skin were cut into the cheeks.

Various internal organs had been stabbed and cut, especially the liver. The left kidney was taken out and removed. Brown noted that the right kidney was pale and bloodless. Part of the uterus had also been removed. These could have served no useful purpose. Brown concluded that the killer had some anatomical and medical knowledge to know where to find the organs and to know how to extract the kidney so carefully. His post mortem report says, "It required a great deal of medical knowledge to have removed the kidney and to know where it was placed. Such a knowledge might be possessed by someone in the habit of cutting up animals."

Two other doctors who were at the post mortem, Drs Sequeira and Sedgwick Saunders disagreed that any skill had been shown by the murderer. When questioned at the inquest, Brown refused to admit any skill to the killer, but affirmed that some anatomical knowledge must have been present.

Part of Eddowes' apron was missing. It had been torn almost in half. The other piece was found at 2.50am by PC Long in the doorway of Wentworth Model Dwellings in Goulston Street. Above this was written a chalk message, which became referred to as the Goulston Street graffito. The apron was stained in blood and was an exact match to Eddowes'. The graffito read:

"The Juwes are the men That Will not be Blamed for nothing."

Thus agreed the report of the Metropolitan Police and the Home Office. The City police reported it as:

Catharine's body lay in front of gate in corner of Mitre Square.

The corner in Mitre Square as it is today.
(Photo: Andy Parlour)

"The Juwes are not The men That Will be Blamed for nothing."

While the words were copied down by hand, requests to have them photographed were refused by the Metropolitan Police, in whose district the writing lay. Superintendent Arnold feared that the largely Jewish inhabitants of the buildings would riot for this would revive the anti-semitism and the whole Leather Apron saga again. He had a man ready with a sponge. Sir Charles Warren arrived on the scene – the only time he actually visited a murder site – and authorised that the writing should be erased straight away for it might inflame the Jewish residents of the area when they rose for work in the next few hours. He had a point, but it remains a mystery why permission was refused for a photograph to be taken.

Interestingly, not all were agreed that this was the work of the Ripper. Arnold thought it a hoax, and Detective Constable Walter Dew felt it was one of many bogus messages which had been written up around the place.

Investigations revealed that Eddowes had returned to

47

Above left: *Wentworth Buildings, Goulston Street, site of the graffito.*

Above right: *Site of graffito as it is today. (Photo: Andy Parlour)*

London with her common law husband, John Kelly, on 28 September. They had been hop picking in Kent. Eddowes went to the Shoe Lane Workhouse to find a bed, and said, enigmatically, "I have come back to earn the reward offered for the apprehension of the Whitechapel murderer. I think I know him." At 8.00am on 29 September, she arrived at Cooney's Lodging House and met Kelly. She took a pair of his boots to pawn in Church Street, and received 2/6d and she used the name 'Jane Kelly'. By 2.00pm, they had used up the money, and Eddowes said that she was going to Bermondsey to borrow money from her daughter, Annie.

Wherever she went, Annie did not see her, and she emerged again at 8.30pm, drunk and disorderly outside 29 Aldgate High Street. She was impersonating a fire engine, and had attracted a small crowd. PC Robinson stopped her trying to sleep there and took her to Bishopsgate Police Station. She was locked in a cell and slept. At 12.15am., she was awake, and singing to herself. At 12.30 she asked when she could be released, to be told by PC George Hutt that she would go when she was capable of taking care of herself. He released her at 1.00am, and she gave her name as Mary Ann Kelly. She added "I shall get a damn fine hiding when I get home." As she left, her last words heard by anybody were, "All right. Good night, old cock."

At about 1.35 am, three men, Joseph Lawende, Joseph Hyam Levy and Harry Harris saw her talking to a man in the entrance to Church Passage, leading into Mitre Square. She had her hand on his chest. The three had stayed late at the Imperial Club, Duke's Place, because of the heavy rain. Only Lawende had taken in the man's features. He saw a man of medium build and sailory appearance with a pepper and salt loose jacket, a grey cloth cap with a peak, and a reddish necker-chief. He was about thirty, 5'7-8" tall, with fair complexion and a moustache, and his appearance was shabby.

There is one more, rather apocryphal description that is difficult to place. Shortly after the death of Sergeant White in 1919, an article appeared in the 'People's Journal' by "a Scotland Yard Man". This claimed that White had been one of the undercover police watching the streets. Officers disguised as working men walked the streets and frequented the public houses. The article refers to a surveillance of an alley off the Whitechapel Road with two undercover men placed there in hiding. White was going in to get their report when he saw a stranger who he felt was rather sinister.

"He was walking quickly but noiselessly, apparently wear-ing rubber shoes which were rather rare in those days....He was about five feet ten inches in height, and was dressed rather shabbily though it was obvious that the material of his clothes was good. Evidently a man who had seen better days....

His face was long and thin, nostrils rather delicate, and his hair was jet black. His complexion was inclined to be sallow, and altogether the man was foreign in appearance. The most extraordinary thing about him, however, was the extraordinary brilliance of his eyes.... The man was slightly bent at the shoulders, though he was obviously quite young – about 33 at the most – and gave one the idea of having been a student or professional man. His hands were snow white and the fingers long and tapering..."

As the man passed White, he tried to engage him in con-versation. The man scowled and said simply, "Good night!". White continued:

"His voice was a surprise to me. It was soft and musical, with just a tinge of melancholy in it, and it was the voice of a

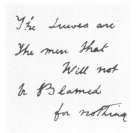

A police copy of the Goulston Street graffito.

man of culture – a voice altogether out of keeping with the squalid surroundings of the East End. As he turned away, one of the police officers came out of the house he had been in, and walked a few paces into the darkness of the alley. "Hello! what is this?" he cried, and then he called in startled tones for me to come.

In the East End we are used to some shocking sights but the sight I saw made the blood in my veins turn to ice. At the end of the cul-de-sac huddled against the wall, there was a body of a woman, and a pool of blood was streaming along the gutter from her body. It was clearly another of those terrible murders. I remembered the man I had seen, and started after him as fast as I could run, but he was lost to sight in the dark labyrinth of East End mean streets."

It is impossible to place this incident with any exactitude in the Ripper sequence of murders. Some suggest it belongs to the Mitre Square killing because of the mention of a cul-de-sac, but this is a piece of floating tradition that, while it might contain a kernel of truth, is difficult to assess (though see Appendix One for possible confirmation that this tradition did take place in Mitre Square) but Donald Rumbelow in his 'Complete Jack The Ripper' states: "Clearly it refers to the Mitre Square murder, as it is the only murder that fits the facts."

'The Illustrated Police News' of October 6th, 1888 carried a column discussing the views of Dr George Savage, who had written an article on 'Homicidal Mania' in a forthcoming 'Fortnightly Review'. He pointed out that some murderers behaved as though suffering from mania, though an actual killer's disease could not be classified as such. He pointed out that infants could show terrible cruelty, such as pulling wings off flies, baking frogs, boring the eyes out of birds and pouring boiling oil over cats. These children might grow up disturbed enough to become killers. There were also cases of people performing terrible deeds whilst not in their right mind, an example being given of a mother who was taking a knife to cut a slice of bread for her infant when she was stricken by an epileptic attack and she cut off the child's legs without knowing what she was doing, and she ended up at Broadmoor. The theories of Professor Benedikt were also discussed, whereby murderers' brains resembled those of bears. The Medical Congress of 1880 gave this short shrift but concurred that the brains of murderers could be of a lower type. The newspaper goes on to say, "The apparently purposeless character of the crimes by which we have lately been shocked goes far to suggest that their perpetrator – assuming for the moment that there has been but one perpetrator – is really one of these unhappy creatures." The Victorians were clearly shocked and perplexed by the cruel and pointless killings. The killer must have been a maniac.

The Fifth Murder

At 10.45am on Friday 9 November, 1888, Thomas Bowyer was sent to 13, Miller's Court to collect the rent. The room was small and dismal, with a contemporary account of it as follows:

"This latter place was a dismal hole seen on a dark, wet, gloomy afternoon. It consisted of one very small room, with a small window, a fire, a chair, and a bed. it was sombre and sinister, unwholesome and depressing, and it was approached by a single doorstep from a grimy covered passage leading from Dorset Street into a courtyard."

Bowyer was an older man, being an army pensioner, who worked for John McCarthy who owned the Chandlers shop at 27 Dorset Street which was situated at the entrance to Miller's

The mutilated body of Mary Jane Kelly(?) taken at Miller's Court.

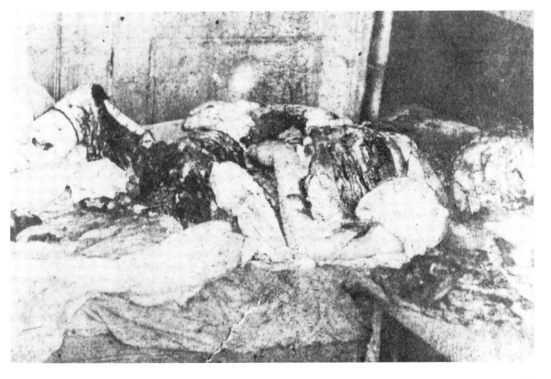

Court. The McCarthys owned all six houses found in this quadrangle. Mary Jane Kelly was six weeks behind with the rent, which was remarkable for those days as landlords were ruthless and callous in collecting their money. It is also slightly odd that Bowyer was sent on the Friday morning on the day of the Lord Mayor's Parade. He knocked on the door and got no answer, and the door was locked. He pushed his hand through a broken window pane and pulled back the curtain, which, in fact, was an old coat hung there for the purpose. The room was small, being 12' by 10', containing a bed, a fireplace with grate, a cupboard , a small table, a disused washstand and a few chairs. The boards were bare and filthy and a cheap print hung above the fireplace, 'The Fisherman's Widow'. Bowyer stepped back with shock, for he could see a mutilated body lying in a pool of blood. He immediately went to John McCarthy, saying, "Governor, I knocked at the door and could not make any answer. I looked through the window and saw a lot of blood." McCarthy exclaimed, "Good God, do you mean that, Harry?" before going to look through the window himself. He returned white faced. "Go at once to the police station and fetch someone there," he ordered.

Bowyer found Inspector Walter Beck at Commercial Street Police Station. Bowyer stammered in shock, "Another one. Jack the Ripper. Awful. Jack McCarthy sent me." Walter Dew was also present and the two men set out to see for themselves, arriving after eleven. Dr Phillips arrived at 11.15, and Abberline was there by 11.30. No attempt was made to force the door until 1.30pm. Abberline was to reveal the reason for the delay. They expected bloodhounds to be brought, for there was talk of Warren introducing them to try to track the killer, and Phillips advised him to wait to test the dogs before anyone else went in. At 1.30, Superintendent Arnold arrived, explaining that the dogs were not available, and he gave orders for the door to be forced. McCarthy opened it with an axe. This, in fact, was an unnecessary act, for though the door locked automatically when shut by a spring lock, it could be opened easily by reaching through the broken window. The key had been missing for some time, apparently.

Phillips was the first person inside, and he tried to suppress details of the mutilation as it was so horrific. All that he said at the inquest was that the cause of death was the severance of the cartoid artery. The large amount of blood on the bed and the floor showed that the body had been moved after the death blow. Some post mortem notes by Dr Thomas

Entrance to Miller's Court, Dorset Street.

Rare photo of Miller's Court.

Bond, Police Surgeon to A Division (Westminster), were found in 1987, and these give a full report of the injuries.

The body was naked in the middle of the bed, with the shoudlers flat, but the body inclined to the left. The head was turned to the left and the left arm was placed across the abdomen. The fingers of the right hand were clenched – possibly showing that the victim had been suffocated before-hand. The legs were wide apart.

The flesh on the thighs and the abdomen had been stripped away and piled on the table nearby. The abdominal cavity had been emptied and the organs were placed at various points around the body – the uterus and kidneys were under the head, the liver between the feet, the intestines by the right side. The breasts had been cut off, one being placed under the head and the other by the right foot (though some press reports at the time wrongly suggested that the breasts were placed upon the table). The intestines were pulled out and placed at the right side. The bed clothing on the far right was heavily bloodstained, and there was a pool of blood about 2 metres square on the floor. There were blood splashes on the wall in line with the bed. The second photograph taken of the body went missing and returned in 1988, sent anonymously to Scotland Yard from someone in Croydon, Surrey. This shows clearly that Kelly's left thigh-bone had been split from the hip downwards, exposing the marrow cavity. This suggests a wound by an axe rather than a knife. N. P. Warren has drawn attention to this quoting from the 'Globe' of 16th February 1891. This describes a visit to the exhibits of the murders at Scotland Yard: "a hatchet by the door... used by the Whitechapel murderer to hack and disfigure the ...poor girl who fell a victim to his fiendish fury in Dorset Street." The hatchet was among the items found in Kelly's room. Knife and axe took its toll on the victim, disfiguring and butchering her completely.

The police also found that a fire had been blazing in the grate that had been hot enough to melt the solder at the joints in the spout and handle of a kettle. The remains of some clothing were found there, including a woman's bonnet, and part of a skirt. Kelly's clothes were draped over a chair at the

Dorset Street looking towards Providence Row Refuge.

55

foot of the bed. Abberline assumed that the fire had been lit to provide illumination, but it is hard to imagine why this risk would have been taken when the candlelight available should have sufficed. The clothes might have been some of those which the prostitute Maria Harvey had left there when she stayed with Kelly earlier. She listed these at the inquest – two men's dirty shirts, a boy's shirt, a black overcoat, a black crepe bonnet and a girl's white petticoat. The overcoat was the only item found in the room by the police, but it is hard to imagine that the other garments alone would have burned for so long with such ferocity. If the bloodstained clothes had been burnt, then they would probably have smouldered. There was no sign of these in the grate.

Kelly was well known in the area, and was about 24 years old. She was attractive, and Walter Dew reports that she was good-looking and often paraded around the area with one or two friends. She never wore a hat and always sported a spotlessly clean, white apron. It is odd that a bonnet was burning in the grate if Kelly did not wear one.

The inquest was held three days later by the coroner Dr Robert MacDonald. MacDonald was in charge of the recently created North Eastern Middlesex district, which administered inquests in Shoreditch and Whitechapel. The inquest, on 12 November at Shoreditch Town Hall did not go smoothly. One Shoreditch parishioner who had been called on jury service complained that as the murder had happened in Whitechapel, the inquest should have been held there. MacDonald answered curtly, "Do you think that we do not know what we are doing here? The jury are summoned in the ordinary way, and they have no business to object. If they persist in their objection I shall know how to deal with them." They did persist, also arguing that Dr Baxter should have performed the inquest. MacDonald replied, "jurisdiction lies where the body lies, not where it was found." As the body lay in a mortuary under his jurisdiction, it was in order for him to preside.

The remarkable thing was the speed of the inquest. MacDonald wrapped it up in half a day! People had expected this to drag out for several days like the others. When Dr Phillips stated his minimalist observation that the cause of death was the severing of the cartoid artery, MacDonald pressed the jury for a decision. The press were surprised at this haste, and the 'Daily Telegraph' pointed out how odd it was "that the inquest should have been closed before an opportunity was given to the relatives of the deceased to identify the body." It was also commented upon that the haste might have neglected to collect the comments of important witnesses that might still have come forward, as one did on the very day of the inquest at 6.00pm. The body was buried on 19 November at Walthamstow Roman Catholic Cemetery. No member of Kelly's family was present at the funeral.

Investigations revealed that Kelly had been observed several times on the night of the murder. Bowyer had seen her talking to a man in Miller's Court on the afternoon of 7 November, whom he described as having a dark moustache and "very peculiar eyes". The man was late twenties and very smartly dressed. Kelly's lover, Joseph Barnett, had moved out of 13 Miller's Court on 30 October over a row about the women that she was inviting home to stay. He mentioned a Julia (possibly the Julia Van Teurney who was living opposite on the night of the murder) and a Mrs Harvey. He kept seeing Kelly and their relationship was amicable. He visited her between 7.30–8.00pm on 8 November, and was possibly seen drinking with Kelly later on in the 'Horn of Plenty', according to a tailor from Dorset Street, one Maurice Lewis. At 11.45pm Mary Ann Cox saw her return with a stout, shabby man in his thirties, with a carroty moustache and a billycock hat. The man carried a quart pail of beer. Kelly was inebriated and she told Mary Ann that she was going to sing. Several witnesses relate that they heard singing from Kelly's room between midnight and 1.00am. She sang, "Only a violet I plucked from my mother's grave..." One neighbour nearly went in to complain at 12.30am.

A key witness turned up on the day of the inquest, at 6.00pm at Commercial Street Police Station. This was George Hutchinson, a labourer from Victoria Home in Commercial Street. He described seeing Kelly in Commercial Street at 2.00am. She called him by name and asked for sixpence. She walked along, and picked up a client near Thrawl Street. Hutchinson watched him by the light coming from the 'Queen's Head' as they walked past. He followed them to Dorset Street and watched them go into 13 Miller's Court. Hutchinson waited across the road for 45 minutes, sheltering from the rain in the passageway by Crossingham's lodging house. His description runs as follows:

"A man coming in the opposite direction to Kelly tapped her on the shoulder and said something to her, they both burst out laughing. I heard her say 'alright' to him and the man said 'you will be alright for what I have told you'. He then placed his right hand around her shoulders. He also had a kind of small parcel in his left hand with a kind of strap round it..... They both came past me and the man hung down his head with his hat over his eyes. I stooped down and looked him in the face. He looked at me very stern..... They both stood at the corner of the court for about 3 minutes. He said something to her. She said 'alright my dear come along you will be comfortable'. He then placed his arm on her shoulder and gave her a kiss. She said she had lost her handkerchief. He then pulled his handkerchief, a red one, out and gave it to her. They both went up to the court together....Description, age about 34 or 35, height 5ft 6, complexion pale. Dark eyes and eye lashes. Slight moustache curled up each end and hair dark. Very surly looking. Dress, long dark coat; collar and cuffs trimmed astrakhan and a dark jacket under, light waistcoat, dark trousers, dark felt hat turned down in the middle, button boots and gaiters with white buttons, wore a very thick gold chain, white linen collar, black tie with horseshoe pin, respectable appearance, walked very sharp, Jewish appearance..."

Abberline later interviewed Hutchinson and felt that his testimony was true.

This was the last person to definitely see Kelly alive. Two other women saw some people in Miller's Court or Dorset Street that could have been Kelly and the killer. Sarah Lewis went into the Court at 2.30am. She saw a man and a woman, and she thought that the man was similar to a man who had

Police ambulance of the time.

frightened her the previous week. Mrs Kennedy went into the Court to visit her parents between 3.00 and 3.30am. She saw an intoxicated man with a dark moustache talking to a woman in Dorset Street, saying, "Are you coming?" and she turned away. Another woman was with her. She also felt that this man was like one who had frightened her in Bethnal Green the previous Wednesday. Just before 4.00am, Sarah Lewis, Mrs Kennedy and Elizabeth Prater, who lodged in the room above Kelly's, all heard a cry of "Murder!".

There were some other witnesses who claimed, amazingly, to have seen Kelly alive the morning after the murder. Caroline Maxwell of 14, Dorset Street, reported seeing her between 8.00am and 8.30am that morning, wearing a green bodice, a dark skirt and a maroon crossover shawl. Kelly had told her that she had "the horrors of drink" upon her. Maxwell told her to have another to steady her stomach, but Kelly said she had tried that but it made her vomit. Maxwell told her "I pity your condition". She saw Kelly again, about an hour later, talking to a stout man in dark clothes and a plaid coat outside the 'Britannia'. The coroner pressed her, believing that she must be mistaken. Maxwell swore she was right, for she was returning some china borrowed from a house opposite. 'The Times' report has her justifying her memory by the fact that it was the time her husband went out to work, and so she was sure of the time. Walter Dew believed that she was a sensible woman of good reputation, but he said she must be mistaken.

Maurice Lewis, the tailor, also said that he had seen Kelly in the 'Britannia' about 10.00am. One other witness, unnamed in 'The Times', also said she saw Kelly between 8.00am and 10.00am on the morning of the 9th.

Some Ripperologists have suggested that the body was not Kelly's at all, but a substitute. The testimony of the witnesses, plus the unrecognisable features of the corpse, coupled with the rushed inquest, with no family members being present to identify the body or see it buried, has made people wonder. Even Colin Wilson, who is not given to conspiracy theories on this matter, has remarked, "At least, the mutilated body found in 13, Miller's Court was buried on that day" when relating the details of Kelly's burial.

Colin Kendall, in an article in 'The Criminologist' Autumn 1988, argued that Maxwell's testimony was trustworthy and that Kelly did not die. Melvyn Fairclough also asserts this in 'The Ripper and the Royals', adding that the substitute was one Winifred May Collis, a young, pregnant housemaid friend. This name is suggested by the problematic Abberline Diaries (see chapter, 'Rogues Gallery') but no record of this person's existence can be found. Also, there was no evidence that the body in 13, Miller's Court was pregnant. John Wilding also thought that Kelly escaped, in his book, 'Jack the Ripper Revealed'.

The Parlours support this theory, and suggest that the body was of one Winifred Collyer. She was born on 17 August 1868 in the parish of St Mark, Kennington, to Henry and Elizabeth Collyer. The 1881 census reveals that the Collyers were living round the corner from Dorset Street, and Winifred was 11 or 12 years old. In the 1891 census, the family had moved and no record can be traced of their whereabouts. It might be the case that she was the Winifred in Kelly's room on the fateful night, and the source for 'Winifred Collis' in the Abberline Diaries was almost right.

The leading question is why someone else died in 13, Miller's Court, and not Kelly. Was Kelly out looking for a client when the girl took up by misfortune with the Ripper, or was Kelly allowed to escape for some mysterious reason?

There is a persistent testimony to the general appearance of the killer – aged in the late twenties or early thirties, stout or broad shouldered, about 5'7", striking eyes, a moustache, dressed in a long, dark coat, and wearing a hat – either a peaked cap, or a felt hat with wide brim (though occasionally a billycock hat or a deerstalker). Some reports have him smartly dressed, cultured and clerkly. Some suggest he was shabbily dressed. There are small differences in the type of apparel and the colour of the moustache on different occasions. We might be dealing with two different men (remembering the testimony of Israel Schwartz) and it is also possible that they deliberately dressed in different guises or wore different coloured facial hair, which might also have been a disguise. If we are dealing with a highly devious, witty, criminal mind, then anything is possible. There is also a recurring mention of the colour red – a red flower, a red scarf, and a red handkerchief.

Five For Sorrow

Who were the Five Victims?

Whitechapel "unfortunates".

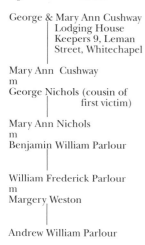

George & Mary Ann Cushway
Lodging House
Keepers 9, Leman
Street, Whitechapel

Mary Ann Cushway
m
George Nichols (cousin of
first victim)

Mary Ann Nichols
m
Benjamin William Parlour

William Frederick Parlour
m
Margery Weston

Andrew William Parlour

The Ripper claimed five victims, all 'unfortunates', working as prostitutes and lodging in various houses or staying with various men in the Whitechapel area. An obvious question is to ask if they knew each other and were connected in any way. If the Ripper were a random serial killer, he could have chosen any women out of the thousands in Whitechapel. He picked five, and five particular ones who all lived very near to each other. Mary Ann Nichols, Elizabeth Stride and Catharine Eddowes were all lodging in Flower and Dean Street in the latter part of 1888. Annie Chapman lived in Dorset Street, and Mary Jane Kelly was in Miller's Court, just off Dorset Street. We are talking about a very small area of Whitechapel, around the corner and across the road from each other. This has led some writers to assume that the women must have been aquainted with one another. They might have been a special group of friends, and something made the killer pick them all off.

We have no definite proof that they were a particular group of friends, though, surely, they would have known each other if only in passing. No one has yet explored their characters and backgrounds to see if there might be anything that might have drawn them together. An examination of their life histories might, indeed, reveal some details that would make them seek out each other's company, thrown together for mutual support in a difficult environment. We shall present a circumstantial case for them being close friends.

Mary Ann Nichols (1845–88)

Mary Ann, or 'Polly' was the daughter of blacksmith, Edward Walker and his wife Ann (née King), of Dean Street. (They had married in 1826 at Lambeth when Ann was only 13 years old.) In 1864, then aged 19, Mary married William Nichols, a printer from Bouverie Street, where they lived for a while. They later lived with her father at 131 Trafalgar Street, Walworth. Between 1874-1880, they lived at 6D Peabody Buildings, Stamford Street, in Lambeth. The couple had five children, Edward John, Percy George, Alice Esther, Eliza Sarah and Henry Alfred.

The first sign of strain in the marriage appeared in 1877 when William eloped briefly with a woman who had helped with Eliza's birth. The eldest son soon moved out and lived with his maternal grandfather and did not speak to William until after his mother's death.

Mary was drinking heavily by 1877, and she left home five or six times. The couple separated in 1880. William had the other children, and paid Mary five shillings a week until 1882, when he heard that she was making a living by prostitution. She summonsed him for maintainance, but lost her case because of her immoral lifestyle.

Her whereabouts after 1880 are very well documented apart from two brief spells from 31 May 1881 to 24 April 1881, and from 12 July 1888 to 1 August 1888. She worked as a domestic help for Samuel and Sarah Cowdry in Wandsworth just prior to 12 July 1888, and she seemed to be getting on fine at first, writing to her father:

"I just write to say you will be glad to know that I am settled in my new place, and going all right up to now. My people went out yesterday, and have not returned, so I am left in charge. It is a grand place inside, with trees and gardens back and front..."

She absconded, later, stealing some clothes worth £3 10s, and the reason might have been drink. The Cowdrys were teetotal.

William (Inker) Nichols, husband of Mary Ann. (Published for the first time from family collection.)

Her introduction to the Cowdrys might have been through the Detective Walter Dew, who was with the Whitechapel CID from 1887. He would have known some of the women. Dew lived in Wandsworth, as did the Cowdrys. Samuel Cowdry was a Clerk of Works at New Scotland Yard, and the two men might have travelled into work on the same train.

Mary might have lodged with the Cushways between 12 July and 1 August 1888. George and Mary Ann Cushway owned a lodging house at 9 Leman Street. Their daughter, Mary Ann, had married George Nichols, William Nichols' cousin. It is possible that Mary Ann Nichols stayed with them when desperate, though they would not have approved of her drinking or soliciting. It would have cramped her style to stay there too long.

Edward John, Mary Ann's eldest son. (Published for the first time from family collection.)

Another possible link between Nichols and the Cowdrys might be through the Manchee family. Sarah Cowdry's maiden name was Manchee, and their niece, Lucy Manchee, stayed with them at the time that Nichols was in service there. Sarah's brother, Daniel Manchee was a renowned mantle maker in the East End, who would have serviced various houses. A family such as the Cushways would probably have done business with him.

By August 1888 she was at 56, Flower and Dean Street, a doss house that allowed men and women to sleep together.

It is interesting that, after her death, her father did not blacken her name but showed her sympathy. Her eldest son always took her side, and her youngest son also stayed with his grandfather at the time of her death. William never denied

The Cowdry's home in Wandsworth where Mary Ann was in service May–July 1888. (Published for the first time.) (Photo: Andy Parlour)

deserting her, and presumably starting the trouble. She was also known as a clean women. Dr Llewellyn commented at the post mortem that her thighs were surprisingly clean for someone of her class.

She had known a secure and comfortable, though not affluent, lifestyle with her husband and children before his adultery turned her to the bottle and a rapidly downward spiral began that led to prostitution.

Annie Chapman (1841–1888)

She was born Eliza Anne Smith. Her father was George Smith, a Lifeguardsman. He married Ruth Chapman, her mother, in 1842 and the family moved to Windsor in 1856.

64

She married John Chapman, a relative of her mother's, and a head coachman, at All Saints, Knightsbridge. They lived in West London until 1881, then moving to Windsor.

She had two daughters, though one died in childhood, and a crippled son. The girl, Emily, died in 1882, and shortly before the death, Annie abandoned the family and moved back to London. She received occasional allowances from her husband until his death in 1886. She lived as a hawker, selling crochet work, matches and flowers. She only occasionally turned to prostitution. Some accused her of alcoholism before she left the family, but other aquaintances said that she was only occasionally drunk.

By September 1888 she was lodging at Crossingham's Lodging House at 35, Dorset Street. According to the 'Times' report, her son had been sent away to a Cripple's Home, and her daughter to an unnamed school in France. Annie had known a secure upbringing and a comfortable life in West London and Windsor before something made her snap and leave home.

Elizabeth Stride (1843–1888)

Elizabeth was a Swede, born to middle class parents, Gustaf Ericsson and Beata Carlsdotter, being known as Elizabeth Gustafsdotter. She had two brothers, Carl and Svante, and an older sister, Anna Christina. They lived at Stora Tumlehed farm near Gothenburg.

Between 1860 and 1862, she was listed as a domestic servant in different parts of Gothenburg. In March 1865, she was listed as a prostitute no. 97 in the area, twice being admitted to hospital with venereal disease. She also gave birth to a stillborn girl.

She came to London in 1866, claiming that she was in domestic service to a foreign gentleman in Hyde Park. However, the Swedish Church in Prince's Square (now Svedenborg Square) has an oral tradition that Stride used to frequent the Gothenburg docks as a prostitute until she met an English sailor and travelled to England with him. He threw her out when he realised that she still went with other men. In 1869, she married John Thomas Stride, living at 67, Gower Street. She later told friends that they had run a coffee shop in Chrisp Street, Poplar (there is evidence that she was admitted briefly to Poplar Workhouse in March 1877).

In May 1878, the steamer Princess Alice sank off Woolwich. She said that her husband and two children had drowned in this disaster, but the only record of the death of a John Thomas Stride was actually in Bromley-by-Bow in 1884 in the sick Asylum, whose last given address was Poplar Workhouse. Also, she did not claim from the subscription fund for relatives and survivors. It is true that the News Agency report of 8 October 1888 mentions the story of the sinking, and seems to believe this, but they were simply telling it as they heard it. She also claimed that her two children were being privately educated in South London at the expense of the Swedish Church, a fact denied by Sven Olsson, their verger. The Parish register of the Swedish Church mentions that in 1880 she was "Helped by the Church because of her husband's illness." (?) Neal Sheldon has located the entry for Liz Stride in the 1881 census. Elizabeth and John Thomas Stride were living at 69, Usher Road, Old Ford Road, Bow. Stride was then aged 34, and she had no children.

Extract from Swedish Church Parish Register 1879. "Gustafsdotter Elizabeth. Housemaid. Helped by the church because of her husband's illness." (Published for the first time.)

From 1885 she lived with Michael Kidney at 33 Dorset Street, though she often left him to get drunk or to see other men. In 1887-1888 she had eight convictions for drunkenness from the Thames Magistrates Court. Witnesses also state that she lodged at 32 Flower and Dean Street on and off since 1882. She was lodging there in September 1888.

The Parlours have traced various traditions about Stride through Sven Evander, the Pastor of the Swedish Church in London from 1956-1981. The Pastor at the time was Johannis Palmer, and the verger, or 'klockare' (bellringer) was Sven Olsson. He was married with two daughters and one of his duties was to look after the reading rooms and the Swedish seamen's mission which were situated in a large 3 storey house on the corner of the square opposite the church. He and his family lived on the top floor. The mission had the unusual right to dispense alcohol 24 hours a day but only to the Scandanavian seamen. Stride was a frequent visitor to the reading rooms where she kept up with the Swedish newspapers. She was known as a highly intelligent woman who spoke English with hardly a trace of an accent. It is also rumoured that she used this venue to pick up Swedish men as clients as she felt easier with them. One of Sven Olsson's duties was to distribute welfare money to the Swedish community and these payments were all entered in an accounts book by the verger. Apparently, Stride often took advantage of this welfare, and she had been to the church for a handout on 20 September and was given one shilling and a Swedish hymn book (It was the custom to give a Swedish Bible or hymn book when giving welfare, and this hymn book was in her belongings after her death. The 'East London Advertiser' of 6 October 1888 mentioned the book; "Michael Kidney, the man with whom Stride lived, identified the Swedish hymnbook as belonging to the deceased. She gave it to Mrs Smith the previous Tuesday saying she was going away. She gave it to Mrs Smith, not as a gift, but to take care of."). The Swedish Church was only 200-300 yards from the spot in Berner Street where Liz's body was found on 30 September.

Michael Kidney said that he believed she was of superior birth to him, and that she was fluent in Yiddish. Everyone knew she was Swedish, even though she spoke such good English. She

Swedish Church Records for 20th September 1888 showing Elizabeth Stride (bottom of list) receiving 1 shilling. (Published for the first time.)

67

The Swedish Seaman's Mission, Prince's Square, Whitechapel. It was here Liz Stride obtained assistance from Verger Sven Olsson who lived on the top floor with his family.

was 45 when she died, as can be ascertained from the Register of Burials for the East London Cemetery Company. She was known as 'Long Liz' as she was tall, and one Thomas Bates, a watchman at 32, Flower and Dean Street, declared that she had been clean and hardworking. She was usually a charwoman, but she went on the streets when she was desperate. Though usually quiet, she would sometimes disappear for a few months and then reappear, and people were glad to see her back.

Stride is difficult to assess. If her stories of running a coffee shop are at all to be believed, then she had known a more prosperous life and lost it all through one reason or another. Even if this was a lie, she was born into Swedish middle-class stock and had a degree of education and intelligence. It is intriguing to note that she had lapsed into prostitution in the early 1860s in Sweden for some reason whether through family difficulties or a character defect. There are missing pieces of information about this woman, but the same pattern emerges of one who had known security and then had lost it.

Catharine Eddowes (1842–1888)

Catharine was born in Wolverhampton, and then moved to Bermondsey when she was two years old. Her father, George Eddowes, was a tinplate worker. Her mother, Catharine, died in

1855 and most of the children in the family went into the Bermondsey Workhouse and Industrial school. Her whereabouts until 1861 are uncertain. Sometime between 1861 and 1863, she left home with an army pensioner, Thomas Conway, who had been in the 18th Irish Regiment. They lived in Birmingham and the Midlands. Though she claimed they had been married, no legal trace of a marriage has been found. She had a tattoo, 'TC' on her arm, and had three children by Thomas; Annie, who was about 23 at the time of the murder, George who would have been about 20, and one other son who was about 15.

They separated in 1880, and she had custody of Annie alone, who would then have been about 15. Annie later claimed that the separation had been caused by drink and her mother's frequent disappearances. Yet, Catharine's sister, Elizabeth Fisher, blamed Thomas' violence. We simply do not know which came first.

In 1881, Catharine lived with an Irish porter, John Kelly, in Flower and Dean Street. She was still with John Kelly in 1888, and they spent the summer hop picking in Kent. They returned on 28 September. On 29 September a pair of Kelly's boots were pawned by Catharine for two shillings and sixpence. The ticket read her name as 'Jane Kelly'. She often used Kelly's name, but we do not know where the name 'Jane' came from. There is, of course, a striking similarity with the fifth victim's name, Mary Jane Kelly.

Catharine's story is slightly different from the other victims. She had known more of a struggle and more poverty early in life, but then there followed a period of comfortable companionship when she raised a family. This came to a sudden end with stories of drink and domestic violence. She, too, had lost something good.

Mary Jane Kelly (1864–1888?)

Mary's early life can only be constructed from various acquaintances and newspaper reports. She was born in Limerick, but moved to Wales as a child with her father, John Kelly. He worked in an ironworks in Carnarvonshire or Carmarthenshire. She had several brothers and a sister. One brother was named Henry, who was said to have joined the Scots Guards. Her mother possibly stayed behind in Ireland.

Mary married a collier, John Davies in about 1879. He died in a pit explosion a couple of years later. She went to Cardiff, exhausted, and convalesced with her cousin and spent time in an infirmary. At some point, she turned to prostitution with the sailors who thronged the port.

In 1884, Mary moved to London, working in a high class West End brothel, driving around in a carriage and she claimed that she had gone to France with a gentleman, seeing Paris. She did not like the country and she returned after a few weeks. At some point early in this period, she might have stayed in the Providence Row Refuge for women, in Crispin Street, near Dorset Street.

No records can be found of her brother in the Scots Guards, although her landlord, John McCarthy, often received letters for her from Ireland, which he assumed were from her mother. The Scots Guards were, in fact, in Ireland in 1888.

There is no record of her marriage to John Davies, despite the fact that the registration of marriages was compulsory in England and Wales from 1875. Davies might have been a common law husband.

Neither can any records of her stay in a Cardiff infirmary be traced. Joseph Barnett, her lover, claimed she had stayed there, "She was in an infirmary there for eight or nine months. She was following a bad life with her cousin, who, as I reckon, and as I often told her, was the cause of her downfall." No records of patients for the Royal Infirmary survive, but according to the South Wales Daily News of 14 November 1888 the authorities did make a search of the records after her death. They found no one under the name of Mary Janet Kelly (her name as reported by some of the press) or Davies for the period 1881-1885. It is possible that she used an assumed name.

Philip Sugden, in 'The Complete History of Jack the Ripper', mentions the suggestion by Ron Bernard of Cardiff, that Mary was resident at 19 Homfray Street, using the census of 1871 and 1881. There resided John Kelly, a coal trimmer, with his wife Margaret and their four children. Mary Kelly was the youngest, aged four in 1871. In 1881, they are all still there. Mary is 'Mary Ann' and she was then said to be sixteen. The parents were born in Ireland, and all the children in Cardiff. There is no local record of Mary's birth in Cardiff between 1865–1867. It is just possible that she was born in Ireland and brought over, but this might be trying to make any Mary Kelly fit the facts. This Mary Ann Kelly is a possible contender, but a more likely one has been traced by the Parlours back to Limerick.

Irish records reveal that there was only one Mary Jane

Kelly born in the Limerick area around the time of the fifth victim's birth. This reference is to a birth in Castletown, Limerick, in 1864, to a John Kelly and an Ann McCarthy. Two brothers are also listed in the Irish records, John Kelly born 1866, and Peter Kelly born 1868. This is very likely to be *the* Mary Jane Kelly, and her mother's maiden name might solve a long standing problem for Ripperologists. Many have wondered why her landlord, John McCarthy, allowed her to be behind with the rent for six weeks. She owed thirty shillings. Landlords were harsh then, and one night's money owed could result in eviction. It might be just about possible that she was offering him sexual favours, but the tendency was for the wives of the landlords to collect the money and keep the records. Others have wondered if Kelly was expecting a large payment because of some blackmail plot she was involved in, or even for being a government informer, and thus she had asked for credit pending her forthcoming wealth. It is highly unlikely that a landlord would have weathered this for more than a fortnight! If John McCarthy was related to her mother, possibly being Mary Jane's uncle, then this might resolve matters. They could have had a familiar arrangement that she paid some rent when she could. Her small room at 13, Miller's Court was built onto the back of number 26, next door to the McCarthy's shop at 27, Dorset Street. It might have been purposefully sectioned off for her. The Irish records reveal that Ann McCarthy had a brother called Thomas. The 1902 'Kelly's Directory' reveals a Thomas McCarthy also in Dorset Street. Was this her brother?

The McCarthy family held quite a presence in Dorset Street. John owned number 27, on one side of the entrance to Miller's Court. In the 1881 census, McCarthy is there with his wife, son, two daughters, and his brother Daniel. The number of people living there increases by 1891. There is another John McCarthy, with wife and son. Daniel has married by this time. According to Kelly's Directory for 1894, Daniel and Ann now live at 36 Dorset Street, running their own chandlery shop. By 1902, a Thomas McCarthy has taken over yet another chandlery shop at 7 Dorset Street. The McCarthy clan became established in that part of Whitechapel.

In the 1881 and 1891 censuses, John McCarthy's place of birth is listed as Dieppe. It is just possible that his parents settled there as emigrants from Ireland at the time of the Potato famine (1845-1850) which would have been around the time of John's birth. Whole families were uprooted and often split up.

This is a surprising link with the tradition, via Joseph Barnett, that Kelly had visited France, and the supposed reminiscences of the painter Walter Sickert, as relayed by his son, Joseph Sickert, to the late Stephen Knight (see Chapter 'The Plot Thickens'). He said that his father had taken Kelly with him to Dieppe where he often painted. She might have had other family in Dieppe, too, as suggested by John McCarthy being born there. Another intriguing twist is seen in the 1891 census, when the new inhabitant of 13 Miller's Court is listed as a Thomas Kelly. Possibly this is just a co-incidence. This might show a Kelly/McCarthy link, though, with another member of the family staying there.

An oral tradition stemming from the Providence Row Refuge might shed more light on her early days in London. In 1860, a priest, Daniel Gilbert, opened a night refuge run by the Sisters of Mercy in the former stables at Providence Row,

Below left: McCarthy family grave. (Published for the first time.) (Photo: Andy Parlour)

Below right: The grave of "Marie Jeanette" Kelly. (Photo: Andy Parlour)

Finsbury Square. This became far too small, and land once used for fairs off Crispin Street was bought, and the present Refuge built in 1868. This was a Catholic initiative to do something for the homeless young women, many of whom had children, and its work still continues today, though men are also admitted. Two other centres are run in the district.

Joseph Sickert said that Kelly had stayed there in 1884, and his father heard that a shopkeeper in Cleveland Street, where he kept a studio, wanted an assistant. Walter told this to a friend, Edmund Bellord, an estate agent, who was also on the Refuge committee. Kelly was recommended and sent to Cleveland Street in the West End, where she met Sickert, and was introduced to his society friends. The Refuge do, in fact, have an oral tradition that Kelly stayed there, but all their records, that were kept in Milk Street, were destroyed in the War. In 1973, an elderly nun there was interviewed by the BBC. She had been a novice at the Crispin Street convent in 1915 "directly opposite where Kelly and Chapman had rubbed shoulders" in the Horn of Plenty. She also remembered being told by an older nun who was resident at the time of the murders, that "if it had not been for the Kelly woman, none of the murders would have happened." In 1988, a BBC Timewatch team confirmed this tradition, as did the convent's solicitor whose family maintained that a maid had been sent from the convent, had absconded and had become a Ripper victim. Our own contact with the Refuge has confirmed that an oral tradition did exist, but the elderly nuns who had been told of this much earlier have all died.

The amazing thing is that the Refuge is directly opposite Dorset Street. Kelly ended her days in Miller's Court, which was off Dorset Street, about half way along. She would have turned into Dorset Street, looked to the right, and seen the Refuge where she had begun her stay!

Kelly's movements in the few years before the murders are attested by her East End aquaintances. She was believed to have gone to the Ratcliff Highway district after returning from France, lodging in St George's Street. The Star claimed that she worked for a Mrs Buki. Barnett thought that she had lived with a man called Morganstone near Stepney gasworks. Just prior to 1886, she lodged with Mrs Carthy on Breezer's Hill. Mrs Carthy claimed that when she had lodged in St George's Street, her previous landlady had gone with her into Knightsbridge to reclaim a box of clothing from a French lady. She was with a mason or plasterer called Joseph Fleming from Bethnal Green,

Providence Row Refuge today. The statue of the Virgin Mary can just be seen above the middle door looking along what was Dorset Street in 1888. (Photo: Andy Parlour)

before she moved in with Barnett. She was in Cooney's Common Lodging House in Thrawl Street, Spitalfields, until she met Barnett on 8 April, 1887. They moved around various lodgings in Thrawl Street, Flower and Dean Street, and Brick Lane, before settling at 13, Miller's Court.

Barnett left her on 30 October 1888, complaining that she had resumed prostitution, and had brought prostitutes to stay, naming a 'Julia' and a 'Mrs Harvey'. He remained friendly towards her, and kept visiting her. He lived at 24 New Street, Bishopsgate, and 21, Ponpool Lane since leaving her. Kelly was also said to have been three months pregnant, though it was not clear if the child was Barnett's. A question mark hangs over whether the corpse in 13, Miller's Court was pregnant or not.

Whatever the exact truth about Mary's upbringing and movements in London, she had had her share of tragedy, known times of family security, possibly mixed in affluent society, and ended up struggling to survive as an 'unfortunate'. She often turned to drink, and could have a fierce temper when inebriated. She was known as 'Black Mary' for this reason. She may be the Mary Jane Kelly fined two shillings and sixpence at Thames Magistrate's Court for drunken disorderliness on 19 September 1888.

Mary Ann Nichols, Annie Chapman, Elizabeth Stride, Catharine Eddowes and Mary Jane Kelly – all women who had known better times and lost themselves in the 'wicked quarter mile' of Whitechapel around Dorset Street. They had not all struggled up from childhood in the squalor of those tenements like many others there. They had come from a more normal life without. Perhaps their tragedy, the sorrow they carried within, drew them together as they met and rubbed shoulders in those few, narrow streets and drank in the local pubs, such as the Horn of Plenty, the Britannia and the Ten Bells. Why anyone would want to take the lives of the five friends is debateable. It is just possible that a client of one might have become involved in their murders, or that a maniac out to kill prostitutes had contact with one of the women, and through her, the other four. It is highly unlikely that these five were picked out by a random killer, though. There had to be some connection. This adds fuel to the fire of conspiracy theories, for there seems to have been a particular motive in singling out these five women.

Commercial Street, Whitechapel, as it is today. The Ten Bells P.H. (centre) where the five victims drank. (Photo: Andy Parlour)

THE NEMESIS OF NEGLECT.

From Hell

Yours truly, Jack the Ripper

A number of letters appeared both during the murders, and afterwards, that claimed to have come from the killer. The name 'Jack the Ripper' was believed at the time to have originated in these letters.

(a) The 'Dear Boss' letter

This was sent on 27 September to the Central News Agency, having been posted in 'London EC'. It was written in red ink, with a postscript in red crayon. It is in a precise, formal, clerkly hand, making it a fairly anonymous style. The letter reads:

> "Dear Boss,
> I keep on hearing the police have caught me but they wont fix me just yet. I have laughed when they look so clever and talk about being on the right track. That joke about Leather Apron gave me real fits. I am down on whores and I shant quit ripping them till I do get buckled. Grand work the last job was I gave the lady no time to squeal. How can they catch me now. I love my work and want to start again. You will soon hear of me with my funny little games. I saved some of the proper red stuff in a ginger beer bottle over the last job to write with but it went thick like glue and I cant use it. Red ink is fit enough I hope ha ha. The next job I do I shall clip the ladys ears off and send to the police officers just for jolly wouldnt you. Keep this letter back till I do a bit more work, then give it out straight. My knife's so nice and sharp I want to get to work right away if I get a chance. Good luck.
>
> Yours truly,
> Jack the Ripper
>
> Dont mind me giving the trade name.
>
> wasnt good enough to post this before I got all the red ink off my hands curse it. No luck yet. They say I'm a doctor now ha ha."

A postcard was sent on 1st October from 'London E'.

> "I was not codding dear old Boss when I gave you the tip, you'll hear about saucy Jacky s work tomorrow double event this time number one squealed a bit couldnt finish straight off. had not time to get ears for police thanks for keeping last letter back till I got to work again.
>
> Jack the Ripper"

The "Dear Boss" letter.

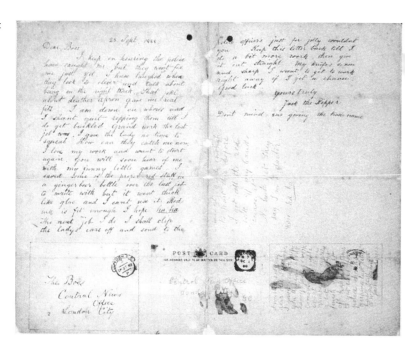

The "Saucy Jacky" postcard.

It was assumed that these were from the same hand. The first was printed in the morning edition of the 'Daily News' on 1 October, and the second was printed in the evening edition of 'The Star' on the same day – though only in part. Both copies were printed in full in the 'Evening News' on 4 October, and the police published a poster with copies of the two letters, hoping for information. (As shown in an earlier chapter, the name 'Jack the Ripper' might have been current in Whitechapel prior to this.) The reference to 'the tradename' is suggestive. 'Jack' was often used of tradesmen, a nickname for one having completed their apprenticeship. Thus 'steeplejack' or 'Jack Tar' for a sailor. A dock worker at Portsmouth, hanged in the 18th century for causing arson was known as 'Jack the Painter'. 'Jack the Lad' and Jack of all Trades' follow on in the same tradition. The killer's nickname was a play on this sort of naming. We should not read anything else into it, despite those who see a reference to the name 'James' – of whom there are a few suspects so named!

It is just possible that the postcard was an imitative hoax as this could have been composed and sent just after reading about the first letter and the double event murders in the morning paper. After 1910, Anderson and Swanson stated that they believed the letters to be a hoax, being the work of a journalist they could identify. Macnaghten, the later Chief of the CID, also believed them to be a hoax. A letter from Chief Inspector John Littlechild has recently come to light which repeats the assertion that the police believed these to be hoaxes, and this names Tom Bullen of the Central News Agency, and implicates Moore, the Chief of the Agency, with their invention.

In 1966, a writer for 'Crime and Detection' reported that he had spoken with a journalist called Best who had worked on 'The Star' during the murders,. This meeting was in 1931, and Best had claimed that he had invented all the Ripper letters to keep interest in the crimes going. He said that a Waverly nib had been used which was flattened to simulate illiteracy and a National School education.

It is interesting, though, that the first letter was kept back until the next murders, and the police at least thought they might be genuine, by issuing a poster. The reference to the ears is apposite, for a section of Eddowes' ear came loose when the body was examined at the mortuary. The ear was cut but not severed completely. Many more hoax letters began to flood in; one, sent to the 'Daily News' was signed 'Ripper' and 'Boss' had been inserted. The City Police chose never to make this public. One Maria Coroner was charged with a breach of the peace on 21 October 1888 for sending hoax Ripper letters to the police and a local paper saying that the killer was coming to Bradford "to do a little business".

Opinions probably varied among the police about some of the letters. A parallel might be drawn with the written messages and the telephone conversations purporting to come from the Yorkshire Ripper in the 1970s. Posters of these were issued and people were urged to phone to listen to the messages to see if they recognised the voice – I had the unfortunate experience of suspecting someone myself, a disturbed drifter I knew of, and I phoned and was relieved that this was not the same man. They turned out to be hoaxes, though. Some people claim attention by such tricks. The police have to give the benefit of the doubt to some material like this just in case it should pay off.

The Parlours have suggested some slightly fresh understandings of the 'Dear Boss' letter by consulting dictionaries of underworld slang, such as 'A Dictionary of Crime' by Jay Robert Nash (Headline). They suggest that 'Boss' was derived from 'boatswain', used as a stronger form of 'sir' and would have been in use in Britain in the 1880s. Thus they challenge the claim that this was an Americanism. 'Fix' meant to place under arrest, and had been used by the police since 1781. 'Fits' meant hysterical laughter. 'Down' could be read as being suspicious of someone. 'Buckled' was to be arrested (as in fastened up).

The possible reading of 'down' might be interesting if this should read "I am suspicious of whores". This might show that the killer knew something about the women he killed that disturbed him.

(b) The Lusk Letter

George Lusk, the chairman of the Vigilance Committee, received a small parcel and a letter on 16 October 1888. The parcel, wrapped in brown paper, contained a cardboard box, three inch square. Inside this was part of a kidney, which had been preserved in spirits of wine. The letter read as follows:

> "Mr Lusk
>   Sor
> ˙I send you half the Kidne I took from one women prasarved it
> for you tother piece I fried and ate it was very nise I may send you
> the bloody knif that took it out if you only wate a whil longer
>   signd   Catch me when
>   you can
>   Mishter Lusk"

Lusk assumed it was a hoax, but he was urged to present it to a doctor for examination. Members of the Vigilance Committee took the object to Dr Wiles' surgery at 56 Mile End Road. It was received by a medical assistant, Mr Reed, who examined it and later handed it to Dr. Openshaw at the London Hospital. Reed pronounced that it was definitely human. Press reports stated that Openshaw had said it was the 'ginny' kidney of a 45 year old woman who suffered from Bright's disease. It has been removed from the body during the previous three weeks. The next day, Openshaw denied that he had said anything except that the kidney was human and was preserved in spirits of wine. The elaboration had probably come from Reed.

Dr. Sedgwick Saunders told the press that the age of a person cannot be told from a kidney without the rest of the body, and he argued that Eddowes' piece of kidney had been in good health. Furthermore, gin left no traces in the kidney.

This settled the matter as a hoax, probably from a medical student with access to dissected organs and preserving fluids.

The case was reopened 22 years later when Major Henry Smith released his memoirs 'From Constable to Commissioner' in 1910. Smith had been Acting Commissioner of the City Police in 1888, becoming Commissioner from 1890-1901. He was in charge of the Mitre Square incident as this was the only murder in City Police territory. He boasted that he knew more about the murders than any man living and that he had narrowly missed apprehending the Ripper as he had seen the bloodstained water gurgling down the sink where he had washed his hands. Aspects of his memoirs are inaccurate and questionable, but of the Lusk kidney he says that he showed it to Mr Henry Sutton, Senior Surgeon at the London Hospital. He claimed that it could not have been from a medical specimen as it did not show sufficient charge with liquid to have come from a typical corpse that had been dead for some time. It also showed symptoms of Bright's disease, and the length of renal artery present fitted with what was left in Eddowes' body.

Dr. Gordon Brown's post-mortem report on Eddowes was discovered in the Corporation of London Records. This states that the kidney was "pale, bloodless, with a slight congestion at the base of the pyramid", which meant that symptoms of Brights disease were present. Bright himself had erroneously believed that this disease was caused by alcohol, and hence the possible sense in the earlier description of a 'ginny' kidney as a colloquialism.

The kidney might well, then, be Eddowes' and that would mean that we have at least one genuine Ripper letter.

Graphologists have studied the letter and reached varied conclusions. C.M. MacLeod suggested it was a man of drive and violence with rudimentary education who might be capable of holding down a job and concealing his savagery. Thomas J. Mann felt that this showed semi-literacy, and the non-phonetic misspellings of 'prasarved' and the dialect 'tother' show an English speaker.

Paul Begg, Martin Fido and Keith Skinner have pointed out that the use of 'Sor' and 'Mishter' reflects 19th century stage customs for showing an Irish accent. It may be that the writer is deliberately playacting, mocking and concealing his true identity with the illusion of semi-literacy. If this man also wrote the 'Dear Boss' letter, then his playacting has mimicked an illiterate Irishman here, while posing as an American before.

Of course, this letter shows a more disturbing side. If genuine, the maniac was going beyond a jest. He was sadistic, depraved, and also cannibalistic. There is the possiblity that these letters have come from two men, who acted as accomplices – hence the different hands? Perhaps there is a hint of desperation in this one, 'Catch me when you can' for the man knows his mind is giving way.

(c) The Liverpool Letters

These were quoted in a book, 'From City to Fleet Street' by J. Hall Richardson in 1927. He had been a journalist for the 'Daily Telegraph' in 1888. The two letters read as follows:

"Liverpool
29th inst.
BEWARE I shall be at work on the 1st and 2nd inst. in 'Minories' at 12 midnight and I give the police a good chance but there is never a Policeman near when I am at work.
Yours,
JACK THE RIPPER"

"Prince William St.,L'pool
What fools the police are I even give them the name of the street where I am living.
Yours,
JACK THE RIPPER"

Without more background information on their date, postmark and appearance, it is impossible to make much of these. Various speculations have been aired about the Ripper being linked with the Minories in Whitechapel or as coming from Liverpool.

(d) The Lees Letter

This was received on 25 July 1889. It reads as follows:

"Dear Boss
You have not caught me yet you see, with all your cunning, with all your "Lees" with all your blue bottles. I have made two narrow squeaks this week, but still though disturbed I got clear before I could get to work -I will give the foreigners a turn now i think – for a change – Germans especially if I can – I was conversing with two or three of your men last night – their eyes of course were shut and thus they did not see my bag.
Ask any of your men who were on duty last night in Picadilly (Circus End) if they saw a gentleman put 2 dragoon guard sergeants into a hansom. I was close by & heard him talk about shedding blood in Egypt I will soon shed more in England.
I hope you read mark & learn all that you can if you do so you may and may not catch.
Jack the Ripper"

This is interesting for it is the only external reference to Lees the pyschic apart from his diaries and the questionable newspaper report of 1895. This is curious, but it is impossible to assess such a letter at such a distance. While this is most likely to be a forgery, it shows that there was some awareness of the Lees traditions circulating.

The letters are inconclusive. Ripperologists are frankly divided over the 'Dear Boss' letter and the Lusk letter. If any are genuine, then they might show the clever, playful mind of a disturbed soul who was throwing out clues, half hoping to be caught. We simply do not know.

Rubber Soles and Blood Hounds

The Police and their Investigations

James Monro in retirement.

Sir Charles Warren remained the Metropolitan Police Commissioner throughout the time of the Whitechapel murders, resigning on 9 November – the date of Kelly's death. He worked with two deputies during this period, James Monro, and Dr Robert Anderson.

Monro was Assistant Commissioner, in charge of the C.I.D. from 1884 until 1888, at the outbreak of the murders. He resigned to be the Head of the Detective Service, an unofficial title. He had resigned because he could not procure complete control of the C.I.D. from Warren. Monro had taken over a new department, 'Section D', which observed the activities of the Fenians. He had direct access to the Home Secretary, and wanted the C.I.D. to have this as well. Tensions with Warren came to a head when Warren vetoed Monro's appointment of Melville Macnaghten as Assistent Chief Constable. In his new post with the secret Detective Service, members of the C.I.D. were encouraged to liaise with him by going behind Warren's back.

Monro took over as Commissioner after Warren's resignation, and served until 1890. He resigned from this position to found the Ranaghat Medical Mission in India, from 1890–1903.

Monro seems to have won glowing praise from many of the men who worked under him – he championed the cause of police pensions, and brought the Fenian dynamite campaigns more under control. He was a difficult character in other respects, and often resigned upon principle.

Dr Robert Anderson was Assistant Commissioner with reponsibilty for the C.I.D and in charge of the Whitechapel Murder Investigation from October 1888 until the possible closure of the file in 1892. He kept his position until his retirement in 1901, when he also received a knighthood. He was a scholar, a theologian and something of a reclusive writer by nature. His contemporaries complained that he was not shrewd and experienced enough in matters of street crime to have been of much impetus in solving the Whitechapel murders, though he was undoubtedly a clever man.

He took his post as Assistant Commissioner on the day of Mary Ann Nichols' murder. He had just been prescribed a month's sick leave by his doctor, and thus he handed the case over to Chief Inspector Donald Swanson. He left for Switzerland on the day of Annie Chapman's death. He returned on 6 October, after the 'Double Event' had taken place. He was told by the Home Secretary and Warren that they expected him to find the murderer and they held him responsible for this. He

Dr Robert Anderson, Head of Met. C.I.D.

replied, "I will hold myself responsible to take all legitimate means to find him."

In fact, he seems to have instigated very little. He recommended that all known prostitutes in the East End should be arrested – this was rejected as totally impractical. He then made it clear that any prostitute could not be expected to be protected by the police. He seems to have thought that this had some impact, stating; "However the fact may be explained, it is fact that no other street murder occurred in the "Jack-the-Ripper" series." This seems to have been a reference to Kelly's murder having taken place indoors!

On 23 October, he wrote to the Home Office, "That five successive murders should have been commited without our having the slightest clue of any kind is extraordinary...." (Here, he includes Tabram as a Ripper victim.) He liaised closely with Monro, and with Swanson, and asked Dr Thomas Bond to review the reports of the victims to assess the state of the Ripper's supposed medical knowledge.

In his retirement, he made various statements which contradicted his earlier remarks about having no definite suspicions. In 'Criminals and Crime' in 1907, he stated that the only people ever at risk were the East End prostitutes, and that the women of the metropolis had nothing to fear "during the weeks the fiend was on the prowl, as they were before the mania seized him, or after he had been safely caged in an asylum."

The story changed in 1910, in a series of memoirs, 'The Lighter Side of My Official Life' which were published firstly in 'Blackwood's Magazine' and then in book form. Here, Anderson claimed that the Ripper was a "sexual maniac of a virulent type" who lived locally and was protected by his people, low-class Jews who mistrusted Gentiles.

He added that he could disclose who the killer was, but fear of libel action prevented him. The book edition changed things slightly, significantly adding the remark:

"the only person who had ever had a good view of the murderer unhesitatingly identified the suspect the instant he was confronted with him, but he refused to give evidence against him." (see further on this suspect in Chapter Innocent until Proven Guilty).

Donald Swanson was placed in charge of the Whitechapel Murders investigation from 1 September to 6 October 1888 when Anderson was away. Upon his superior's return, Swanson was desk officer in charge. He worked well with Anderson and the two remained friends after retirement. Swanson witnessed

Anderson's will, for example. Swanson disagreed with making public announcements about former police investigations, and the only reference to his views on the Ripper is in the 'Pall Mall Gazette' of 7 May 1895. This feature comments that Swanson believed that the Ripper was now dead, and thus his identity had been known to the Yard.

Besides this, Swanson pencilled notes in the margin of Anderson's 'The Lighter Side of My Official Life". These was not discovered until 1980 when the book came into the hands of Swanson's grandson, and they were published in the 'Daily Telegraph' in 1987. Swanson added that the witness would not bring evidence against the suspect because he was also a Jew and his death would weigh upon his conscience. Swanson then names Kosminski as the suspect, and wrongly asserted that he died soon after being sent to an asylum. It is likely that he mixed two different Jewish suspects up. This man, Kosminski, a mentally ill Jew, was also mentioned as a suspect by Macnaghten (see further in Chapter Innocent until Proven Guilty).

The most famous policeman on the case was Inspector Frederick George Abberline. He was in charge of the detectives on the ground, reporting to Swanson. He had joined the Metropolitan Police in 1863, and became a sergeant in 1865. He was involved in Fenian surveillance, in plain clothes, in 1867, and he married Martha Mackness. A year later she died aged 26 of consumption. He was promoted to Inspector in 1873 and worked with H Division in Whitechapel. He married Emma Beament in 1876, and was promoted to Local Inspector in 1878, being transferred to A Division, and then to Scotland Yard in 1878. He became Inspector First Class in 1888, and then Chief Inspector in 1890. He retired in 1892, working as a private agent, until settling in Bournemouth in 1904. He died in 1929.

Abberline had an excellent knowledge of the East End from his many years there and was a natural choice to head the men on the ground. He seems to have been denied some information during the investigations, however, as when the press asked him which organs had been taken from Annie Chapman, he said that he had not seen the medical report!

Abberline's theories about the killer have naturally aroused deep interest. The 'Pall Mall Gazette' in 1903 interviewed him about the trial of George Chapman, who had been accused of poisoning his wives. Abberline said that he felt that this man was a likely suspect – "I have been so struck with the remarkable coincidences in the two series of murders that I have

Inspector Frederick George Abberline.

MATHEW PACKER TELLS A STRANGE STORY TO THE POLICE.

not been able to think of anything else for several days past...."
– and the only reservation he expressed was that Chapman was
23 at the time of the murders, whereas witnesses reported a
man in his early thirties. Later on, the paper published his
views that the Yard had never believed the Ripper to have died,
and there is no proof that he had been sent to an asylum.
Abberline's views thus contradict those of his direct superiors.

Abberline was involved in the Cleveland Street investigation in 1889 of the homosexual brothel. His uncharacteristic
delay let important witnesses escape across the Channel. Some
see a sinister turn in his retirement from the force in 1892, the
year that the Ripper case seemed to be closed. Could Abberline
have been paid off for services rendered, to cover up the
crimes? Could the killer have been highly connected? We must

be careful, though, for he was entitled to retire on full pension, even though he was only 49, by the terms of the 1890 Police Bill. Policemen ever since have some times taken advantage of this, to have more leisure years and a chance to earn extra income.

Two other officers were intimately connected with the crimes, George Godley and Walter Dew. Godley had joined the Metropolitan Police in 1877, and he served in J Division (Bethnal Green) in 1888. He was present at Nichols' inquest with Abberline. The 'Police Review' said of him, after his retirement, "Called in each case from his bed while the bodies were still warm, Mr Godley's knowledge of this series of crimes is perhaps as complete as that of any Officer concerned."

Dew joined the Metropolitan Police in 1882 and was posted to X Division, Paddington Green, before transferring to H Division (Whitechapel) in 1887, for the C.I.D. he had the nickname, 'Blue Serge' for wearing his best suit while on duty. He lived across the river in Wandsworth. He was promoted to Inspector in 1906, and became famous for apprehending Dr. Crippen.

Each of the murders brought new fears and ideas in turn. Hysteria mounted and the police were pilloried for their impotence. Nichols' murder was thought to be the work of a blackmail gang at first, and police investigations were limited to questioning local residents to see what they had seen or heard on the night. Chapman's death led to the sending out of a large group of detectives to interview locals and to bring in any suspicious characters. Mobs gathered outside police stations, and they yelled "Murderer!" at anyone arrested, even for petty offences. John Pizer ('Leather Apron') and a disturbed man called William Henry Piggott were both taken into custody. Pizer could provide alibis, and was released on 12 September. Piggott claimed that he had received hand injuries from being bitten by a woman when he tried to help her. His rantings led to his incarceration in an asylum.

After the scandal of the 'Double Event', Warren sent every available policeman into Whitechapel to reinforce the 546 constables, 29 inspectors and 44 sergeants already present. A house-to-house search of the Spitalfields area continued for three weeks, and every doss house was scoured. A handbill was given out, "Police Notice to Occupier", which urged anyone with suspicions of anyone "to communicate at once with the nearest police station". This had little positive affect, but a torrent of gossip and rumour poured forth.

POLICE NOTICE.

TO THE OCCUPIER.

On the mornings of Friday, 31st August, Saturday 8th, and Sunday, 30th September, 1888, Women were murdered in or near Whitechapel, supposed by some one residing in the immediate neighbourhood. Should you know of any person to whom suspicion is attached, you are earnestly requested to communicate at once with the nearest Police Station.

Metropolitan Police Office,
30th September, 1888.

Printed by M'Corquodale & Co. Limited, " The Armoury," Southwark

The press besieged Warren. 'The Times' complained of "the inability of the police to properly cover the whole of the ground within their jurisdiction". Letter writers complained of the lawlessness in the East End, and the "bands of thieves who almost hourly committed robberies in broad daylight with impunity". Ideas and suggestions flooded into the press and the Yard. The Yard was receiving 1,200 letters a day at one point!

Mr Frederick Wallasey wrote to 'The Times' suggesting that a special force of plain clothes detectives should be sent out on bicycles at night to move speedily and noiselessly around. Mr L. R. Thomson suggested that the soles of police boots should be made of a noiseless material such as India rubber. Mr Percy Lindley wrote in suggesting the use of bloodhounds:

"Sir – With regard to the suggestion that bloodhounds might assist in tracking the East End murderer, as a breeder of bloodhounds and knowing their power, I have little doubt that, had a hound been put upon the scent of the murderer while fresh, it might have done what the police have failed in. There are doubt-less owners of bloodhounds willing to lend them if any of the police – which, I fear, is improbable – know how to use them."

Warren was under considerable pressure to use blood-hounds, and he staged a demonstration in Hyde Park on 8 October. At 7.00am, two hounds, Barnaby and Burgho, were presented by their owner, Edwin Brough of Scarborough, and they tracked a man for a mile after he was given a head start of fifteen minutes. The following morning, the tests were repeated twice, with Warren acting as the hunted man! The press reported, erroneously, that the dogs had become lost, and Warren was the subject of derision. This had happened on a completely different case, but Warren's reputation was so low that no one would, or could, listen. It was also reported that Warren had acquired the two dogs for police service, though their owner denied this the next day.

Flamboyant suggestions were received by the Yard. One man suggested that a special force of policewomen should be recruited and sent out in plain clothes, for there were no policewomen in 1888. (Interestingly, Amelia Brown of Peck-ham claimed in the 'Sunday Chronicle' of 1949 that she had been sent out as a decoy, and given a police whistle for her protection!). One person suggested that female dummies should be positioned around the East End, with their arms and legs made of powerful springs, which would be released by rais-ing the chin or pressing the throat. The killer would thus be entangled while a sound like a police whistle might be sounded from the machine. Such Heath Robinson ideas were not taken seriously! A saner solution was suggested when one writer proposed that an advertisement should be placed in the press as follows:

"Medical Man or Assistant Wanted in London, aged between 25 and 40. Must not object to assist in occasional post mortem. Liberal terms. Address stating antecedents. PTR [Please to reply] NAME STREET."

Dr. Forbes Winslow was a specialist in mental disorders and he offered his services. He wanted to set up a dozen decoys around Whitechapel in female clothing. These should, ideally, be wardens of mental hospitals and asylums so that they could recognise a maniac and be best placed for restraining him. Inquiries should also be made to all the asylums of the land about escaped lunatics. He speculated that the killer was a well-to-do madman living in the West End who went out to kill while in the grip of an epileptic attack of some kind. (Amazingly, Wilson received a chillingly prophetic letter from one Mr Lungi, stating his opinion that another murder would happen on 8 or 9 November in Clapham or the West End, as this was Lord Mayor's Day.)

The police did put out undercover agents posing as locals and even as women! Detective Sergeant Robinson of G Division (Clerkenwell) wore a heavy veil, petticoats and skirt. He took his place at Phoenix Place, St. Pancras, after midnight on October 9th. He was accompanied by Detective Sergeant Mather in plain clothes. They were keeping watch on a courting couple across the street in a doorway. They thought that the man was behaving suspiciously. A cab-washer called William Jarvis passed by and took them for a pair of voyeurs. "Wot yer muckin' about'ere for?" he shouted. Sergeant Robinson stepped forward, lifted his veil and replied that he was a police officer. Jarvis cursed, "Oh, a rozzer, eh?" and he hit Robinson in the eye!

Another incident involved a young journalist from Bow who dressed up as a woman to try to glean some information. Police Constable Ludwig was suspicious of his gait, and cried, "Just a minute, you're a man, aren't you?" Then he asked, "Are you one of us?" The journalist replied, "I don't know what you mean exactly but I'm not a copper, if that's what you're referring to." Two hours later, he had managed to talk himself out of police custody.

There was also rivalry and tension between the City Police and the Metropolitan Police, in whose territory the body of Catharine Eddowes was found. The press commented that the City Police were less secretive and more forthcoming than the Metropolitan Police, and differences of opinion emerged over the Goulston Street graffito. If the floating piece of tradition about Sergeant White is to be placed in Mitre Square, then this was particularly sensitive as White was working undercover on City territory. It seems that the City police also used undercover police on Metropolitan territory. The 'Times' of 2 October 1888 reveals City involvement with "several plain-clothes constables being ordered on the beats in a district which has now become so notorious. Instructions were given to the constables to watch any man or woman seen together in suspicious circumstances..." In fact, two such men were near Mitre Square, on the night of Eddowes' murder. They were on duty in Windsor Street, about 300 yards away. They heard of the murder five minutes after the discovery of the body, and immediately searched the houses in their area.

The exasperation with the police led to the setting up of various local Vigilance groups. One of the first had Mr J. Aarons as the secretary of 16 local traders, who offered a reward and raised money by public subscription. The Mile End Vigilance Committee wrote to the Home Office about a reward and received the following reply:

> "I am directed by the Secretary of State to acknowledge receipt of your letter of 16th, with reference to the question of the offer of a reward for the discovery of the perpetrators of the recent murders in Whitechapel, and I am to inform you that had the Secretary of State considered the case a proper one for the offer of a reward, he would have at once have offered one on behalf of the government, but that the practice of offering rewards for the discovery of criminals was discontinued some years ago, because experience showed that such offers of reward tended to produce more harm than good. And the Secretary of State is satisfied that there is nothing in the circumstances of the present case to justify a departure from this rule.
>
> I am, Sir,
> Your obedient servant
> G. Leigh Pemberton "

This caused resentment and the Vigilance groups thought that they were being treated in a high-handed manner. A number of individuals had put up rewards – Samuel Montagu, MP for Whitechapel, the Lord Mayor and the Corporation of London, the Officers of the Tower Hamlets Militia, and Angela Burdett Coutts, who personally offered a pension for life of £1 per week. The government's reluctance was seen as shameful, and evidence of their disregard for the poor of the East End. The Home Office were following a precedent established after 1884, however. The government used to offer rewards of £100 for the conviction of a felon, but false denunciations to collect the reward money had stopped this. Discretionary rewards could still be given if the person collecting the money did not provide the evidence that convicted. Clearly, the Whitechapel murders were not such a case. (Payments were made to underworld informers, however, to try to gather information. The police accounts listed "incidental expenditure in the apprehension and conviction of criminals".)

A pardon was, however, offered on 10 November, "to any accomplice, not being a person who contrived or actually committed the murder" who gave information leading to arrest. Henry Matthews, the Home Secretary, explained to the Commons that there were special circumstances surrounding Kelly's death that suggested more than one man was involved. He was prepared to offer a pardon where various degrees of guilt in a case could be established, and all other routes to prosecution had failed. The Home Office Permanent Secretary had strongly advised taking this course of action, fearing that it would make the public more hysterical to believe that there was more than one Ripper at large, and that the police would be admitting failure. It is not clear what the different circumstances were surrounding Kelly's murder, that Matthews referred to.

William Henry Weston, Andy's great-grandfather, patrolled the streets as part of the Vigilance Committee. (From family collection.)

One of the most well known presidents of a Vigilance committee was George Akin Lusk. He was a local tradesman who had built up a building and decorating business with his wife, Sarah, who died in 1888. He employed a group of men, specialising in restoring music halls. He lived in Mile End, and later moved to Bow. He was elected president of the Whitechapel Vigilance Committee on 10 September in the Crown public house in Mile End Road. He drew attention to himself by writing to the 'Times' and was convinced that his house was being watched by a bearded man. He asked for police protection thereafter. He used his workmen as his team, including Andy's great-grandfather William Henry Weston, getting them to patrol the streets at night. He organised a petition which was sent to the Queen, asking for a reward to be offered, with no result.

The women of the East End also organised a different kind of petition. They wanted the police to close down the worst of the brothels:

"To Our Most gracious Sovereign Lady Queen Victoria.
Madam:
We, the women of East London, feel horror at the dreadful sins that have been lately in our midst and grief because of the shame that has befallen the neighbourhood. By the facts which have come out in the inquests, we have learned much of the lives of those of our sisters who have lost a firm hold on goodness and who are living sad and degraded lives. We call on your servants in authority and bid them put the law which already exists in motion to close bad houses within whose walls such wickedness is done, and men and women ruined in body and soul.
we are, Madam, your loyal and humble subjects."

Psychics became involved, too. A medium from Cardiff reported that she had summoned the ghost of Liz Stride up in a seance with five other persons, on October 6th. The ghost had described her middle-aged assassin and given an address in Whitechapel, saying that he was a member of a gang of twelve. Another medium from Bolton, claimed that the Ripper was a farmer, with a dark moustache and scars behind his ears. The journal, 'Light' stated that the dead should not be called upon to do Scotland Yard's job for them, and any medium reporting to the police would be pilloried and maybe even locked up for wasting police time!

The most interesting psychic involved was Dr. Robert James Lees. He lived in Peckham in 1888 and had Kier Hardie, the radical socialist, as a friend. He was a philanthropist and a respected medium. He ran a Spiritualist Centre in Peckham and gave private consultations. It was alleged that he had come to the notice of Queen Victoria in the late 1860s when he contacted the spirit of Prince Albert. Thereafter, he was a frequent visitor to Windsor Castle. There is no documentary proof of this connection.

Lees' diaries, preserved at Stanstead Hall, contain references to the Whitechapel murders.

"Tuesday 2nd October. Offered services to police to follow up East End murders – called a fool and a lunatic. Got trace of man from the spot in Berner Street. Wednesday 3rd October. Went to City police again – called a madman and fool. Thursday 4th October. Went to Scotland Yard – same result but promised to write to me."

Lees claimed that his involvement began after the death of Annie Chapman. He dreamed of the killing in a precognitive dream, and was convinced that he would be instrumental in stopping the murderer. The strangest and most elusive tale of Lees' involvement comes from the Chicago 'Sunday-Times Herald' of 28 April 1895.

This stated that Lees had caught a glimpse of the killer on the top of an omnibus. Seventeen murders later, Lees was finally asked for assistance by the police and he followed a psychic trail to the house of an emminent physician. He had trained at Guy's, was a convinced vivisectionist, and had a wife and a son. When questioned, he admitted that he occasionally had lapses of memory, and he had once come home with a bloodstained shirt. Proof was found in the house and a medical court of enquiry was held and he was committed to an asylum in Islington under the pseudonym, 'Thomas Mason, 124'. He was still alive in 1895, although the public had been told that he had been buried in a Kensal Green cemetery. The source was said to be a "Dr. Howard of London" who had been a member of the court of inquiry.

Dr. Howard did, indeed, exist, but when the story came to his attention, he vigorously denied it. The story was probably a hoax by the Chicago Whitechapel Club which met at the rear of the newspaper offices. Lees, though, never did deny it, and variants of it were told by him. One such had him following the killer from the omnibus to his home. Another had the Queen instructing him to assist the police if there should be another murder. Thus the pyschic trail was followed with a Scotland Yard official. The body of a beggar who died in Seven Dials was buried in place of the insane doctor. Lees was then asked to leave London for five years, owing to the embarrassment caused to the doctor's wife, and he was given a pension during this time. His daughter, Eva, later showed visitors evidence that he had received a pension, and a gold cross in the family's possession is said to have been a gift from the grateful women of Whitechapel.

Cynthia Lee, who knew Lees from 1912, claimed that she had heard him tell various versions of the tale, reporting this in the Autumn 1970 issue of 'Light'. No trace can be found of any documentary evidence of Lees' involvement with the police. No relevant material is in the Home Office or the Yard.

Some have speculated that the emminent doctor was Sir William Gull, the Royal Physician, who trained at Guys and was an ardent vivisectionist. His home at 74, Brook Street in the West End would fit the description of the house in the tale.

There was a Thomas Mason in Islington at the time, of Bookbinders' Alms Houses, Balls Pond, Islington, who was in the Islington Infirmary until his death in 1912. He was not registered as being in any lunacy ward or asylum.

For some time, the police were searching for a left-handed killer. This came from Dr. Llewellyn's remarks that the bruising on Nichols' throat was from a thumbmark. He thought that a man had thus stood in front of her, steadied the jaw with the right hand and then cut the throat with the left hand, from left to right. This would have been extremely clumsy as a manouevre.

There is evidence that the Ripper strangled the women before cutting their throats. Chapman's tongue was purple, and Eddowes' was swollen. Kelly's throat was too disfigured to tell what bruising there might be, but her fists were clenched, as were those of Chapman and Stride. Clenched fists can be a sign of strangulation. The 'Lancet' of 29 September 1888 concurred that Chapman had probably been asphyxiated before she was cut. This would explain why there was not so much blood found with the body.

One theory of the method of operation of the Ripper is that he held the women from behind as they were preparing for anal intercourse – a common prostitute's trick to prevent conception – and then he would have strangled them, pushing their faces against the wall in the process. This would explain some of the bruising. This is suggested by Professor Cameron based upon a case in 1968 where a woman had been strangled and then had her throat slashed. He felt that an attack from the front would have been awkward and would have had to have been left-handed when studying the wounds. This is supported by Donald Rumbelow in 'The Complete Jack the Ripper'. However, the victims' backs, not their fronts, were bloodstained, and the flow of blood from the cartoid artery was always beside or under the neck and shoulders, suggests that the Ripper stood in front of the victims. He would have seized them by the throat and strangled them, pushed them down with their head to the left, and would have drawn the knife toward him. The bloodflow would thus be away from him. This suggests a right handed killer. This convincing method has been offered by Paul Begg, Martin Fido and Keith Skinner, and Cameron himself allows that the contemporary victim he studied might have been cut while lying on the ground, approaching from the head end and dragging the knife to the left.

The Scotland Yard files became available to the public in the Public Record Office at Kew in 1976. (It seems that one researcher, Leonard Matters, had access to them earlier, as well as the BBC.) A number of papers are missing, and various items were taken by souvenir hunters to about the second decade of this century. Various Ripper and Crippen related documents were removed and some were returned in 1987. About a hundred papers from the 'Suspects' file went missing about ten years ago. This refers to Folios 32-135 which were present in 1976, and were used by BBC researchers in 1973. They refer to a file of suspects in MEPO 3/141, which would have contained these folios. The bulk of the file contained reports on suspects brought in by the police for carrying black bags, having foreign accents, troubling women, or even for talking about the Ripper in public houses. There was also a collection of reports from the separate divisions listing all persons detained in connection with the murders.

PUNCH, OR THE LONDON CHARIVARI.—September 22, 1888.

BLIND-MAN'S BUFF.

(As played by the Police.)

"TURN ROUND THREE TIMES,
AND CATCH WHOM YOU MAY!"

It is easy to be frustrated with the police from such a distance before the skill of forensic science was established. Finger printing, blood samples, thread comparisons and so forth might have led them to a conviction. Social inequality, and a natural mistrust of the police by many of the East End, hindered matters further.

GHASTLY MURDER

IN THE EAST-END.

DREADFUL MUTILATION OF A WOMAN.

Capture of Leather Apron

Another murder of a character even more diabolical than that perpetrated in Buck's Row, on Friday week, was discovered in the same neighbourhood, on Saturday morning. At about six o'clock a woman was found lying in a back yard at the foot of a passage leading to a lodging-house in a Old Brown's Lane, Spitalfields. The house is occupied by a Mrs. Richardson, who lets it out to lodgers, and the door which admits to this passage, at the foot of which lies the yard where the body was found, is always open for the convenience of lodgers. A lodger named Davis was going down to work at the time mentioned and found the woman lying on her back close to the flight of steps leading into the yard. Her throat was cut in a fearful manner. The woman's body had been completely ripped open, and the heart and other organs laying about the place, and portions of the entrails round the victim's neck. An excited crowd gathered in front of Mrs. Richardson's house and also round the mortuary in old Montague Street, whither the body was quickly conveyed. As the body lies in the rough coffin in which it has been placed in the mortuary —the same coffin to which the unfortunate Mrs. Nicholls was first placed—it presents a fearful sight. The body is that of a woman about 45 years of age. The height is exactly five feet. The complexion is fair, with wavy dark brown hair; the eyes are blue, and two lower teeth have been knocked out. The nose is rather large and prominent.

Innocent Until Proven Guilty

Contemporary Suspects

The press and police reports at the time of the Whitechapel murders reveal that a number of people were listed as suspects.

(1) 'Leather Apron'

John Pizer, nicknamed 'Leather Apron' was the first, a Jewish slippermaker who wore a leather apron for his trade and had sharp knives for cutting the leather. He did abuse and threaten prostitutes, but he never cut them. He had solid alibis for the murders and was released from police custody. The finding of a leather apron at the site of Annie Chapman's murder fuelled these rumours, until it was shown that this belonged to a young man lodging at 29 Hanbury Street. The suspicion of Pizer sparked off a surge of anti-semitism, with mobs shouting at Jews, throwing stones through their windows, or beating people up. A common cry was, "No Englishman would commit murders like these!" 'Leather Apron' was still being used as a nickname for the killer as late as the night of the Double Event. J. Best said to Stride and the stranger with her, "That's Leather Apron getting round you." as the rain lashed down.

Whitechapel and Spitalfields had Jewish immigrants living there in large numbers since 1880, and they had moved into an overcrowded and poor area, with the former residents fearing for their jobs and fearing that Yiddish speakers in foreign clothes would swamp their area. Some of the Jewish families were chronically poor, and lodging houses or shelters for poor Jews were established. Other Jews kept clean houses and began to establish businesses. They were seen by many of the authorities as a very closed community who would have probably have kept any suspects in their own care rather than trust them to the police.

(2) Aaron Davies Cohen

Chief Inspector Swanson's notes in his copy of Sir Robert Anderson's book reveal that he suspected an insane Jew of the murders. He names him as Kosminski, but gets some of his facts wrong. He says that the man died soon after going to Colney Hatch asylum, having been sent to the Whitechapel Workhouse Infirmary first. Kosminski lived on for a number of years. His suspect, in reality, was probably one Aaron Davis Cohen who was brought before Thames Magistrates Court on 7 December 1888 as a lunatic wandering at large. He was sent to the Whitechapel Workhouse Infirmary for observation where his rages and anti-social behaviour led to his incarceration in Colney Hatch Lunatic Asylum where his poor behaviour continued. He was fed by tube and eventually died on 20 October 1889. Swanson wrote:

> "The only person who ever saw the murderer unhesitatingly identified the suspect the instant he was confronted with him; but he refused to give evidence against him because the suspect was also a Jew and also because his evidence would convict the suspect, and witness would be the means of murderer being hanged, which he did not wish to be left on his mind.... And after this identification which suspect knew, no other murder of this kind took place in London."

It is difficult to assess this charge, based in part upon Anderson's suspect. It is hard, too, to unravel the truth in Anderson's statements made later in life, when his comments during the murders suggested that the police had no real clue who the killer was.

Jews were certainly possible suspects. Major Smith, the Acting Commissioner for the City of London Police in September 1888, sent samples of shochet knives used in Jewish ritual slaughter to be pathologically tested and compared with the wounds found on Catharine Eddowes. They were shown to have definitely not caused the wounds, and the Jewish Chronicle expressed thanks at this observation.

The 'Times' for 12 September 1888 might give the origin for the Anderson/Swanson suspect. This describes the identity parade which involved John Pizer, 'Leather Apron'. The witness was one Emmanuel Delbast Violenia, who had seen a man arguing with a woman in suspicious circumstances and then threatening to do for her with a knife. Pizer was picked out immediately, but when Violena was taken to view Chapman's body, he could not identify her as the woman that he had seen. Thus he did not give evidence against Pizer. Pizer was the only Polish Jew known to have been arrested by the police. He could be the basis of the mixed up stories circulating later.

(3) Doctors and Medical Students

Doctors or medical students also came under suspicion because of the belief that a surgical knife had been used and some medical or anatomical knowledge was present in the killer. In fact, any doctor carrying his black bag, once a symbol of healing and succour, was a potential mob target. One was followed until he visited a house to help deliver a baby as he had said he was doing. Swanson reported to the Home Office on 19 October 1888 that three insane medical students were being investigated. Two had been traced and one had gone abroad. Abberline's report suggests that this man was a John Sanders, and he believed, wrongly that he and his mother had gone abroad. In fact, Sanders had been committed to Holloway Asylum in Virginia Water in 1887. Major Smith also mentioned investigating an insane medical student who was reputed to pass off polished farthings as sovereigns (remembering the farthings found by Chapman's body).

(4) Dr Morgan Davies

A Fellow of the Royal College of Surgeons, based at the London Hospital in 1888. In November of that year, Robert D'Onston Stephenson was sharing a room with a patient in the London Hospital when he claims that he watched Davies giving a graphic representation of how he thought the Ripper murdered his victims, grabbing them from behind and sodomising them before cutting their throats. Stephenson wrote for the 'Pall Mall Gazette' and was informed by the editor, W. T. Stead, that medical reports revealed that the Ripper had sodomised his victims. (This was wrong, and the Ripper had probably not approached them from behind, either.) Stephenson then began to watch Dr Davies as a suspect, helped by George Marsh, an unemployed ironmongery assistant. They even went to Scotland Yard. Marsh claimed that Stephenson was a fuddled, habitual drinker and his testimony could not be trusted. The two had signed an agreement that they would share any reward money equally, and Marsh later said that he had only done this to get a sample of Stephenson's handwriting, suggesting that he might be a suspect himself. The police did not seem to take this seriously. While some of the missing police files refer to Stephenson, nothing is mentioned about Dr Davies in their records.

Sir Melville Macnaghten –
suspected Druitt.

(5) The Macnaghten Memoranda

A major source of contemporary police suspicions was revealed in the Macnaghten memoranda. These are the notes of Sir Melville Leslie Macnaghten, the Assistant Chief Constable of the CID from 1889-1890, and the Chief Constable from 1890–1903. His memoranda were written in response to reports in 'The Sun' about a new suspect. There are two extant versions of his notes, which differ slightly, and a third has been described but has not been traced. Macnaghten begins by discussing the suspect Thomas Cutbush who was named as such in 'The Sun' on 13 February 1894.

Cutbush lived in Albert Street, Kennington, and was thought to have contracted syphilis in 1888, having paranoid delusions afterwards. He had worked as a canvasser for a tea firm in The Minories in the East End, but he abandoned this and wandered about at night. His whereabouts during the Whitechapel murders were unclear. He was detained as a lunatic in Lambeth infirmary in 1891 but escaped. He later assaulted two women, stabbing them in the behind with a knife. He was arrested and sent to Broadmoor. Macnaghten points out that his knife was different from the Ripper's, that he did not attack like the Ripper, and it is hard to imagine that he would have been quiet for a couple of years and then started to behave in such a way again.

Macnaghten then lists three suspects whom he claims were more seriously considered by Scotland Yard. Macnaghten relied on memory rather than notes and records, and some details are mixed up.

His three suspects were Montague John Druitt, Aaron Kosminski, and Michael Ostrog.

Druitt is described thus by Macnaghten in the Scotland Yard version of his notes:

"A Mr M. J. Druitt, said to be a doctor & of good family, who disappeared at the time of the Miller's Court murder, whose body (which was said to have been upwards of a month in the water) was found in the Thames on 31st Dec. – or about 7 weeks after that murder. He was sexually insane and from private info I have little doubt that his own family believed him to have been the murderer."

(The Lady Aberconway version calls Druitt a doctor unequivocally, and gives his age as of about 41 years of age – he was actually a barrister and teacher, and was 31.) We have no idea what the private information was that he claimed to possess.

Kosminski is described as follows:

"Kosminski, a Polish Jew, & resident in Whitechapel. This man became insane owing to many years indulgence in solitary vices. He had a great hatred of women, specially of the prostitute class, & had strong homicidal tendencies; he was removed to a lunatic asylum about March 1889. There were many circs connected with this man which made him a strong 'suspect'."

Of Ostrog, Macnaghten writes:

"Michael Ostrog, a Russian doctor, and a convict, who was subsequently detained in a lunatic asylum as a homicidal maniac. This man's antecedents were of the worst possible type, and his whereabouts at the time of the murders could never be ascertained."

Kosminski and Ostrog are not as intriguing suspects as Druitt.

Contemporary drawing of Kosminski.

(a) Kosminski

Kosminski was a Polish Jew who came to England in 1882 and worked as a hairdresser. He was treated at Mile End Old Town Workhouse Infirmary in 1890 where it was recorded that he had been insane for two years. He was dismissed into the care of his brother until he was placed in Colney Hatch Lunatic Asylum in 1891. One witness at his certification said:

"...he goes about the streets and picks up bits of bread out of the gutter and eats them, he drinks water from the tap & he refuses food at the hands of others. He took up a knife and threatened the life of his sister. He is very dirty and will not be washed...."

Colney Hatch records state that his condition had lasted for six years and resulted from self-abuse. He had calm and erudite periods, with occasional bouts of moroseness and violence until he became incoherent and demented, being transferred to Leavesden Asylum for Imbeciles, suffering from aural and visual hallucinations, where he died in 1919.

Kosminski can be dismissed as a mentally ill man who cannot be linked to the murders in any definite way. His violence only once involved a threat with a knife, and once a threat with a chair while in the asylum. This was not the mind that could so mutilate the women.

Michael Ostrog – suspect.

(b) Ostrog

Ostrog was a confidence trickster and a thief who spun yarns about his past and used many aliases. He was 5'11" with dark brown hair, grey eyes, and wore a clerical style suit. He was sometimes described as a Russian, a Russian Pole or a Polish Jew. He claimed that he was a former surgeon in the Russian navy, or a member of the Imperial Guard, and he was forced to leave Russia on account of killing a man in a duel. The earliest definite trace of his movements in England is in 1863, when as 'Max Gief' he was convicted of swindling hoteliers in Oxford and sentenced to ten months imprisonment. He was in and out of court and prison over the years to follow, and could certainly ingratiate himself with the rich, putting on a cultured voice and wearing smart clothes. In 1887, he was arrested for stealing a metal tankard, and was found wearing cricket clothes and carrying a black, Gladstone bag. He was described as gentlemanly in bearing. In October 1888 he failed to report to the police when on a ticket-of-leave parole. The 'Police Gazette' said of him, "Special attention is called to this dangerous man." His subsequent career is uncertain. In 1939, a letter written by Basil Thomson claimed that he had heard mention of Ostrog in Paris where he was suspected of being the Ripper, and was also known as Konovalov. However, Konovalov was a totally different man, a junior surgeon suspected of killing a woman in Paris in 1887 and of a woman in Russia in 1891. He was arrested in Petrograd and died in an asylum.

The police were looking for Ostrog as a dangerous con man at the height of the Whitechapel murders, but there is no evidence to link him to the killings. His appearance could have fitted the sightings of Ripper witnesses, and he was a play actor, with different guises and identities. He was a crook, but never a killer, as far as we know. The mad behaviour of the Ripper showed rank insanity or a hidden motive that cannot be traced in a man such as Ostrog.

(c) Druitt

Druitt was educated at Winchester and New College, Oxford, graduating in 1880. He was thirty one at the time of the Whitechapel murders. At Winchester, he was an accomplished debater, championing Wordsworth as a defender of Protestantism, speaking in favour of the French Republic, and also defending the fashions of the 1870s as being attractive and utilitarian. His one recorded failure was as an actor when he played Sir Toby Belch in a school production of 'Twelth Night'. The college magazine reported, scathingly, "But of the inadequacy of Druitt as Sir Toby Belch, what are we to say?" He was sufficiently respected to be made Prefect of Chapel in his final year.

He was a keen sportsman, particularly at cricket, playing for the school First Eleven at Lord's in 1876. He taught at Mr Valentine's school in Blackheath from 1880, and was admitted to the Inner Temple in 1882, showing an unusual delay. Many would enrol at one of the Inns before leaving University. It is just possible that he made preparations to study medicine for a

Montague John Druitt (note the striking resemblance to Prince Eddy!)

year, following in his father's footsteps, but then changed course. He was called to the Bar in 1885, attached to the Western circuit. He had chambers at 9, King's Bench Walk in the Temple. He was honorary treasurer and secretary for Blackheath Cricket, Football and Lawn Tennis Company. He worked as a special pleader, supplementing his work as a teacher. He did not often have to appear in court, and could either act as a runner dealing with various documents for other barristers, or took on cases of poorer clients. This would sometimes involve waiting at the court for a case to be brought to him for a pittance. There would often be lines of barristers trying to earn a living in this way. This was known as 'the Dock Brief', deriving from the Dock labourers who would assemble each morning hoping that there might be work for them. He obviously had to supplement his income from teaching. He was dismissed from Mr Valentine's school on about 30 November 1888, for being in "serious trouble at the school", the circumstances of which are unknown. Some have wondered if a homosexual assault was involved on a boy, but we have no evidence. He was last seen alive between 1 – 3 December 1888. His body was pulled out of the Thames on 31 December, by a waterman, Henry Winslade. This was near Thorneycroft's Torpedo Works at Chiswick. He had been in the water for about a month. Four large stones, £2.17s.2d. in cash, two cheques for £50 and £16, a pair of kid gloves, a silver watch on a gold chain, a white handkerchief, and two rail tickets were found in his pockets. One ticket was a first class half-season from Blackheath to London, and the other was a second half return from Hammersmith to Charing Cross, dated 1 December.

Macnaghten claimed that Druitt was the most likely suspect later in his career. On 2 June 1913, he told the Daily Mail that he joined the Yard two months after the Ripper committed suicide! In his memoirs, 'Days of My Years', in 1914, he returns to the suicide theme:

> "Although... the Whitechapel murderer, in all probability, put an end to himself soon after the Dorset Street affair in November 1888, certain facts, pointing to this conclusion, were not in the possession of the police till some years after I became a detective officer...."

What these "certain facts" might have been has caused much speculation, and Macnaghten said that he had destroyed any papers relating to this. The Daily Mail report of 2 June 1913 adds:

"I have destroyed all my documents and there is now no record of the secret information which came into my possession at one time or another."

Such wanton destruction would be very odd for a senior police officer, as commented by H. L. Adam, writing earlier this century. Macnaghten's daughter, Lady Aberconway, suspects that his tale of destroying evidence was told to silence his cronies at the Garrick who were always pestering him about the Ripper.

It would be important to establish that Druitt was a suspect before Macnaghten's tenure to make him more worthy of consideration. G. R. Sims wrote, in the 'Referee' in 1902 that the man who was found drowned in December 1888 was considered a suspect in his lifetime. However, Sims was an associate of Macnaghten, and might be relying upon his memoirs. That this was the prevalent view at Scotland Yard at the time is also confirmed by the Crimes Club tour of the Whitechapel sites, which Conan Doyle joined in with in 1905. They were guided by Dr. Gordon Brown, the City of London Police Surgeon, who had examined the body of Catharine Eddowes. He challenged the belief at the Yard that the Ripper was a homicidal maniac doctor who was found drowned in the Thames. He argued that the killer had been a highly disturbed sexual pervert. A fascinating oral tradition claims that the police told a Chairman of the Vigilance Committee that the Ripper had committed suicide in 1888. This man was Albert Bachert, who was Chairman in 1890. He badgered the police about the Whitechapel murders until he was told about the suicide. This tradition stems from Dr Thomas Dutton. Dutton was a doctor in Aldgate at the time of the murders, and he died in 1935. He supposedly wrote copious notes on famous crimes of his day, 'Chronicles of Crime', which were seen by Donald McCormick in 1932, and used in his 'The Identity of Jack the Ripper' in 1959. A Miss Hermione Dudley claimed to have possession of the Chronicles in 1935. The oral tradition about Bachert might well be true, but we do not have enough evidence to substantiate this.

On firmer ground is a report in the 'Bristol Times and Mirror', 11 February 1891, that an unnamed West of England MP declared that the Ripper was the son of a surgeon and that he committed suicide on the night of the last murder. The Littlechild Letter, mentioned in the next section, names a different Ripper suspect, but also mentions the tradition that the killer had committed suicide. This letter dates from 1913, again under possible Macnaghten influence, but this shows that the suicide theory was gaining widespread belief in police circles by this time.

One final source for the strong belief that the Ripper had drowned has been traced by the Parlours. This is in a manual about the constitution and principles of the Metropolitan Police that was published in 1929. This was by J. F. Moylan, the Receiver for the Metropolitan Police District and the Metropolitan Police Courts. This office was parallel in authority with that of the Commissioner of Police, both being directly under the Home Secretary. Moylan was thus a very senior figure. He had been at the Home Office from 1905-1918, and had been Receiver from 1919. He wrote:

> "The dynamite campaign practically ceased after 1885, but 1887, the Jubilee year, was full of anxieties for the C.I.D. and its Special Branch. Next year, 1888, came the series of fiendish murders in Whitechapel popularly attributed to "Jack the Ripper", a name that first appeared as the signature to a bogus letter which was treated as possibly authentic and given undue publicity by Scotland Yard. Notwithstanding the peculiar character of these murders, both as regards locality and victims, there was a general scare, many believing that Satan, or perhaps Cain, was revisiting the Earth. Feeling ran very high against Scotland Yard and the C.I.D. for their failure to lay hands on the murderer, who, it is now certain, escaped justice by committing suicide at the end of 1888."

It is worth asking if so firm a set of views could have come from Macnaghten's influence alone?

Druitt might have been the subject of police enquiries before his body was found purely on the basis that he had gone missing. His brother, William, discovered this on 11 December 1888. The note found in his rooms suggested that he was suicidal, and as suicide was then a criminal offence, it would have been enough to have mounted a police search. Donald Rumbelow wonders what might have been found in Druitt's chambers if the police organised a search. Could surgical knives have been found that would have implicated him? Rumbelow then recounts how he was given a broken post mortem knife by Miss Dorothy Stroud. She had been assistant editor on 'Sporting Life' in the thirties, and her editor, Hugh Pollard, is said to have shown her a case with two knives in which was heavily bloodstained inside. He said these were the Ripper's knives. He let her keep one of them. Pollard had been a gun expert who had worked with the Yard earlier, and it is just possible that he acquired the knives from the police. Rumbelow's knife was examined and found to be a 19th century post mortem knife that was used for ripping upwards. Could this have been found in Druitt's belongings, and have constituted the "certain facts" mentioned by Macnaghten? But this is pure speculation.

It is important to explore what is known of Druitt's character and circumstances to try to weigh up the evidence against him. Could this man have been the Ripper?

The first point to note is that he could have acquired some medical knowledge. Though Macnaghten wrongly describes Druitt as a doctor, his father, William Druitt was. William was a member of the Royal College of Surgeons from 1849, as well as his father before him and some cousins. William practised in Wimborne, Dorset, he died in 1885, only months after Montague was called to the Bar and took rooms at 9 King's Bench Walk. We can speculate that Montague picked up some rudimentary knowledge from his father, possibly attending operations or autopsies that his father conducted. He would certainly have had access to surgical knives. He might have started to pursue medical studies in 1880, and might have dallied with a return to them after he was failing to achieve anything as a barrister. Rumbelow wonders if Macnaghten was not actually so mistaken by calling Druitt a doctor. He wonders if Druitt was one of the two unnamed medical students who were questioned as suspects early in October. This might explain why he laid low before killing Kelly the next month. Possible, but just speculation.

Then there is the state of Montague Druitt's mind. His mother, Ann, suffered terrible depressions and delusions after her husband's death in 1885. She attempted suicide in 1888, and by July of that year she was certified as insane, being taken to the Brooke Asylum, Clapton, and later to an establishment in Brighton. She was finally transferred to the Manor House Asylum, Chiswick, in May 1890. She died there on 15 December. The root of the problem might have been hereditary diabetes which can induce such melancholy. Her mother committed suicide, and her sister attempted it. The death of her husband, and then of Montague, made matters far worse. The notes regarding her death certificate say that she had had "brain disease" for 21 months, which would have been since her son's suicide.

Montague left a letter, addressed to Mr Valentine, found by his brother, William, saying that he feared "Since Friday I felt

I was going to be like mother and the best thing for me was to die." Macnaghten's claim that his family suspected him of being the murderer and that he was sexually insane cannot be tested. (Rumbelow wonders if he was a repressed homosexual who was impotent with women, drawing upon the graphologist's reports on the Lusk letter and modern cases of sexual killers who have taken out their rage and frustration against women for reasons of impotency.)

Druitt's finances at the time of his death are also a mystery. He had struggled to make it as a barrister, borrowing against a legacy of £500 to pay for board, examinations and various fees before being called to the Bar in 1885 (he borrowed about half the amount). He was unable to make a living as a barrister. He had previously taken employment in 1880 at the school in 9, Elliot Place, Blackheath, a small school with 42 boarders, three resident staff and seven servants. The cheques found upon his person were probably final payments from the school, from whence he had been dismissed after term ended on 1st December. Druitt left £1,300 in his will, roughly equivalent to £58,000 today. This is amazing, given his struggles and the legacy he drew from in 1885. His father's will had left so little to him, and to two of his other brothers, whereas his mother received all income and rents from the estate, his older brother William inherited the property, and his sisters received £6,000 each so long as they did not marry before they were 21. Their father probably believed that he had already given a fair share to the boys for giving them their education. Where did Montague get so much money? His pay as a schoolmaster, and his income as a special pleader cannot account for this. Did he receive some special pay-off for his services in the Whitechapel murders?

Montague left what seems to have been a suicide note, and yet, he had travelled all the way to Chiswick to commit such an act. There were deep enough and accessible enough stretches of the Thames nearer to Blackheath. He also had a return ticket to Hammersmith, which is odd if he was seriously contemplating suicide. He was finely dressed, which has led some to wonder if he was on his way to meet someone, although a suicide's turn of mind can perform like this, going to the grave in one's best array! It is possible that he was meeting someone, who then murdered him.

Druitt would have had little difficulty travelling to and from Blackheath during the murders. The last train from Cannon Street was at 11.40pm, with one at 12.25am from London Bridge. The earliest one in the morning was at 5.10am from Cannon Street, and this is the one he would have had to take. The murders occurred in the early hours. Alternatively, he could have travelled back to King's Bench Walk easily, via Embankment or Fleet Street. He could have easily left the school at weekends to return for duties on Monday, and some of the murders were in vacation time. His cricketing record is illuminating, for MCC records show that on 1st September, the day after Polly Ann Nichols was murdered, Druitt was playing in Canford, Dorset. On 8 September, 1888, Druitt played for Blackheath at 11.30am. This latter engagement would have been possible, but it is usually thought highly improbable that he would have travelled all the way to Dorset after being up for most of the night and killing a woman. However, the Parlours have checked the timetables for trains from Waterloo that summer. The earliest one to Bournemouth was at 5.30am, with the next two at 5.50am and 6.25am. These reached Bourne-mouth at about 8.30am, 9.08am and 10.25 am respectively. Canford is just West of Bournemouth and could be reached by a branch line in about 45 minutes. The first two trains would have allowed him to get there in good time to play cricket, and to have had time for sleep on the journey.

Another oddity is that his brother, William, stated at the inquest that there were no other relatives when his two other brothers, three sisters and mother were also alive.

Did he want to spare them the embarrassment of publicity, or of any suspicion that Druitt was involved in the murders?

There are two other peculiar traditions surrounding Druitt. Montague's cousin, Dr Lionel Druitt, emigrated to Australia in 1886. He had worked, briefly, at a surgery in the Minories in 1878 or 1879. He is the alleged author of 'The East End Murderer – I knew him' which was first mentioned in a letter from a Mr A. Knowles in 1959. He claimed to have seen the booklet in Australia, and that it was published by a Mr Fell of Dandenong in 1890 (interestingly, Dr Druitt lived in Dandenong Road). However, no one has yet been able to trace any copy, or any details of this having been printed.

The Minories has raised interest because of the Liverpool letters where the 'Ripper' claims that he will be at work there. Lionel Druitt was not resident there then. Druitt would have had no connection as far as is known.

There is a tale that the painter Walter Sickert was lodging in a room in London some years after the murder. He was told by his landlady that the previous occupant was Jack the Ripper! The man was a young veterinary student who was consumptive and delicate in appearance. He would often stay out all night, returning about six in the morning and then he crept out to buy the first edition of the morning newspaper. Traces were found in his fireplace of his burnt suit that had been blood-stained. His health deteriorated and his mother came from Bournemouth and took him back home where he died three months later. One source has suggested that Sickert told this tale to Macnaghten.

This is a garbled account if it is supposed to relate to Druitt. His family did live in Bournemouth, but he was not a veterinary student, and his mother was hospitalised at the time of the murders. If this has come from Sickert, then it could be a tease for his black humour liked to shock.

Tom Cullen in 'The Crimes and Times of Jack the Ripper', published back in 1965, was the first attempt to provide biographical information on Druitt, identifying Macnaghten's suspect with the reports of the drowned barrister in the press of the time, such as the 'County of Middlesex Independent' of 2 January 1889, and the 'Southern Guardian' of 5 January:

> "SUICIDE IN THE THAMES – Dr. Diplock held an inquiry at the Lamb Tap, Chiswick, on Wednesday of the body of a gentleman named Montague John Druitt [sic], 31 years of age,which was found by a waterman floating in the Thames off Thorneycroft's, on Monday. The pockets of the deceased were found to contain stones. The jury returned a verdict of "Suicide during temporary insanity."...."

> "SAD DEATH OF A LOCAL BARRISTER: An inquiry was on Wednesday held by Dr Diplock, at Chiswick, respecting the death of Montague John Druitt, 31 years of age, who was found drowned in the Thames.The deceased was identified by his brother, a solicitor residing in Bournemouth, who stated that the deceased was a barrister-at-law, but had recently been an assistant at a school in Blackheath. The deceased had left a letter, addressed to Mr. Valentine, of the school, in which he alluded to a suicide. Evidence having been given as to discovering deceased in the Thames – upon his body were found a cheque for £50 and 16 in gold – the Jury returned a verdict of "Suicide whilst of unsound mind."....."

Cullen was the first person to supply background information on Druitt, especially his father's surgical profession, and this aroused new interest in Druitt as a serious suspect. Cullen also speculated that Druitt might have been familiar with the East End through the work of Toynbee Hall which was opened in the East End as a centre for recreation and education to assist the local people. New College undergraduates had flooded into the area earlier to help with charity work, and many of them now visited Toynbee Hall regularly, some of them having been Druitt's collegemates. 'Tobacco parliaments' were held where social questions were heatedly debated. Fabian Socialists were often present at these debates, such as Shaw and the Webbs.

Druitt was subsequently championed as a suspect by Martin Howells and Keith Skinner in 'The Ripper Legacy'. They argue that he was homosexual, and moved in the same social circles as J. K. Stephen and Eddy. His mother's insanity in July1888 was the catalyst that began his deranged decline and sparked off the killing spree. They speculate that an Oxbridge group conspired to kill him so as not to disgrace their social set. Again, this is pure speculation.

Druitt is worthy of more attention, particularly if it can be established that he was the subject of a police enquiry in his lifetime, and if it can be shown that he had connections with other highly placed suspects such as J. K. Stephen. However, without more evidence, he remains yet another suspect, who might just have been a suicide victim because of depression and fears surrounding his mother's health. The fact that he died at the end of the Whitechapel murders might be mere co-incidence.

(6) The Littlechild Letter and Francis Tumblety

One further piece of contemporary evidence needs to be surveyed that has recently come to light. This is the 'Littlechild Letter', written by Chief Inspector John Littlechild, typed and dated 23 September 1913. This was written to G. R. Sims and was purchased along with other papers of Sims' by a collector of crime ephemera. Stewart Evans discovered this, and has written about its possible suspect in 'The Lodger – the Arrest and Escape of Jack the Ripper'. Littlechild states:

> "I never heard of a Dr. D. in connection with the Whitechapel murders but amongst the suspects, and to my mind a very likely one, was a Dr. T. (which sounds very much like D.) He was an American quack named Tumblety and was at one time a frequent visitor to London and on these occasions constantly brought under the notice of police, there being a large dossier concerning him at Scotland Yard. Although a "Sycopatia Sexualis" he was not known as a "Sadist" (which the murderer unquestionably was) but his feelings towards women were

remarkable and bitter in the extreme, a fact on record. Tumblety was arrested at the time of the murders in connection with unnatural offences and charged at Marlborough Street, remanded on bail, jumped his bail, and got away to Boulogne. He shortly left Boulogne and was never heard of afterwards. It was believed that he committed suicide but certain it is from this time the "Ripper" murders came to an end....."

Francis J. Tumblety was born c 1833 in Canada, his family emigrating to Rochester, New York shortly afterwards. He was remembered as a newspaper seller in 1850, and then he left. He returned in 1860 calling himself a doctor. He dressed elegantly and had an aristocratic bearing. One witness thought that his 'qualification' had come from a time working in a Detroit Drug Store. He moved around, always wary of being caught out as a fraud. In 1860, he was in trouble in Toronto when a patient, Mr Portmore, died. An autopsy blamed him for "atrocious treatment" and he was accused of manslaughter. He fled to Boston. He restricted his cures to herbal remedies, and, for a time, was successful with the 'Tumblety Pimple Destroyer'. He was feted by the press for his herbal cures. He was wrongly arrested under suspicion of the assassination plot against President Lincoln, because he was using an alias, 'Blackburn' that was unfortunately the same as that of a Confederate spy who was being hunted down. He was cleared, and his connections with the military led to his flirtation with becoming an army surgeon, but he withdrew, claiming that a poor turn of health had led to his need for a European vacation to recuperate.

Tumblety arrived in Liverpool in 1888. There were no checks on foreign doctors' credentials then and he was free to practise as he wanted. We know that the Yard contacted the San Fransisco police asking for a sample of Tumblety's handwriting in October 1888, and this was forthcoming in November. The 'New York Times' of 19 November 1888 reported that Tumblety had been arrested under suspicion of the Whitechapel murders. This wrongly claimed that he had been found innocent of this charge – the truth was that there was not enough evidence to charge him. He was charged under the Criminal Law Amendment Act, 1885, which dealt with sexual offences to do with prostitution and procuring. This also made homosexual and other 'unnatural' acts illegal between consenting adults. We do not know exactly what he was charged with; Tumblety was known to hate women and avoided their company. He had said at a dinner party in America that he would sooner poison his guests than put them in the company of women, whom he called "cattle". There were suspicions of his involvements with young boys before he crossed the Atlantic.

Bail was set at $1,500 and this was met by two gentlemen. Tumblety then fled to Boulogne. On 24 November, he sailed on La Bretagne for America under the alias 'Frank Townsend'. He was watched by the New York police, but Chief Inspector Thomas Byrne stressed that he was just keeping a trace on him, for there was no actual proof that he was the Ripper. The 'World' on 4 December, stated that a Scotland Yard detective had been sent across to watch him, as a barman revealed in an interview. The 'St Louis Republican' of 22 December revealed that Inspector Andrews of Scotland Yard had been sent to trace Tumblety, and half a dozen men were working with him. The presence of Yard detectives pursuing enquiries across the Atlantic was confirmed in the London 'Pall Mall Gazette' of 31 December.

Tumblety slipped by the watching police and detectives. He disappeared and was not heard of again until he published a denial of all the accusations and slanders made about the Whitechapel murders in 1889. There were claims that murders in Jamaica and Nicaragua at the end of December 1888 and in January 1889 suggested that Tumblety had fled there. The death of Carrie Brown in 1891, in a New York dockside hotel, rekindled speculation. She had been strangled and slashed with a knife. There were cuts and stab wounds all over her, and the killer might have been trying to cut out her abdomen but her struggles prevented him, though the doctor performing the autopsy, Dr Jenkins, contradicted himself at the trial of the supected murderer later, saying that the woman had been strangled first and then mutilated. Thus, this was not a serious attempt at opening the stomach. Ameer ben Ali, an Algerian Arab, was accused of the murder, and he had a room across the corridor from Carrie. However, a man seen earlier in her company was also reported near the scene of the crime.This man looked foreign, was in his thirties, and had a large moustache, wearing a large black, derby hat. Ali was found guilty of second degree murder and was sentenced to life imprisonment. Bloodstains had been found in the hallway between the two rooms, and inside his door, but he always protested his innocence. Later, it seemed that the stains might have appeared after the police investigated the premises, and Ali was released.

Tumblety spent the last ten years of his life with his elderly niece in Rochester, New York, wintering in the south. When in St Louis, he took ill and was treated by the Sisters of Mercy, taking a room in their hospital under the assumed name, 'Townsend'. He died on 23 May 1903.

Tumblety is a possible suspect. He was a flamboyant character, who was 5' 10" with black moustache. He had a hatred of women, and, presumably, of fallen women in particular. He was in the area of Whitechapel during the murders, possibly staying at 22 Batty Street, according to Evans and Gainey in 'The Lodger'. It is possible that James Monro referred to him when he stated, "the Ripper was never caught, but he should have been." His papers were reckoned by his son to contain a "very hot potato" on the subject, which might have been the fact that the police had the Ripper in custody and then let him escape. However, there is no real evidence to convict the man. He is just one more of the eccentric and disturbed individuals who came under suspicion in the country at the time. That he had been involved in some sexual misdemeanor is true, as suggested by the Littlechild Letter, and his charge. There was no evidence that he was a sadistic killer. The only charge of manslaughter he had against him was because of medical maltreatment.

What is interesting is Littlechild's claim that Tumblety committed suicide soon after his escape. This was mistaken, but it is a possible reference to the Druitt tradition that had become garbled. This might, ironically, strengthen the case proposing Druitt as the killer!

The Parlours have pointed out that as Littlechild was Head of the Secret Department from 1883–1893, which was the forerunner of the Special Branch, with special interest in Fenian activities, it is possible that Tumblety was pursued and watched because of suspected Fenian connections, and that the Whitechapel connection was a suitable cover. Tumblety did refer to himself as a great Irish patriot, and had held meetings in the States to rouse support for the Irish cause. This might have been another example of posturing, but the Fenian connection remains tenable.

(7.) George Chapman

The American connection produced one more suspect. In 1903, Severin Klosowski, alias George Chapman, was arrested and tried for the murder of three of his wives. According to H. L. Adam, who wrote 'The Trial of George Chapman' in 1930, Abberline had told Inspector George Godley at the time, "You've got Jack the Ripper at last!" As Godley helped Adam to prepare the volume, it is likely to be true. (Though we might wonder if Abberline had mixed up Klosowski with earlier police suspect, Kosminski.) Godley also asserted that Abberline had gone out of his way to question Chapman's first wife, Lucy Baderski, about his whereabouts during the time of the murders. She is said to have claimed that he was out till the early hours and she had no idea what he was doing. It is fairly certain that they did not know each other then, and so this evidence is highly questionable. They met in a Polish club in Clerkenwell, and according to Lucy's brother, their courtship was very brief. They were married in 1889.

Chapman was born in Poland, and was an apprentice surgeon from 1880-1885, a student at the Hospital of Praga in Warsaw from 1885-1886, and a Junior Surgeon in 1887. In June of that year, he came to England. and turned his hand to hairdressing. He made his living as a barber or as a publican thereafter. He ran a basement shop under the White Hart on the corner of Whitechapel High Street in 1890. By this time, he was living with Lucy Baderski. She gave birth to a son in April, and they emigrated to New Jersey (probably in the Whitsuntide of that year). Lucy returned in February 1891, giving birth to a daughter, Cecilia, soon afterwards.

Chapman returned early that summer, and cohabited with another woman, Annie Chapman (of no relation to the second Ripper victim). It was then that he adopted her surname and started to call himself 'George Chapman'. He kept his own premises in Tottenham for a few years, and then worked as a barber or as a publican in such diverse places as Hastings, the City, Bishops Stortford, Lambeth and Southwark. He came to trial for being a poisoner and wife killer.

Annie Chapman left him in 1894 over his womanising, and in 1895 he had taken up with a Mrs Mary Spink, falsely claiming that she was married to him. They moved to Hastings in 1896 and he used her money to run a hairdressing business. He soon began to beat her and to take up with a servant girl, Alice Penfold. He decided to poison Mary, and in April 1897 he bought an ounce of tartaremetic, a metallic poison, which he slowly fed to his wife. They moved in 1897 to the Prince of Wales public house in Bartholomew Square, and she died by the end of the year. Her death was put down to natural causes.

Chapman hired a new barmaid, Bessie Taylor, and they began a relationship. In 1901, she developed similar symptoms and she died in the February. Her death was also put down to natural causes. In August 1901, he hired Maud Marsh as his new barmaid, moving to the Crown in Borough High Street. By summer, he was carrying on with a new barmaid, Florence Rayner. In October, Maud died of the same condition as the other two women. This time doctors traced a poison in her body, and the previous two women were exhumed and investigated. He was hanged on 7 April 1903.

Suspicions about him being the Ripper began with the publicity surrounding the trial, as can be seen from the 'Daily Chronicle' of 23 March 1903. This report stresses the similarity of Chapman's appearance with that of the Ripper – he carried a black bag and wore a peaked, 'P. and O.' cap. The reason for Lucy's abandonment of him is also given. Apparently, a row started in the New Jersey shop, and he pushed her down on the bed and pressed his face against her mouth to keep her from screaming. A customer chanced to enter, and he let her go. She noticed a long knife under the pillow and genuinely feared for her life. In 1902, she was traced by Detective Sergeant Arthur Neil and she picked Chapman out of an identity parade. He claimed that he did not know her, but she replied, "Ah, Severino, don't say that! You remember the time you nearly killed me in Jersey City!"

The 'Pall Mall Gazette' questioned Abberline, and he pointed out that the murders ceased here when Chapman left, but similar incidents began when he arrived in America. Abberline made mistakes. He thought that Chapman was living at George Yard at the time of Martha Tabram's death – he was not. He was elsewhere in the Whitechapel area. Abberline also seemed to believe the reports of organ selling, repeating the story about an American enquiring for specimens for sale, as told by the coroner Dr Wynne Baxter. The British Medical Journal of the time refuted this connection, stating that the doctor in question was highly respected and no large sum was offered. The doctor had left the country eighteen months before the murders began.

The American incident is that of the murdered prostitute Carrie Brown, which Tumblety was also suspected of, on the night of 23-24 April 1891. However, Chapman was still living in Whitechapel on 5 April 1891, according to the census. Chapman's son had died the month before. It is not known exactly when he left for America, but it is just possible that it was in April and that he was the killer of Carrie Brown, but this is unlikely. His appearance as foreign with a large moustache would fit, but this is very general. (Philip Sugden, in 'The Complete History of Jack the Ripper', has pointed out that

Chapman was about 23 at the time of the Whitechapel murders, and that most witnesses put the killer in his early thirties or late twenties, and that we do not know how long he had carried the black bag, or how long he had worn the sailing cap. The cap might have been acquired during his time in Hastings, when he started sailing.) Chapman was also fond of Americanisms after his trip to New Jersey. He appealed, during his trial, as a man who was "born in 1865 in the County of Michigan, USA." The Americanisms of the 'Dear Boss' letter might have lent support to his identity as the Ripper, but he had only acquired these after 1891!

The strongest objection to Chapman being the killer is his method of operation. He acted as a poisoner and serial killers do not usually change their method midstream. While he was violent to Lucy, this was a domestic situation and a precedent cannot be proven from this. Chapman was a womaniser who made attachments for a period and then rid himself of the women to attach himself to someone else. This was not the way of the Ripper who seemed to have picked the victims up casually and then murdered them horribly and without any sexual involvement. While it is possible that he was the Ripper, and Sugden feels that he is a stronger suspect than Druitt, Kosminski or Ostrog, it is yet another case of a crook and a killer who was around at the time and the case remains unsolved.

The Parlours have chanced upon some fascinating oral traditions about Chapman and his first wife, Lucy Baderski, through a mutual friend, David Brown, another East End emigre. David happens to be the great-grandson of George Chapman. He interviewed his mother, Cecilia Brown – Chapman's grand-daughter – in January 1997, then aged 86. She said that her mother, Cecilia Przygodzinski – Lucy Baderski's daughter – never told her or the rest of the family anything about the execution of Chapman until her engagement. Her fiance was asked, "Do you realise that you'll be marrying the granddaughter of a murderer?" The fiance replied, "I'm not marrying her grandfather. I'm marrying her!" The children had presumed that their grandfather had died early, before learning this news. They knew that Lucy and their grandfather were Polish born, and that they had been to America for a short time. Lucy's daughter said that she did not have much schooling, and that she left at 12, rather than 14, because of the difficulties she faced when Chapman was executed in 1903. Lucy had worked in a factory, for a time, making men's trousers. Her daughter used to go there straight

Severin Klosowski, alias George Chapman.

from school and she used to sew on buttons from an early age.

The only time that Chapman's daughter saw her father was when he was in prison, and he was hiding under the bedsheets. She presumed that he was ill and was in the prison infirmary. The remarkable thing was that he was still using an American accent and claiming that he was an American citizen!

A model of Chapman was exhibited in the Chamber of Horrors in Madam Tussauds until a fire damaged this exhibit and many others. Cecilia Brown's sister-in-law, Queenie, went to see him and she said how surprised she was to see "such a weedy little man." He was not tall and handsome as she had expected, after all the stories about him attracting the women. His secret appeal lay in his posing as a Polish aristocrat. He used to stand up whenever a strange woman entered the room, and with a click of the heels and a low bow, he would kiss her hand and enquire of her name.

George Chapman's daughter, Cecilia with her husband, Albert Przygodzinski, October 1908. (Published for the first time, from family collection.)

It seems that Chapman had had another child by Lucy, but the baby had died. Lucy's daughter had been allowed to dress it like a doll before it was buried!

Lucy Baderski left for Brazil, with her new husband, after running the Polish Club as the caretaker for a time. Her daughter did not get on with the step-father, and she stayed in London. She married an ex-Prussian cavalryman, Albert Przygodzinski, who bore a sabre scar on his foot. He had been born on the border of Poland and Germany, and he came to England when he was 25. He was a tailor and a designer, working for the department store, Peter Robinson's. He would often travel to Paris, to check out the latest fashions. Her own daughter was born in 1910.

Cecilia Brown recalls a succession of older, colourful characters from the Polish community at the turn of the century. When she lived in Walthamstow, there were constant visitors. There were the two Sophies, and a bachelor known as 'Pidgeon' for his Polish name meant 'bird'. Pidgeon used to mend the police boots at the Police Station in Leman Street. He survived into the years of the Second World War, and was so terrified of the bombs that he once hid underneath a horse!

Mr and Mrs Stanislaus Rauch were also mentioned. Mrs Rauch was Lucy Baderski's sister, and she was one of the witnesses at the trial of Chapman. The Rauchs lived in a well-off area and did not really mix much with Lucy and her family. Lucy's granddaughter speaks of them having twins just after she was born, and they would play together. She had a vivid and frightening memory of having to see Mr Rauch in his coffin, and to kiss him on the forehead, noticing cotton wool stuffed up his nose!

This intriguing section of oral history tells us a few previously unknown details about Chapman but tells us nothing about whether he might have been the Ripper or not.

Severin Klosowski m. Lucy Baderski 1889

one son b.1890 d. 1891   Cecilia b. 1892

                        m. Albert Przygodzinski 1908

                        Cecilia b.1910

                        m. Arthur Brown 1932

                        David b. 1940

(8) 'Jill the Ripper' and Sherlock Holmes

Another speculation at the time of the murders was that the killer might have been a woman, for she would have been able to approach the women without them feeling threatened. This was first suggested by the Reverend Sydney Godolphin Osborne in a letter to the 'Times', arguing that she was an abortionist, thus explaining her anatomical knowledge. This was not taken seriously by the police, but Sir Arthur Conan Doyle thought that a male killer might have disguised himself as a woman with an apron, for a midwife in a bloodstained apron would not arouse any undue suspicion.

Conan Doyle had an interest in the Whitechapel murders after visiting an exhibition in Scotland Yard where he saw the 'Dear Boss' letter and the postcard written in red ink. In 1894 he suggested to an American journalist how Holmes might have gone about solving the murders. Holmes would have noted the clerkly hand of the 'Dear Boss' letter, and also the Americanisms, 'Boss', and 'fix it up'. Holmes would have had the police advertise the handwriting, with a feature on significant letter formations, and invite response. (The writing was placed on posters, in fact, to no avail.) Conan Doyle also joined a group for a tour of the murder sites.

To conclude this chapter, the notes, interviews and memoirs of detectives involved at the time or soon afterwards reveal that various people came under suspicion, and some policemen clearly had their pet suspects. One can almost imagine them at the Yard placing their bets on different characters that came to their attention.

POLICE THE ILLUSTRATED NEWS
LAW COURTS AND WEEKLY RECORD

No. 1,292.   SATURDAY, NOVEMBER 17, 1888.   Price One Penny.

SKETCHES OF THE SEVENTH EAST END CRIME.

THE SEVENTH HORRIBLE MURDER BY THE MONSTER OF THE EAST END.

THE SEVENTH VICTIM!
PICKED OUT FOR SLAUGHTER BY THE EAST-END FIEND.
FROM DESCRIPTIONS GIVEN BY HER INTIMATE FRIENDS.

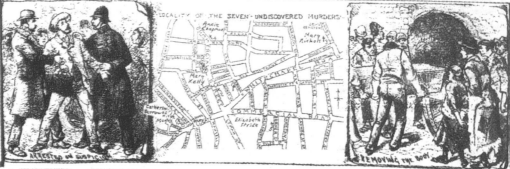

LOCALITY OF THE SEVEN UNDISCOVERED MURDERS.

Rogues Gallery

Recent Suspects and Theories

The Mysterious Dr Stanley

The first story to be told to try to solve the Ripper murders after the years surrounding the events was in an article in 'The People' of 26 December 1926 by Leonard Matters, who published the book account in 1929 as 'The Mystery of Jack the Ripper'. Matters was an Australian journalist who had become editor of the Buenos Aires 'Herald'.

Matters claimed to have seen an article in a Buenos Aires Spanish language journal by a former student of a Dr Stanley who heard his dying confession in a Buenos Aires hospital. Stanley was supposed to be a distinguished doctor at 'X' Hospital in London and he devoted his life to the study of cancer. He had a son called Herbert or Bertie who had contracted syphilis from Mary Kelly on Boat Race night, 1886. He died, and Stanley set out to have his revenge. Once the woman and her friends were dead, he left for Buenos Aires.

Matters also claimed to have heard from a Mrs North who had known Stanley in 1888. She lived in Chelsea, but frequented the cafe Monico in Shaftesbury Avenue, where she met the doctor and played dominoes. She noticed how he listened in to conversations, and he broke off an appointment to see her as he had to visit the graves of his wife and son.

This cannot be substantiated, and no Dr Stanley can be traced, though it is possible that Matters was using a pseudonym. Colin Wilson was contacted by a Mr A. L. Lee of Torquay saying that his father had met Dr Stanley, and that he was believed to be the Ripper. Michael Harrison recalls the tale from his childhood (he was born in 1907) that the Ripper was a "venereally infected son of a royal surgeon."

It is possible that these surgeon stories are part of the tradition surrounding Sir William Gull as the Royal Physician, and various street gossip and tall tales about medical men would have passed around. The Ripper was suspected of being a doctor very early on, from the observations of those conducting post mortems on the victims that the killer showed some surgical and medical knowledge. The 'Dear Boss' letter shows how this had become sensationalised, "They say I'm a doctor now ha ha" One Scotland Yard file of suspects was of doctors and policemen.

Dr Pedachenko

This sounds a far-fetched account of Russian Secret Police involvement. The Ochrana, the Czarist Secret Police supposedly set up Dr Alexander Pedachenko, a well known criminal lunatic to them, to murder the women so as to discredit the Metropolitan Police, as they were tolerating a large number of emigres hostile to the Czar. Once Warren had resigned in disgrace, Pedachenko was smuggled back to Russia, and was sent to an asylum.

The sources for this tale were an article seen by Donald McCormick, and the contents of 'Things I Know' by William Le Queux in 1928. This draws upon an alleged manuscript that had been dictated by Rasputin, and information from the Ochrana. McCormick also claimed to have seen a copy of the Ochrana Gazette for January 1909, that cannot be traced, which claimed that Pedachenko was an alias of Vassily Konovalov, the murderer of the Parisian woman in 1886.

There was a Dr Pancheko who was a supplier of poisons. He was arrested and was sentenced to 15 years in jail for aiding a murder in 1911. Whether this is the same man as the apocryphal Pedachenko is not certain.

Dr Stowell's 'S'

1970 sparked off a renewed interest in the Ripper murders. An article appeared in the November issue of 'The Criminologist' by Dr Thomas Edward Alexander Stowell. Stowell wrote this near the end of his life – he was born in 1885. He did not name his suspect, only calling him 'S', after his own initial, in fact. 'S' was a gentleman who had contracted syphilis in his youth, and in its final stages, he had suffered delusions, being sadistically aroused by watching deer being dressed. This led to the killings as his warped sexual passions exploded. Stowell claimed that Sir William Gull, the Royal Physician, was rumoured to have been seen in the streets of Whitechapel, and was there to certify 'S' as insane. He speculated that 'S' had been captured after the 'Double Event' and had escaped, to kill again. The old Lees story about the medium tracking down the Ripper to a West End mansion was repeated – but this time openly associated with Gull, for he claimed that he was told this by Gull's daughter.

"Mrs Acland's story was that at the time of the Ripper murders, her mother, Lady Gull, was greatly annoyed one night by an unappointed visit from a police officer, accompanied by a man who called himself a medium and she was irritated by their impudence in asking her a number of questions which seemed to her impertinent. She answered their questions with non-commital replies such as 'I do not know,' "I cannot tell you that,' 'I'm afraid I cannot answer that question.'

Later Sir William himself came down and in answer to the questions said he occasionally suffered from 'lapses of memory since he had a slight stroke in 1887'; he said that he once had discovered blood on his shirt...."

Stowell interpreted the bloody shirt as evidence that Gull had been examining the killer. Gull was further implicated by Stowell's claim to have been told, by Gull's daughter, Caroline Acland, that her father's diary contained a reference, "Informed Blank that his son was dying of syphilis of the brain." (although Gull died before Eddy).

This caused a sensation when the 'Sunday Times, carried an article a few days later by Magnus Linklater, entitled, 'Did Jack the Ripper have Royal Blood?', suggesting that 'S' was Prince Albert Victor ('Eddy') the Duke of Clarence. Stowell denied this in a subsequent BBC interview, and wrote to 'The Times' in the same vein. He died shortly afterwards. Colin Wilson recalls meeting Stowell back in 1960 after he had written a series on the Ripper for the 'Evening Standard'. Stowell wrongly believed that Wilson thought Eddy was the Ripper, and confided that this was, indeed, the identity of his suspect. Wilson also recalls Stowell's claim that he had been invited to see some papers of the late William Gull soon after his death in 1931, which revealed that Eddy had not died of influenza in 1892, but of advanced syphilis. The invitation was supposed to come from Caroline Acland. There are obvious inaccuracies here. Gull died in 1890, and Acland in 1931. Caroline had died before her husband, and Stowell, as an executor, had no need to be granted permission.

This rambling story is difficult to assess, but one must remember that this introduced a whole new dimension – a possible royal connection, the possible involvement of Gull, a possible cover up. Stowell was a family friend of the Aclands and Theodore Dyke Acland had appointed Stowell one of the trustees of his will, bequeathing him a Pre-Raphaelite painting.

Stowell's article opened the flood gates for various new theories and studies. The Eddy theory was given dramatic verve in Frank Spiering's 'Prince Jack', published in the USA in 1978 He claimed to have seen a copy of Gull's notes from the period, which were kept in a portfolio in the New York Academy of Medicine. These cannot be traced, though the reference number he gives does correspond to their filing system, and it is a portfolio of papers relating to Gull and Acland. The personal notes are not there and no one knows anything about them at the Academy. Spiering claims to have his own copy of the notes, which he chose not to use in his book (!) and these are held by Paul Harrison, presumably awaiting publication.

Court circulars of the time reveal that Eddy was not in London during the murders. When Nichols was killed, he was at Danby Lodge in Yorkshire. When Chapman was killed, he was at the Cavalry Barracks at York. When Stride and Eddowes were murdered, he was at Abergeldie, Scotland, and even the Queen recorded in her journal that he lunched with her on the 30th. When Kelly was killed, he was at Sandringham.

Though clearly nowhere near the murder sites, his name continued to be linked with the Ripper saga, as revealed in Stephen Knight's 'The Final Solution' (see next chapter) where his supposed illegitimate child is the subject of the cover up.

James Kenneth Stephen

Michael Harrison, in 'Clarence' in 1972 suggested that Stowell's 'S' was not the Prince, but perhaps someone close to him, James Kenneth Stephen, his former tutor. Harrison thought it likely that there had been a homosexual affair between the two men and Stephen killed the women on birth-days of the Royal family and pre-Christian festivals. He wrongly assumed that there were ten Ripper victims, and worked out an elaborate system of dates around this. One recent book has tried to revive the Eddy theory, having him commit the murders with an accomplice, J. K. Stephen. 'Murder and Madness – the Secret Life of Jack the Ripper' by Dr David Abrahamsen claims to be based upon "heretofore unrevealed information from Scotland Yard", a claim which the Yard denies. This builds upon the Stowell story, and adds the idea that a homosexual bond had developed between Stephen and Eddy. As Eddy left Cambridge and entered public life, Stephen grew insanely

James Kenneth Stephen in his early Cambridge days.

jealous and wanted to do something that would unite the two together. Eddy's condition and delusions were fed by Stephen, and the murders began.

The biggest nail in the coffin of this book is that Eddy could not have been involved directly, as demonstrated above. There is no definite evidence of a homosexual link between the two men, though this is plausible.

Perhaps it is time to explore the character and possible role of James Kenneth Stephen.

J. K. Stephen was educated at Eton where he excelled in debate and sports, being a formidable player of the Wall Game

131

and an adept cricketer. He was known as a 'water-bob' for his rowing ability. He went to King's College, Cambridge and became President of the Cambridge Union in 1880. He was a member of the elite group, the Apostles. He was tutor to Eddy from 1883-1885, and was called to the Bar June 25th 1884. He became a Fellow of King's in 1885. A. C. Benson wrote some reminiscences of the young J. K. at Eton:

> "....but he was so entirely unlike other boys that, once seen, it was impossible to forget him. He had a very big head with fine, clear-cut features, large and rather terrific eyes, a strong expressive mouth and a solid chin.... He gave the impression of enormous strength."

Benson also remembers how he felt in the presence of J. K.:

> "I was not, I remember, exactly at ease with him, though I felt it was a great honour to be selected as his friend. I was always over-shadowed by a sense of his cleverness, quickness, and ability....."

J. K. was a member of the illustrious Stephen family of lawyers. His father, Sir James Fitzjames Stephen was a judge on the Queen's Bench until he retired due to ill health in April 1891. J. K.'s elder brother, Herbert had chambers at 4, Paper Buildings in the Inner Temple, and from 1889-1927, he was Clerk of the Assize for the Northern Circuit. Harry Lushington Stephen was called to the Bar in 1885, and kept chambers at 3, King's Bench Walk. He was on the South Wales circuit before becoming Judge of the High Court of Calcutta from 1901-1914.

A respectable legal career loomed for J. K., but an accident in Felixstowe in 1886 seemed to halt that path. He was staying with friends for the New Year, possibly John Cobbold who he was at Cambridge with and who lived at the Lodge, situated on a clifftop to the east of Felixstowe, and the home of the Cobbolds. J. K. was riding along the bridal path which ran along the cliff top before turning inland by the railway track. The riders stopped at the Mill and spoke with millowner John Bloomfield. J. K. was interested in the steam engine that powered the Mill. A shrill whistle from one of the dock trains caused J. K.'s horse to lose its footing, and its rider was thrown onto his head. J. K. was eventually returned to London, to the family home at De Vere Gardens, and was attended by the family physician, Sir William Gull. J. K. seemed to recover after a few months, and published a newspaper, 'The Reflector' which ran for seventeen weeks. J. K. found some work through his father on the South Wales circuit.

*Sir James Fitzjames
Stephen, c1859, on his
appointment to Newark
Crown Court.*

Virginia Woolf, his cousin, wrote that he would come
rushing into their house and behave in a strange manner. He
rushed into the nursery at 22 Hyde Park Gate and pulled a
blade from a swordstick and plunged it into a loaf of bread.
Another time, he urged Virginia and her mother to accompany
him to his room in De Vere Gardens. Virginia was to pose for
him, for he believed he was a great artist and was euphoric. He
painted her on a small bit of wood, and she later reflected, "I
suppose madness made him believe he was all powerful." He
was also known to ride around for hours in a hansom. Woolf
recalls a time when Dr Savage had spoken with him, and he
came into breakfast saying, "Savage has just told me I'm in
danger of dying or going mad." and he laughed. Woolf also

133

Felixstowe Mill.

mentioned his poetry recitals, "This great mad figure with his broad shoulders and very clean cut mouth, and the deep voice and the powerful face – and the very blue eyes – this mad man would recite poetry to us; "the Burial of Sir John Moore", I remember; and he always brings to mind some tormented bull; and also Achilles – Achilles on his pressed bed lolling roars out a deep applause." His health in 1890 was still a cause for concern, as revealed in a letter by Leslie Stephen to his stepson, George:

> "We are uncomfortable about Jem. He lies in bed all the morning and seems unable to rouse himself to anything. I got him to come and play billiards on Saturday. We then proposed a walk on Sunday, but when the time came, he could not be roused to come out. It is very sad."

134

One of his poems, 'The Splinter', reveals his mood swings at this period of his life. He got a splinter in his toe and this made him withdraw to his room in deep depression. Food and the papers were brought, to no avail. Then, something snapped him out of it:

"But, oh; at last
A lady passed
Beside my chamber casement,
With modest guise,
And down-cast eyes
And fair beyond amazement:
She passed away
Like some bright fay
Too fair for earthly regions,
So sweet a sight
Would put to flight
The fiend and all his legions!
And I, that noon in winter,
Forgot the cruel splinter."

The Blue Boar Inn, Cambridge

In moments of lucidity and high spirits, he might still have picked up some work with his brothers on the circuits, and he was painting on and off.

He subsequently returned to Cambridge in October 1890 where he took rooms at the Blue Boar Inn, 18 Trinity Street. He advertised as a tutor, spoke at the Union, gave lectures, and published two slim volumes of his poetry, 'Lapsus Calami' and 'Quo Musa Tendis?' culled from various sources over the years. In 1891, he also published a pamphlet, Living Languages, in defence of the teaching of compulsory Greek at the Universities. An advertisement placed by him in 'The Cambridge Review' of May 14 1891 reads thus:

"Mr J. K. Stephen, M.A., late Fellow of King's,......... Coaches Gentlemen for all Law and History Examinations, and prepares candidates for the Whewell Scholarships. Several vacancies for this term and the Long Vacation. – apply to 18, Trinity Street."

He advertised further in October of the same year.

Michael Harrison's 'Clarence' published a pamphlet which was circulated by J. K. in Cambridge and London after May, 1891. This was protesting about the views of his family doctor, Dr Savage, who persisted in claiming that J. K. was of unsound mind, and would end up with a breakdown which might result in violent behaviour. The pamphlet states that J. K. had arranged separate examinations by Sir Andrew Clark, Dr

"Cambridge Review",
October 15th 1891.

1891-1892.

Law Tripos, History Tripos, Law and History Special, Whewell Scholarship, Bar Examination, Inns of Court Scholarships.

MR. J. K. STEPHEN, M.A., late Fellow of King's College, Barrister at Law, late Clerk of Assize on the S. Wales Circuit, Senior Whewell Scholar, 1880, Senior in History Tripos, 1881, Law Tripos, 1882, will READ with gentlemen for the above Examinations at 18, Trinity Street, from October, 1891, to June, 1892.

Hughlings Jackson and Dr Hack Tuke between October and December 1890. He was found to be in good health. Savage then asserted that it was unwise for his patient to travel to London, Cambridge or Paris, and should convalesce in a quiet place for some months. J. K. deliberately went to London, Cambridge and Paris. (Interestingly, the 1891 census reveals that he had taken new chambers at 5, Paper Buildings, and thus he intended to carry on some form of legal career.)

He opened a letter from Savage in May 1891 which predicted that over the next six months he would become more eccentric, dressing oddly, spending wildly and becoming exhausted and depressive. The pamphlet rejects this. However, interestingly, towards the end of 1891, his manner and dress had become more eccentric and he was expelled from his London club.

His behaviour became more erratic. A sign of his decline might be seen in a report of the Cambridge Union of October 1891 when it was remarked that J. K.'s debate "lacked something of its usual brilliance" but there were cries of "No, no!" when J. K. announced that he felt he was too old for debating. In November 1891, he was found naked, singing and screaming in his room. Dr Lawrence Humphrey, J. K.'s usual Cambridge doctor, of 3, Trinity Street, wrote in his report of J. K.'s admission to hospital, "This morning in an attack of violence he threw his looking glass out of the window into the street and stood naked in his bedroom, smiling, all the furniture and clothes in disarray around him. He declined to move and was under the delusion that there was a warrant out for his detention."

His eldest brother, Herbert, was sent for, and he took J. K. to St Andrew's Hospital in Northampton – J. K. was apparently under the delusion that he was to enjoy a trip out into the countryside. The hospital was, in fact, an asylum, and J. K. was certified. He spent periods of cheerfulness mixed with deep depression. His state worsened when he was told of Eddy's death in January 1892. He refused food, and died on 3 February, shortly after 4.00pm in the presence of his mother, Lady Mary Stephen and Herbert and Harry. His death certificate reads, under 'Cause of death', "Mania, refusal of food, exhaustion". His will left only £87.12s.11d. as can be expected from an ill, erratic worker who lost money through his disasterous 'Reflector' venture.

Stephen's close association with Eddy has been the fertile ground of speculation. That they were close and fond of each other is clearly true. J. K. made him his protege at Cambridge, and controlled his dress sense and circle of friends. The impact of the news of Eddy's death is also clear testimony to the bond between the two men. This might have involved some homosexual liaison, but maybe no more than in an Upper Class, public school manner of showing affection. One of his poems mentions a 'Mr. B' which might have been a reference to Oscar Browning, who tutored the young J. K. at Eton. Browning was dismissed for assumed over familiarity with the boys:

"When I had firmly answered "No",
And he allowed that that was so,
I really thought I should be free
For good and all from Mr. B,
And that he would soberly acquiesce:
I said that I would be discreet
That for a while we should not meet;
I promised I would always feel
A kindly interest in his weal;
I thanked him for his amorous zeal,
In short, I said all I could but "yes"....."

The poem ends with an unwanted tryst:

"He advanced before I could retire,
And I suddenly felt to my great alarm,
The grasp of a warm unlicensed arm,
An embrace in which I found no charm;
I was awfully glad when he let me go."

This hardly sounds like the pleasant memories of a willing, homosexual encounter! It is not clear what did happen in the case of Browning. A fellow Master at Eton, Mr Wolley-Dod, complained to the Head Master, Hornby, that Browning had

137

told him that one of his pupils, Curzon, should be paid more attention, because he was good looking. Browning claimed to have said that the boy was clever. The truth seems to be that Browning's teaching styles, and considerate manner of running his House, roused opposition and jealousy amongst the more traditional, older Masters. J. K. would have come under the considerable influence of Browning at Eton and was a member of his House. Browning was also at King's College when J. K. went up there in 1879. Browning was still present when J. K. returned to Cambridge in 1890! Benson wrote, in 1876, "J. K. Stephen, Sir Cecil Spring-Rice, Mr. C. Lowdry (Head of Tonbridge), Archdeacon Burrows, Lord Curzon, were all strongly under the influence of Mr Oscar Browning."

We have on record a poem poking fun at Browning for his obesity:

"O. B., Oh be obedient
To Nature's stern decrees,
For though you be but one O. B.
You may be too obese."

J. K. was also capable of attraction and obsession with the opposite sex. He fell head over heels in love with Stella Duckworth, the half sister of his young cousins. He fell for her when staying with his uncle, Leslie Stephen, one summer at Talland House. He became obsessive and she did not return his love. Woolf recalls, "we had orders to tell him, if we met him in the street, that she was away, staying with the Lushingtons at Pyports." His attraction to beautiful women can also be glimpsed in the extract from 'The Splinter', above. He once spoke in a Cambridge Union debate on 13 May 1879 in support of the motion, "That this house desires to express its sympathy with the movement for the higher education of women." This is all significant, for J. K. has all too often been cast as a bitter homosexual and woman hater. The misogyny is seen in other poems of his, such as 'In the Backs', where he sees an ugly looking woman:

"Loose-hipped, big-boned, disjointed, angular.
If her anatomy comprised a waist,
I did not notice it: she had a face
With eyes and lips adjusted thereunto,
But her round mouth no pleasing shadows stirred,
Nor did her eyes invite a second glance....."

He ends with these sentiments:

"I did not like her: and I should not mind
If she were done away with, killed or ploughed.
She did not seem to serve a useful end:
And certainly she was not beautiful."

Then there is 'A Thought':

"If all the harm that women have done
Were put in a bundle and rolled into one,
Earth would not hold it,
The sky could not enfold it,
It could not be lighted nor warmed by the sun;
Such masses of evil
Would puzzle the devil
And keep him in fuel while Time's wheels run.

But if all the harm that's been done by men
Were doubled and doubled and doubled again,
And melted and fused into vapour and then
Were squared and raised to the power of ten,
There wouldn't be nearly enough, not near,
To keep a small girl for the tenth of a year."

These outbursts must be seen in the wider context of his life and feelings. The violence might be only black humour, or a melancholy mood. Thinking such thoughts does not mean that someone would necessarily commit them, just as a Tarantino might make violent films but be a very gentle person in real life. We cannot read too much into these, though people try to do so. J. K. has been proposed as the Ripper because of an unsound mind and a supposed homosexual hatred of women. These things cannot be proven and he seems to have been a far more complex character. Joel Norris in 'Serial Killers' has suggested that J. K.'s accident caused a lesion in the limbic area of the brain which might be a primary cause of sexual murder. We simply do not know.

J. K. was just under six feet high, broad shouldered, with dark hair and piercing, sparkling blue eyes. He was cultured and dandified, a trickster and a wit. He could fit many of the descriptions of the Ripper – especially the one given by Sgt. Stephen White – and he had the sort of mind to leave demented clues such as the Goulston Street graffito and the Ripper letters.

His strong physique and black moods might have led to a killing spree, but we have no evidence of this. His highly placed connection with Eddy and the Royals might have sucked him into a conspiracy as a willing pair of hands to act 'for Queen and country' as he was a fierce Royalist and Conservative. He was also connected with Sir William Gull, whose name has often been implicated with a cover up. If Stephen is to be seriously considered as a suspect, we would have to link him with a government conspiracy that involved murdering the women. Ideas and new evidence about this will be discussed in later chapters.

James Maybrick

James Maybrick was a Liverpool cotton broker who died in May 1889 as a result of arsenic poisoning. He was an addict, and used arsenic as well as amounts of other substances such as strychnine as a stimulant and as an aphrodisiac. This information was ignored at the trial of Florence Maybrick in 1889, when the judge, Sir James Fitzjames Stephen, the father of J. K. Stephen, was losing his mind and had not got a full grasp of the facts. Florence, an American, had admitted her adultery with another cotton broker, Brierly, and this prejudiced the court against her, suggesting that she had a motive to kill her husband. She was sentenced to hang, commuted to life imprisonment and the matter raged in the press of the day. Many felt that there had been a gross miscarriage of justice. Florence was released fifteen years later, and reprieved. She went to America where she died in 1941.

Maybrick's name had never been suggested as a Ripper suspect until the appearance of a Jack the Ripper diary in May 1991. This was in the hands of a scrap-metal dealer, Michael Barrett, who said that he had been given it by a drinking partner, Anthony Devereux. Devereux had refused to disclose any more information about it, and he had died in August 1991. Devereux's family said that they knew nothing about any such diary. Internal evidence showed that the diary purported to be that of James Maybrick, for his Liverpool home, Battlecrease House, was mentioned, along with Florence, her lover, the children, Bobo and Gladys. There were plays on the name 'Sir Jim' and 'May', too. Barrett suggested that the diary might have been found in Battlecrease House when some electricians were pulling up the floorboards. The electricians, and the owner of the house, deny any such knowledge.

The diary is written in a Victorian picture album, which has the first 48 pages torn out with a knife. Faded images and gum traces suggest that these pages once held photographs or postcards. The rest of the 63 pages are filled with a spidery scrawl which intersperse details of Maybrick's life with accounts of the killings, from April 1888 – May 1889. The motive for the killings is vengeance for Florence's adultery. Her sin is projected onto the five unfortunates.

Barrett approached Doreen Montgomery of Rupert Crew Literary Agency and Shirley Harrison was contacted to discuss writing this up as a book, containing the diary entries. Initial enquiries to the British Museum and to antiquarian booksellers did not show any obvious signs of forgery, and Robert Smith bought the publishing rights in 1992. A group of Ripper-ologists, including Donald Rumbelow, Melvyn Fairclough and Martin Howells, were asked to examine the diary, and were to hold confidentiality. Various tests were undertaken, such as graphology, which suggested that the work revealed the mind of a serial killer, and preliminary ink tests that established that the ink type was consistent with the late nineteenth century. Similar letter formations were pointed out in the 'Dear Boss' letters. Research into Maybrick's life revealed that the dates mentioned showing his whereabouts in the diary could not be contradicted by any known information discovered about Maybrick elsewhere. The research also discovered a previously unknown fact, which is not mentioned in the diary, that Maybrick had had a lover in the East End much earlier in his life and so he would have been acquainted with the Whitechapel area.

In 1993, however, Warner Books in the USA and 'The Sunday Times' called in their own experts before publishing a book, and a serialisation, respectively. They concluded that it was a forgery. Their handwriting comparisons denied there was any similarity with the Ripper letters, and migration tests on the ink suggested that it was composed between 1912 and 1933, though others questioned the reliability of such a test. Handwriting analysis also showed that there was not enough variation in the entries, as though they were deliberately written by the same person at one sitting.

In July 1994, Barrett published a confession in the 'Liverpool Daily Post' but this was retracted by solicitors. He had confessed to buying a special ink, from the Bluecoats Art Shop, Diamine black manuscript ink and they have confirmed that they sold some of this. It contained irton salts and nigrosine as colouring matter, and chloroacetamide as a preservative. Chloroacetamide was not used before 1974, and the Warner investigation submitted six ink samples to Analysis for

Industry, headed by Dr Diana Simpson. She found chloroacetamide in the samples. Later tests at Leeds University might
dispute this – they found the substance but blame this on
contaminated equipment. But what does this prove? Also
when the diary was shown to Alec Voller, Diamine's own
chemist, he denied that the ink used was theirs. However, Mike
Barrett claims that he did not use the ink neat, but added
certain substances such as sugar and water.

Disputes also raged over the signature on Maybrick's will.
The Warner/Sunday Times experts claimed that the handwriting did not match that of the diary, and that this was the same
with the signature of the marriage certificate. The supporters
argued that the signature was a forgery by Maybrick's brother.
The problem seems to be with an erroneously transcribed copy
of the will in notes by the lawyer Alexander MacDougal in 1891.
A copy of the original on file at Somerset House shows up these
errors.

It seems that Barrett still holds to his confession in a sworn
affidavit.

Certain details about the diary do not add up, either. If
Maybrick really wanted to keep a diary then why use an old
photograph album with its absorbant pages unsuited to ink and
why tear out the contents of one already in use? Victorian
albums can be easily found in antiquarian booksellers. A forger
would probably find a partially used copy, and have to tear
material out to make it useable and anonymous.

The style is derivative of the Ripper letters, as follows:

"Sir Jim with his shining knife,
cuts through the night,
and by God,
does he not show his might ha ha "

The diary is rambling and does not clearly tell any details
about the murders that could not have already been found out
from books, contemporary press reports, or police files
released since 1987 – though some details could be interesting
if interpreted in a certain way, if the diary dates from an earlier
date. In fact, there are errors. The most glaring is that the diary
describes Kelly's breasts as being placed upon the table. They
were not, though that is what press reports of the time said.
They were placed one under the head and one by the right
foot. The apologists for the diary plead that Maybrick was in
such a frenzy during this murder that his memory of exact
events was clouded. This is special pleading par excellence!

If this is the diary of the Ripper, it is a disappointing product, lacking substance. A killer would have poured out much more of his heart in the confessional of its pages. The fact that the entries seem to have been written in batches also points to a forgery. The diary is undoubtedly a fake, and it is sad that so many respected Ripperologists seemed to throw in their lot with it. There were shameful attempts to reread 'The Juwes' as 'The James', or to see the inverted V cuts on Eddowes as a letter 'M'. No less an authority than Colin Wilson wrote in the foreword to 'The Diary of Jack the Ripper'; "Maybrick is far and away the most likely Ripper candidate so far."

The diary is clever in that good homework has been done about the character and life of Maybrick (much could have been gleaned from the excellent book 'The Poisoned Life of Mrs Maybrick' by Bernard Ryan, first published in 1977), but it did not convince. Paul Begg discussed the possibility with me that it might be a clever forgery by someone linked with the Maybrick family, earlier this century, to discredit the memory of James, possibly from the 1920s as there is an oral tradition that youths ran past Battlecrease House then shouting 'Jack the Ripper!' Melvyn Harris has pointed out that the idea of using Maybrick – at a later date – might have been derived from Michael Harrison's 'Clarence' where he speculates that Sir James Fitzjames Stephen was lacking in judgement at Florence Maybrick's trial because he was so overcome with the news that his son was the Ripper. Thus, Florence could be claimed as another Ripper victim, after a manner of speaking!

A final detail is the Maybrick watch which came to light. This is a gold watch made in 1846 and purchased from Stewart the Jewellers of Wallasey in July 1992. They had had it for at least five years. It was bought by Albert Johnston and he reported in June 1993 that he had found names scratched on the inner case. There were the initials 'J. Maybrick', the phrase, 'I am Jack' and the initials of the five victims. Tests upon the scratches have so far suggested that they are probably quite old, and might have been made in the 1880s. No more tests seem to have been carried out in the light of the likelihood that the diary is a forgery.

The case for the diary is reopened in Paul Feldman's book 'Jack the Ripper: The Final Chapter', amassing new evidence of Maybrick's movements at the time, showing that he would, or could, have been in the Whitechapel area when the killings took place, and also more information about his East End mistress and five illegitimate children who used the name

'Maybrick'. More examples of Maybrick's handwriting have been found and surveyed. The facts remain that the diary's handwriting is not identical, and it is a frustrating document – full of accurate details about Maybrick's family, fairly accurate details about the murders, but a poor, vaccuous account of the killer's mind. If this really is the Ripper's diary, we could have hoped for something better!

Robert D'Onston Stephenson

Stephenson was mentioned in the last chapter for his suspicions about Dr. Morgan Davies, which were completely unfounded. In 1994, Melvin Harris proposed Stephenson as a serious suspect in 'The True Face of Jack the Ripper'. He felt that Stephenson possessed all the characteristics necessary for the murderer; a gentle and cultured appearance; physical strength; callousness and awareness of surgery; and his presence in Whitechapel during 1888.

Stephenson sometimes called himself Dr Roslyn D'Onston, a title that might have been purely self-styled, though he had studied medicine in Paris. He fought for Garibaldi in Italy and claimed that he had acted as a military surgeon. He was fired from a post with customs in Hull in the 1860s, and moved to London where he wrote for the 'Pall Mall Gazette'. He wrote flamboyant pieces about the Whitechapel murders. He was known as a heavy drinker and abuser of drugs. He might be the Robert Stephenson who was charged at Thames Magistrates Court in June 1887 for assault, and the Stevenson charged with indecent assault in October 1888.

He began an interest in occult studies, being influenced by the rambling mysticism of Bulwer Lytton, and had links with the Theosophical Society.

In 1930, a journalist, Bernard O'Donnell, interviewed Vittoria Cremers, an American and the widow of Baron Louis Cremers. She was an active member of the Theosophical society in the 1890s and she met Stephenson when he was living with the occultist Mabel Collins. The two went into business with her as the Pompadour Cosmetics Company in Baker Street. Collins and Cremers put up the money and Stephenson provided the recipes and potions.

Cremer's reminiscences contain references to Stephenson's character and behaviour which are the real grounds for Melvin Harris' suspicions. These rest upon the general air the man had of being gracious and unassuming which masked the orror beneath, and the tales of magical belief and heartless haracter. She recounts how she watched him making the sign f an inverted triangle on his door, invocation protection gainst a mysterious presence. He told her about his days ighting for Garibaldi, having to hack off limbs without the use f anasthetic, and then swopping scalpel for sword as he gutted he enemy. Cremers commented that she felt he had a heart of lint as she heard him recount these stories.

On another occasion, a girl had been made pregnant and hen abandoned. Stephenson asked for a handkerchief belonging to her and then went off to avenge her. Fifteen months later e returned, saying that he had dipped the handkerchief in the nan's blood and had thrown it into her lap.

Stephenson also repeated the ideas about the Ripper pproaching the women behind, much as he says he had heard rom Dr Davies. He acted this out on Cremers and she was rightened. She also noted that he made the sign of an inverted riangle over her as he came in front of her. Her real suspicions vere roused when she ventured into his room one day and saw ome blood-encrusted ties in a black box. She did not mention his to him, but later, he told her how he had heard that the Ripper concealed organs from the dead women under his eckties. Mabel Collins also harboured suspicions, apparently.

A garbled version of these tales was published in the 'East Anglian Daily Times' by Pierre Girouard. This stated that he ad met a 'Baroness K.' (obviously Cremers) and he added the letails that Stephenson had been struck off the register, that he ived in the Harrow Road at the time of the murders, and that e made his living by selling perfumes and lecturing on the occult. The discovery of the ties led to his being sent to the USA vhere he had died in a New York hospital and confessed his guilt.

Harris feels that the reference to the hospital confession is onfused with that of the Norwegian seaman, Fogelma, a leluded man who 'confessed' to being the Ripper before he lied.

Stephenson seems to have abandoned his occultism in the 1890s, writing a book on the Gospels in 1904, which was a earned and serious contribution to Biblical studies.

Harris speculates that he had had a conversion experience and found release and forgiveness for the dark secret he must have harboured.

The combination of the heart-hardening experience of war, barbaric surgery and the black arts convinced Harris that

145

this man was a prime suspect. He feels that Stephenson's theories about Dr Davies were a bluff to cover up his own guilt. His book is a fascinating read and it carefully assembles the Cremers material, but it is based upon hearsay that cannot be substantiated. Stephenson was another crook and conman who might have been the killer, but there is no definite evidence or clear motive. He must simply take his place in the roll call of possible suspects.

Charles Dodgson (Lewis Carroll)

Richard Wallace's 'Jack the Ripper: "Light-hearted Friend" uses knowledge about Charles Dodgson's private life from his earlier work, 'The Agony of Lewis Carroll' to propose that he might have been the killer. This research is based upon the originals of Dodgson's diaries in the British Library, noting the passages crossed out in pencil by his family, or only half erased as the diaries were edited. That Dodgson was a disturbed character is clear enough, but he is known to have been in Eastbourne with Isa Bowman in his rented summer house for several weeks from August 31st 1888. Trains ran through the night, however, and he often took the opportunity to travel to London to visit the theatre. Dodgson commented that the journey – of just under two hours – was faster than that from Christ Church, Oxford, to London. This is just another playful theory with a disturbed individual who might have been around at the right time.

'Prisoner 1167'

One of the most recent theories is a reworking of an older idea. 'Prisoner 1167' was James Kelly, who came to London from Liverpool and escaped from Broadmoor. He remained on the run until the 1920s when he turned himself in. John Morrison first suggested this Kelly as the Ripper in the 40 page photocopied manuscript, 'Jimmy Kelly's Year of the Ripper Murders 1888', a copy of which is kept in Whitechapel Library. His basic idea was that Mary Kelly might have travelled to Liverpool after leaving Wales, because of the strong Irish community there. She might have lived with James Kelly and then left him, descending to her life of prostitution in London. James would have sought her out, once having escaped from jail, and sought his revenge. Pure speculation and assumption, but the recent book by Jim Tully 'The Secret of Prisoner 1167, Was This Jack The Ripper?' builds on this, claiming to have Home Office documentation that shows that James Kelly was considered as a suspect at the time of the murders. Interesting, but just another suspect in the rogue's gallery.

As this chapter and the roll call of suspects draws to a close, it might be worth reflecting what sort of material would constitute proof, so far from the period in time. The vast array of Ripper books which propose this person or that person and argue their case are interesting and worthwhile for they advance the debate and present new evidence. None of them prove anything, though. If any artefact or writing is discovered that purports to name the Ripper, one must immediately enquire of its provenance. If it has come from reputable sources and can be considered a genuine document through dating techniques and comparisons with other extant handwriting, then it is worth listening to. The appearance of dubious diaries such as the Abberline and Maybrick diaries should warn scholars to approach such material with great caution. Consider their provenance – the Abberline material held by Joseph Sickert and the Maybrick diary handed to Barrett by a drinking companion. Materials found in Yard files, the vaults of Buckingham Palace, or in the private papers of people connected with the murder enquiry are immediately worthy of a second glance.

Until such material might come to light, we have to look at the known evidence and tackle the clues and try to piece together the most plausible solutions. The Parlours have one or two new pieces of evidence and suggestions that help to assemble the jig saw puzzle in a different way. This material will be presented in the next chapter.

'After The Deed'

POLICE NOTICE.

148

The Plot Thickens

Was there a Royal Conspiracy at Work?

Andy Parlour remembers his father saying, "The old King had those women killed" when he was a youth. This was a reference to Edward VII. Various oral traditions about the Queen's son or other royals seemed to have circulated in the East End. What might they have been based upon?

The close proximity and probable friendship of the Ripper's five victims has caused some to think that there was more than a lustful, serial killer on the loose. Perhaps there was a deliberate attempt to silence these women who knew something that was dangerous, something sensitive that would have damaged the reputation of a gentleman, or maybe even someone higher. Conspiracy theories are often criticised by Ripperologists for being marvellous flights of fancy, inventing associations and motives without any evidence. We can all play at guessing the Ripper, and making up wild tales of intrigue. But can we take any of them at all seriously?

The first major conspiracy theory came from Joseph Gorman Sickert, born in 1925. His story was presented in a BBC documentary in 1973, and extended and written down in Stephen Knight's 'Jack the Ripper: The Final Solution' in 1976.

Joseph claims that he is the illegitimate son of the painter Walter Sickert. His mother was Alice Margaret Crook, whom Sickert believes was the secret daughter of Prince Eddy. Thus he claims a famous painter as a father, and a royal grandfather. Traditions and stories were handed down to him about the Ripper – and the secret that had to be covered up.

Joseph Sickert told Stephen Knight that the Ripper story had its origins in Cleveland Street. This was an artistic centre, a Bohemian collection of alleys and streets where convention was flouted and radicals such as Morris and Shaw had links. Joseph claimed that his father had a studio there at 15 Cleveland Street in the period near the start of his career when he was apprenticed to the painter Whistler. His mother, he claimed, had been brought up in a Workhouse, and her congenital deafness gave her an added disadvantage. She was overprotective of Joseph, and he felt that she harboured a dark secret. He also claimed that Walter Sickert had taken him on one side when he was only fourteen and confided the full story to him.

Number 22 Cleveland Street was a confectioners and tobacconists where the young assistant was Annie Elizabeth Crook, also known as Cook. Mary Jane Kelly also worked in the shop with her. Prince Eddy visited Sickert who introduced him to the artistic community and expanded his cultural education. Princess Alix had chosen Sickert for this task, as he was attractive, only four years Eddy's senior and his family had been painters to the Royal Court of Denmark earlier, from whence she hailed. He met Annie on one of his visits and a love affair began. Annie had modelled for Walter. When Annie gave birth to a baby girl, Sickert paid Mary Kelly to look after the child in the basement of 6 Cleveland Street where the two women lodged. Kelly obliged because Sickert was responsible for bringing her from a refuge for poor working women, through a lawyer friend. A secret Catholic wedding ceremony was arranged at St Saviour's private chapel, with Kelly as a witness. Sickert married Ellen Cobden in 1885 and travelled frequently to Dieppe to paint. When Eddy was away, Annie, the child, and sometimes Kelly, would accompany him – it was from this French experience that Kelly was to call herself, playfully, Marie Jeanette.

Too many knew who Eddy was, and rumour spread. When Whitehall heard this, Lord Salisbury acted quickly to hush the matter up. Yet more Royal scandal would be damaging enough, but a marriage to a Catholic, with a child, would have sowed the seeds of revolution. There was a police raid on Cleveland Street and two people were taken away – Eddy and Annie. Sickert claims to have witnessed this when walking out one day. A staged fight between strangers took place further down the street while two hansoms drew up, one turning into nearby Tottenham Street, and the other stopping at number 6. Two men went into Sickert's studio, bringing Eddy out, and a man and a woman went into Annie's basement flat. Annie was confined in institutions until her death in 1920. Mary Kelly had the care of their child, and she fled to the East End for safety. The child was Alice Margaret, and they hid in a convent for some time. The child was eventually returned to Sickert, who had her cared for by some relatives until finally he took her to Dieppe. Kelly settled in Whitechapel and confided in her gin-hag friends. They had to be silenced and Salisbury, a leading Freemason, chose Sir William Gull, the Royal Physician, another Mason, for the task, as he had performed discreet abortions to protect the Royals before, and would happily certify someone insane for the same reason as, so Sickert claimed, he had done with Annie Elizabeth Crook. The plot was Masonic, to protect the throne, and was not inspired by the Palace itself.

Sickert claimed that there were three men involved in the killings – Sir William Gull, John Netley the coachman, and Sir Robert Anderson, assistant Commissioner of the Metropolitan Police. Anderson was another Mason, and Netley had been driving for the Royals and for Gull. He had, it was claimed, driven Eddy on his secret visits to Cleveland Street. Netley traced the whereabouts of the women, and Gull enticed them into the coach, feeding them black grapes that were poisoned to induce unconsciousness. Most of the actual murders were performed in the coach, and Anderson helped as a lookout, though later, Walter Sickert was also said to be involved.

Netley had to carry the bodies to the sites where they were found. All the women knew each other, except, maybe for Eddowes, who was killed in mistake for Kelly.

The mutilations were supposedly in accordance with Masonic ritual, as a warning and a threat to any others who might challenge the throne and those of the Brotherhood. Stephen Knight researched Freemasonry and provided copious references in 'The Final Solution' before going on to write his later book, 'The Brotherhood'.

Freemasonry has had a long and complex history, from simple beginnings as a fraternity of tradesmen in the Middle Ages to protect the quality of workmanship and to regulate prices. It was a form of Trade Union, with a strong Christian doctrinal stance. The movement changed over the years and grew more esoteric and encouraged free thinking and occultist notions until by the 18th century, it was a secret organisation which it was very difficult to become a member of. Highly placed people were eager to join its ranks, and preferment might follow if they did so. Today, there is more openness, and the majority of masons, at the lower levels, are hard working, charitable people. The rituals at these levels, such as the Entered Apprentice, are more Christian in content whereby God is the 'Great Architect'. In the highest levels, of the Royal Arch, the concept of God undergoes a profound change. The divine name, Jah-Bul-On is, in fact, a composite of 'Yahweh' (or 'Jehovah') from the Old Testament, Ba'al, from Near Eastern mythology (and one of the names given to the devil in the New Testament!), and Osiris, the Egyptian fertility god. Thus, Jah-Bul-On can be seen as a pagan deity and some Christians assert that one cannot belong to the Church and to Freemasonry.

Walter Richard Sickert.

The Roman Catholic Church only lifted the ban upon joining in 1975, and much suspicion still remains.

What is significant is that Royal Arch level members are bound by oath to support each other and keep any secrets necessary, including any involvement in crimes such as murder ("that a companion Royal Arch Mason's secrets, given in charge as such, and I knowing them to be such, shall remain as secure and inviolable in my breast as in his own, murder and treason not excepted...").

There are various myths told to relate the origins of Freemasonry and the building of Solomon's temple is central to most of these. The story is told of the murder of Hiram Abiff, the master-mason of the Temple. He was killed in the holy place by three apprentice masons, Jubela, Jubelo and Jubelum. They were known as 'The Three Ruffians' in English Masonry, but as the 'Juwes' elsewhere. The men fled, but were discovered near the Joppa coast and were killed in revenge.

Sickert claimed that various details in the Whitechapel murders point to Masonic involvement:

(a) The mutilations of the women are suggestive of Masonic threats and legends.

(b) The throats were cut from left to right. In the ritual of the Entered Apprentice, a 'penal sign' is made of a left to right hand movement across the throat. It is also generally recognised that the women's throats were cut after they had been strangled. There was no necessity to cut them besides a warped cruelty or some form of symbolic warning. Nichols' throat seems to have been cut after the mutilations to her abdomen.

(c) The stomach was torn open and the intestines were lifted out and placed upon the shoulder. In Masonic lore, the killers of Hiram Abiff were killed "by the breast being torn open and the heart and vitals taken out and thrown over the left shoulder". This has become the chief instruction for dealing with wayward Master Masons. This was done in the case of Chapman, being placed upon the left shoulder, by design. Eddowes had the intestines placed upon the right shoulder. Nichols was torn open, but the intestines were left inside. Stride had her throat cut, but with no further mutilations because the killer was disturbed about his business. Kelly was butchered and disfigured beyond recognition, but she was certainly torn open.

(d) The cuts on Eddowes' face were caused by removing two triangular flaps of skin. Triangles are a sign of Masonry.

(e) Kelly's death is similar to that in Hogarth's engraving, 'The Reward of Cruelty'. This is a caricature of the Medical profession, though Hogarth was a Mason, and various symbols appear in his work. In this picture, the victim is laid out on the table with a cable around the throat, signifying the cutting of the throat. The victim is being facially mutilated. One surgeon is cutting at the eyes. The stomach and the abdomen has been ripped open and some vital organs removed. In one version of the drawing, the man's left hand is over his left breast. One surgeon is skinning the feet with a scalpel.

Kelly's body was laid out on the bed, with facial mutilations – ears and nose cut off – the throat cut, the abdomen ripped open, vitals removed. Her left arm lay across her breast as did that of Chapman. Kelly also had her legs and feet skinned.

Hogarth has three surgeons at work. Three is seen as a perfect number in Masonry, and three killers were seen to have revenged Abiff by killing the Three Ruffians. Sickert had three men involved – Gull, Netley and Anderson/Sickert.

(f) Chapman's missing rings were said by some reports to have been placed at her feet with the farthings. The Pall Mall Gazette stated, "the murderer had pulled off some brass rings which the victim had been wearing and these, together with some trumpery articles which had been taken from her pockets, were placed carefully at the victim's feet." Knight felt that if this report was true, the rings might have symbolised the two hollow brass pillars that stood at the entrance to Solomon's Temple, the construction of which was overseen by Hiram Abiff.

(g) The Goulston Street graffito refers to the 'Juwes' and could be a hint that the Masons were behind the killings for those in the know. Also, a piece of Eddowes' apron was left at the scene. This was used to wipe blood from the killer's knife, but the apron was also a Masonic symbol.

Sickert and Knight provided an original and striking theory. There are some major historical difficulties with some aspects of it, though:

(1) Annie Elizabeth Crook

Investigations with the Record Keeper of the Greater London Record Office about Annie Elizabeth Crook, or Cook, reveal that the address given on Annie's daughter's birth certificate in 1885 was indeed 6, Cleveland Street. The father's name and occupation are left blank, intriguingly. A rate book for the same address of 1888 show that the flat was held by one Elizabeth Cook. However, between 1886 and 1888, numbers 4–14 Cleveland Street were pulled down and replaced by blocks of flats. If the Elizabeth Cook in the new flats was the same woman as Annie, then the rate books show that she lived there until 1893, long after Sickert says she was dragged off by the authorities in 1888. Neither is there any evidence that Annie Crook was constantly institutionalised until her death. In 1889 she was admitted to the Endell Street Workhouse, together with her daughter, Alice Margaret. In 1894 she was in prison. Her daughter was sent to a camp for two weeks, so Annie must have received fourteen days. In 1902, the daughter was admitted to St Pancras Infirmary suffering from measles and Annie's address was given as 5 Pancras Street. 1906 saw Annie back in the Workhouse, as did 1913. She died in the lunacy ward of the Fulham Road Workhouse in 1920. The records of her death list her religion as Church of England, and not as Roman Catholic.

(2.) St. Saviour's Chapel

The whereabouts of St. Saviour's Chapel, where the Prince and Annie were supposedly secretly married, is unclear. The only St. Saviour's Church, now Southwark Cathedral, has no records of any such marriage between 1880 and 1889. There was a St. Saviour's Infirmary in Osnaburgh Street, just off Euston Road. It no longer exists and no records exist of the chapel to the infirmary.

(3.) Could Sir William Gull have been involved?

It has been doubted that Sir William Gull would have been fit enough to travel around in a cab, helping to kill the women. It is often assumed that he suffered a stroke in 1887. The Dictionary of National Biography says of Gull, "In the autumn of 1887 he was attacked with paralysis, which compelled him to retire from practice; a third attack caused his death on 29 Jan. 1890." Dr Thomas Stowell wrote that Gull had suffered "a slight stroke in 1887", receiving the information from Gull's daughter. Apparently, Gull became paralysed, but did not lose consciousness, "but fell on one knee and was able to walk to the house with assistance." Gull's son-in-law, Theodore Acland stated that Gull continued to take an active part in public work, serving on the Senate of the University of London until 1889. He might not have seen patients any longer, but he was not incapacitated. He was still included on the Medical Register of 1888 and 1889.

Sir William Withey Gull.

Details given in the 1892 edition of Wilks and Bettany's 'Biographical History of Guy's Hospital' state that Gull suffered a slight paralysis of one side in 1887, from which he made good recovery and seemed quite normal. Later, most people record that he had three epileptiform attacks, which he recovered

*Gull's Home and Practice,
74, Brook Street.
(Photo: Andy Parlour)*

from quickly, but on 29 January 1890, he had a seizure and fell
into a coma (though his death certificate only records two
attacks, the second of which made him comatose.) Gull, therefore, could have been involved from the point of view of his
physical abilities if he had strong assistance, but it seems highly
unlikely that so prominent a person would have 'gotten his
hands dirty' on the streets. He might have been one of a cabal
masterminding the operation. As the Royal Physician he is
bound to have been brought into any conspiracy. More background on Gull and the longevity of accusations made against
him can be found in the next chapter.

(4.) Anderson and Warren as suspects?
　　Sir Robert Anderson seems a highly unlikely Ripper
suspect for he only took over as Assistant Commissioner on the
day of Nichols' murder, and immediately went off to Switzerland on a month's sick leave, returning just after the double
event of Stride's and Eddowes' deaths took place.
　　Sir Charles Warren, as Metropolitan Police Commissioner,
was said to have been in on the conspiracy. Warren was also a
Mason, along with Salisbury. There is one piece of suspicious
behaviour which cannot satisfactorily be accounted for. The
only time when he actually visited a murder site in Whitechapel
was when he heard of the Goulston Street graffito. He insisted
that the writing should be removed straight away, fearing that
it would cause a riot amongst the thriving Jewish community of

the area, who would be rising for work very shortly. This might have been understandable by itself, but he also refused permission to photograph the writing. One Dr Thomas Dutton claimed that he had actually photographed the writing, and that Warren had even the prints destroyed! If he really saw the Masonic clue with the word 'Juwes', then he would have panicked and acted in this way.

Warren resigned suddenly the day before Kelly's murder, but it was not announced until 9 November, causing a delay at Miller's Court. There were reasons for his resignation. A struggle for power had been going on between the Home Office and the Metropolitan Police Commissioners for some years. Warren had written an article defending his police procedures in 'Murray's Magazine' but had not had this cleared with the Home Office. The Home Secretary felt it necessary to invite Warren's resignation, and he offered it. The timing might have been deliberate, or co-incidence.

Knight refers to the 'Protocols of Zion' to explain Warren's involvement. The Protocols are controversial documents, with some arguing that they are fakes. If they are ancient and Masonic, they might be of worth in this study. The Eighth Protocol states, "The services of the police are of extreme importance to us, as they are able to throw a screen over our enterprises, invent reasonable explanations for discontent among the masses, as well as punish those who refuse to submit." Warren might have been involved in the conspiracy, but his reaction to the 'Juwes' incident is the only possible piece of evidence.

(5) Could the Masons have been involved?

Many of the details linking the mutilations with Masonic lore and oaths are impressive and possible. The supposed symbolism of the rings might be far fetched, though, for it is not clear what happened to them. Chapman bore marks on her fingers that showed that she had been wearing two, maybe three, brass rings. Newspaper accounts on the day did not mention them – only the coins were mentioned at first. Later newspaper accounts add the detail of the pile of rings by her body. The rings might have been stolen by a mortuary attendant, for that matter, and were probably worthless curtain rings often worn by such 'unfortunates'.

The oaths said by initiates are as follows:

"These several points I solemnly swear to observe, without evasion, equivocation, or mental reservation of any kind, under no less penalty on the violation of any of them, than that of having my throat cut across, my tongue torn out by the root, and buried in the sand of the sea at low water mark, or a cable's length from the shore, where the tide regularly ebbs and flows twice in 24 hours..."

The three Juwes express these oaths thus:

"Jubela: O that my throat had been cut across, my tongue torn out, and my body buried in the rough sands of the sea, at low water mark, where the tide ebbs and flows twice in twenty-four hours...
Jubelo: O that my left breast has been torn open and my heart and vitals taken from thence and thrown over my left shoulder...
Jubelum: O that my body had been severed in two in the midst, and divided to the north and south, my bowels burnt to ashes in the centre and the ashes scattered by the four winds of heaven..."

While there are striking parallels with the mutilations of the women, we must point out that an obvious Masonic mutilation is missing – the cutting out of the tongue. This is odd, and the other savage wounding shows that the killer(s) were not just coolly carving the women up in Masonic style, almost with textbook in hand, but they were wild and deranged. There was a frenzy involved that was quite sadistic.

Some question the interpretation of the word 'Juwes' as this was not a term used in English Masonry – although a mid-nineteenth century Masonic Manual does use the term. ('A Manual of Freemasonry' by Richard Carlile) Also, the material featuring Hiram Abiff and his killers was said to have been dropped from the ritual of English lodges early in the 19th century, so it is doubted that senior Masons would have known about them by 1888. However, senior Masons can be presumed to have had a learned interest in the history of the Craft and must have had access to material relating the tale of Hiram Abiff. It must also be remembered that the American Mason, William Morgan, had published 'Freemasonry Exposed' in 1826. Material was available for those with sufficient interest. While the modern rituals of the entrance to the third degree mention the three killers as 'ruffians', as the tale of Hiram Abiff is re-enacted symbolically with the initiate being pushed down, covered with a shroud and then pulled up ('resurrected'), it is evident that Masons of a higher standing are aware of the Juwes material. In their book, 'The Hiram Key ' (Arrow), Christopher Knight and Robert Lomas relate how, one month, when they had recently progressed through the early degrees, there were no new initiates. The Master of the Lodge told the full story of the Juwes to them, to fill the time!

A Mason friend of the Parlours has looked at the above details and has commented that some of the mutilations do seem to show some knowledge of Masonry, though it is rather haphazard. He also noted that the left arm placed over the breast (in two of the victims) is in the oaths of the fifth degree, and would not be generally known by anyone of the level of Master Mason down. The term 'Juwes' is usually withheld information until you reach higher degrees, moving from Lodge to Chapter level. It would have been meaningless to any but more senior Masons of the time.

The point must be made, though, that something in Sickert and Knight's scenario, here, does not ring true. Highly placed Masons might endeavour to silence five prostitutes because of sensitive information that they held. Would they really bother to mutilate them in such a way as a warning to others? Such poor women had no knowledge of Masonic matters. If a message like the 'Juwes' was meant as a part of this warning, then it was relatively useless, erudite and comprehensible only to the highest ranking Masons.

It would make more sense if it could be shown that the killer(s) left various Masonic clues to point to their paymasters, both covering their backs and having a joke at their expense. Then the 'Juwes' message would have really stung!

(6) Could Walter Sickert have been involved?

Sickert grew up in artistic circles, with his parents counting the Holman-Hunts, the Burne-Jones and the Morris family among their friends. He studied at King's College School until 1878, and tried his hand at the stage, playing at Sadler's Wells in 'A Midsummer Night's dream' in 1880. He eventually turned to painting, and enrolled in the Slade School in 1881 under Alphonse Legros and Whistler. By the age of 22, in 1882, he had a wide and influential circle of friends and he had become engaged to Ellen Cobden, the daughter of a famed radical politician, Richard Cobden.

The claim that Sickert kept a studio at 15 Cleveland Street cannot be substantiated. His recorded studios were at 13, Edward Square, Kensington in 1884 until his marriage to Ellen in 1885. Number 15 was demolished in 1888 to make way for a Nurses' Institute. The Post Office Directory has it listed as unoccupied from 1885-1887. Various buildings were listed as unoccupied but still used, to avoid paying rent, as with number

19 – being used as a brothel – but listed as unoccupied in the Directory. Sickert did keep his studio separate from his home, and it is possible that he kept rooms in Cleveland Street. He was at the start of his career and might have benefited from the extra free accomodation, but this is only a possibility.

Sickert was said to have been fascinated by Jack the Ripper. One story relates that he joked around with a group of women at the time of the Whitechapel murders, saying that he was Jack the Ripper. This was in Copenhagen Street, and they fled in terror. Some trace an influence in his paintings of murders, such as 'The Camden Town Murder', and there is a recurring study of prostitutes, such as 'The Hollandaise'. Joseph Sickert also found various clues in his paintings. In 'Ennui', there is a portrait of Queen Victoria which contains what is thought to be a dove. Joseph says it is a gull, an oblique reference to the Royal Physician. The painting 'Blackmail' shows a woman with glazed eyes, and part of her nose is missing. Joseph sees a reference to Kelly's death, here.

However, Walter Sickert's wit was also well known, as stated by Osbert Sitwell," The jokes, the quips, the seriousness, the fun, the acting.... the disguises, the beards, the dancing, the declaiming, all those things... " His alternative title for 'The Camden Town Murder' was 'What shall we do for the rent?' If we did not read the term 'Murder' in the title, it would appear to be a moment of intimacy between a man and a woman. His study of nudes was because of their naturalness, capturing their light and warmth. He drew and painted naked women in various situations because he despised the studio nude. A picture should represent "someone, somewhere, doing something."

Sickert led an adulterous lifestyle, and he separated from Ellen in 1896, divorcing her in 1898. Ellen wrote to him expressing her scattered hopes that he might have changed his lifestyle and have been faithful to her. Sickert replied, "It is quite true that I have not been faithful to you since our marriage, & it is equally true that during the two years since we have parted I have been intimate with several women. I have chosen my mode of life, & I am unable to alter it..." His rakish life would fit in with the role described by Joseph, courting the favours of such young women as Annie Crook and Mary Kelly, and it is not hard to imagine him as a part of the West End brothel scene. One possibility that occurs to us is that Walter Sickert might have been the anonymous father of Alice Margaret Crook, and not Eddy. This is plausible, and might explain the grains of truth in Joseph Sickert's story.

7) Did John Netley exist?

Netley was real enough and lived from 1857-1903. His existence was tracked down by a BBC team checking on Sickert's story. He was baptised in the chapel of the St. Marylebone Workhouse. He was employed as a carriage or van driver to several wealthy familes in the Kensington/Paddington area, possibly including William Gull, living at 74, Brook Street and Sir James Fitzjames Stephen at 32, De Vere Gardens. We cannot say for certain, though. He had gained a reputation for reliability and he used various stables, lodging nearby, such as the stables at Albert Mews situated between Victoria Grove and Canning Place, Kensington, within a stone's throw of the Stephen family.

Netley died in an accident when the wheel of the horse-drawn van he was driving, clipped and mounted a high kerb on a pedestrian island in Park Road near to the junction of the Clarence Gate entrance to Regents Park at the Baker Street end. An eye-witness at the inquest recounted how Netley was thrown from his seat and he hit the cobblestone road. He was trampled by the horses hooves and his head was crushed by the wheels of his own van. The Coroner returned a verdict of accidental death and advised that drivers should have safety straps fitted. It is unknown if he ever married, or had any children. He was buried in a pauper's grave. (Knight takes two earlier newspaper accounts from 1888 and 1892 as referring to Netley. The first features an unnamed cab driver, and the second one a driver called Nickley who tried to drown himself. These references might have had nothing to do with the real Netley.) A final thought on Netley; records reveal a 17 year old coachman from the Hyde Park Gate area, who might well have worked with Netley sometimes. His name was Arthur William Ripper!

(8) Druitt's death and Masonic connections?

The Sickert/Knight tradition does not mention any Masonic connection with Druitt's death, though there is a claim that Druitt was used as a scapegoat by the police to cover the real killers. There are various indirect links between Druitt and Eddy – his brother was in the same regiment as Frank Miles, whose brother was Eddy's equerry; Miles lived at Tite Street, across the road from Macnaghten and near to Whistler (whom Sickert visited often); and a former tutor of Eddy's, Canon John Neale Dalton, had been educated at the Blackheath school where Druitt taught, and might have kept up influence in the place. Druitt's death is odd in so far as he had stones in his pockets and had been carrying a return ticket – he was both a strong swimmer and had obviously planned to return that day. The Parlours have toyed with Masonic links by comparing Druitt's death with Roberto Calvi, president of Italy's Banco Ambrosiano, and involved in banking deals with the Vatican, thus being known as 'God's banker'. He was found hanging from a rope tied to scaffolding under Blackfriars Bridge on 18 June 1982. Around his neck was a symbolic 'cable-tow' and his pockets were filled with chunks of masonry. He was near water 'where the tide ebbs and flows'. In Italy, the logo of Freemasonry is a Blackfriar. Masonic involvement was strongly suspected in his death.

Druitt was found with chunks of masonry in his pocket, in the Thames, 'where the tide ebbs and flows'.

Apparently, Joseph Sickert claimed that he had made up the Masonic conspiracy in a Sunday Times article in 1977. He still held to his claims to be descended from Annie Crook and the whole story of the marriage with the Duke of Clarence. He was to reaffirm the Masonic plot later on, though, when a new book appeared by Melvyn Fairclough, 'The Ripper and the Royals' in 1991. He claimed that he had made the earlier denial to protect the reputation of Walter Sickert. The main thrust of the new book revealed the material in the supposed Abberline diaries and various papers which Sickert said he possessed, and that Knight had not used. The Abberline diaries purport to be the diaries of Inspector Abberline. These are three leather-bound volumes covering the period 1892-1915.

The first mention of them was in the Evening Standard of 21 April 1988. Sickert has no documented proof that Knight had seen these, and most people regard them as forgeries. Many of the details of the victims come from Neal Sheldon's article in 'True Detective', and minor errors are reproduced. Even Abberline's own initials are reversed. Fairclough has said that he no longer believes that the diaries are genuine.

Joseph Sickert claimed, in the foreword to 'The Ripper and the Royals' that Knight had distorted some of the material, and they had quarrelled. He wanted to set the record straight with the new account. 'The Ripper and the Royals' develops the earlier story by having a gang of conspirators. Anderson was involved, though not actually on the streets in the killings. He was gathering information for Warren and helping with the cover up. Lord Euston and Lord Somerset were somehow involved in the plot, though neither Sickert nor the diaries revealed how. They had been present in the East End on the nights of the killings, though. Then there was a mysterious 'John Courtenay' who was supposed to work as a 'batman' to the leader of the Ripper gang. He was supposed to have met his death by an accident with a tram in 1936. Fairclough could not trace this man, or his accident, in any records, though he noted that Courtenay was the family name of the Earl of Devon's family. The other member was a surprise, for it was Winston Churchill's father, Randolph Churchill.

Churchill had quarrelled with Bertie in 1876 over his brother, the Marquess of Blandford. Blandford had an affair with Lady Aylesford and when her husband returned from India and started divorce proceedings, Bertie sided with him, calling Blandford a 'blackguard'. Bertie and Randolph did not speak again until 1884, when Randolph returned from Ireland. They renewed their friendship and became close confidants. By 1886, when Churchill had become Chancellor of the Exchequer and Leader of the House of Commons, he was Bertie's principle political advisor. Churchill was also a close friend of Gull, ever since Gull had been called in to give a second opinion about his wife's treatment for typhoid in 1882. Gull's daughter had also married the son of Sir Henry Wentworth Acland, who was the family physician to Churchill's father.

Churchill was something of a cultured rogue, thinking himself the equal of kings as a member of the aristocracy and he could show black moods, foul temper and impatience, so that the Queen commented about him, "So mad and odd."

One problem is that the Grand Lodge denies that Churchill was ever a Mason. This is surprising for someone of his social standing at the time, and there are no extant photographs or paintings of him in any regalia. Fairclough believes that he has unearthed evidence that Randolph was a Mason. The library at Freemason's Hall records that a Rudolph H. Spencer was initiated in 1878 into the First Lodge of Ireland. The following year he was passed into the Westminster and Keystone Lodge. There is no mention of a Spencer in the Irish archives, though. Spencer could have been an alias for Churchill, for he and his brother often used 'Mr Spencer' when travelling abroad 'Rudolph H. Spencer' and 'Randolph H. Spencer Churchill' are not too dissimilar. Also, the 1953 edition of 'The Pocket History of Freemasonry' by Fred L. Pick and G. Norman Knight, an official Masonic publication, lists Randolph as a member!

Sickert also implicated Blandford, though with no exact detail. Blandford died at Blenheim in 1892. He was found in his

Lord Randolph Churchill.

laboratory by the housekeeper, with "a terrible expression on his face."

The diaries also claim that Abberline suspected and interviewed J. K. Stephen. Stephen revealed that Eddowes was killed in mistake for Kelly, and that there was no connection between Eddowes and the other women. The other four were in the blackmail attempt. There was also a volume of Vanburgh's plays with the diaries, and one had some notes in the same hand as the diaries. J. K. Stephen's name was written at the end of the prologue to 'The Confederacy'. Churchill's name, Eddy's, Netley's and Gull's were also scribbled throughout the play.

A final twist in the diaries is the claim that Mary Kelly did not actually die. Someone was killed in her place and she was allowed to escape. Abberline felt she was a police agent at some point in the saga, and a letter he was supposedly sent from a relation revealed that Kelly's real name was O'Brien, and that a letter had been sent by her from Canada in January 1889 after her supposed death. The diaries mention a mysterious Winifred May Collis, aged 20, who had known Kelly from service in Cleveland Street, and who had gone to stay with her in November 1888 because of an unwanted pregnancy. She was never heard of again. Collis was thus suspected of being the poor girl who was killed in 13, Miller's Court.

An O'Brien connection has not been traced, and Barnett never mentioned any alias that Kelly used. We have found an adequate reference to a Mary Jane Kelly born in Limerick as mentioned earlier. There is no record of any Winifred Collis, either.

Fairclough interviewed Ellen May Lackner, Sickert's cousin, who confirmed some of the details of his story, showing that there was some kind of family tradition. She mentioned that their grandfather, William Crook, had been educated at Eton with his cousins, who were of the Stephen family, but he was disgraced for marrying beneath his station. Stephen, Sickert, Eddy and Annie Elizabeth Crook, Mary Jane Kelly. The connection is constantly repeated. According to Sickert in 'The Ripper and the Royals', it was J. K. Stephen who introduced Eddy to Annie. Stephen was in love with Eddy, and he thought a woman would deflect him from other homosexual attentions that he would be moving into (at 19, Cleveland Street?).

It is difficult to know what to make of Sickert's stories. There is a good deal of confusion and contradiction, and both Knight and Fairclough had to struggle to make a logical sense of his reminiscenses. Some details have been disproved, and the diaries are very untrustworthy. Perhaps there are examples of conflation and mistakes – the raid on Cleveland Street could be mixed up with that on the brothel in 1889. However, there are some persistent facts that demand attention. Sickert was the first to draw attention to the Cleveland Street connection. His grandmother did live at number six for some time. There was a tobacconists and confectioners in the street which has now been taken over by the Middlesex hospital. The view that Kelly had been sent from a Refuge to assist at the shop is backed up by the curious oral tradition stemming from Providence Row. Sickert was also the first to draw attention to the existence of the driver, John Netley, and the possibility of a Masonic link with the killings. The members of his final Ripper gang are all credible, and would have been the kind of individuals involved in any such conspiracy. There is also the insight that Eddowes might have been killed in mistake for Kelly, which could illuminate a longstanding Ripper mystery, as will be revealed in the last chapter. His source is also the first full blown account of Kelly's possible substitution and survival, which looks very likely when all the facts of the case are surveyed. Perhaps Sickert is related to the painter, and did receive some garbled bits of information along the way. We feel he is not just after 'a fast buck', though something of that could have crept into the proceedings at various points. Ripperologists who have spoken with him find him confused but genuine. When parts of the diaries were proven to be untrue by presenting certain facts to him, he seemed genuinely shocked and let down. Perhaps there are some glimmers of truth even in these. It should also be noted that Fairclough interviewed Ellen May Lackner, Sickert's cousin, who confirmed some of the details of his story, showing that there was some kind of family tradition.

Another oral tradition has come to light in recent years concerning Freda Thomson, an old lady who recalls being told that the murders were linked to "The Queen's son, the Duke of Clarence". When pressed about this discrepancy, wondering if she meant 'grandson', she was insistent that it was the Queen's son – which would have been Bertie, the Prince of Wales. The tale involved a marriage to a prostitute, and the police were keeping watch over the house were she lived in Fitzroy Square. She did not know what had happened to the prostitute. The story had stemmed from her grandfather who was with the City Police CID and he was allegedly called to Mitre Square when Eddowes was found. (Though she referred to this as 'Mitre Court', which is the designation used in the Macnaghten memoranda, interestingly.) Her father was present also, then aged 14, as he was a runner for Reuters.

Freda's maternal grandmother also had a story about this murder. As a young woman, she was walking through Mitre Square, taking food to a cousin who worked at the nearby Royal Mint. She saw a man in a cape and a large, black hat, as in the Sandeman's Port advertisments. He looked at her and said, "It's alright. I don't want your sort!" and then walked away.

Later on, there were 'Toffs' in the Square, knocking the residents up, getting them to swill the blood away, after the body had been taken.

It is difficult to assess folk stories like this, but they show that there were variants of the Sickert theory at large, earlier this century. The tradition of 'the Queen's son' is interesting, and Bertie and Eddy seem to become confused and conflated in the various versions.

In 1993, John Wilding's 'Jack the Ripper Revealed' was published. This was the first new conspiracy theory after variations of the Sickert story. Wilding believes that there was a royal pregnancy and a blackmail attempt, but it was between Kelly and Bertie, not Eddy and Annie. One inconsistency in the Sickert story is that it is hard to imagine that the royal child would have been spared or allowed to be taken by Kelly, and then given over to Sickert to make arrangements for. If 6 Cleveland Street had been raided in 1888, it is inconceivable that the child would not have been taken with her mother. Kelly, as a confidant, and a witness to the supposed wedding, would also have been taken and incarcerated, surely.

We know from Barnett's account that Kelly had been in the West End soon after her arrival in London, working in a high class brothel. Wilding gives a fullsome account of Bertie's personality and womanising and it is clearly possible that the two met in such a brothel, or possibly at a wild party in his Watling Street flat. If Kelly did become pregnant by him, or became pregant by another man, and claimed it was the Prince's after a liaison with him, she might have tried to procure financial support from Bertie to escape her squalor. The reaction of the Palace would have been a curt denial and any Royal finding out about this claim would have been thrown into panic. A blackmail attempt might have followed, as Kelly espied the key to a fortune. Thus the plot and the tracking down of her known confidants. The idea of Kelly being protected at the end was also explored, as Wilding speculated that Gull met Kelly, concerned for the well being of the royal child. A switch was made and Kelly escaped.

The Ripper was actually two men, J. K. Stephen, and that other Ripper suspect, Montague John Druitt. Wilding felt that J. K. was passionately loyal to the Throne, and of striking physique, well equipped for the job of silencing the women. He was also a wit and a joker, and Wilding claims to trace anagrams in the Ripper letters and the Goulston Street graffito.

The graffito can be read as:

"F. G. Abberline. Now hate M. J. Druitt. He sent the woman to hell."

Wilding says that a list of names can be traced in about half of the 170 letters in the Liverpool letter; "Charles Warren. Annie Chapman. Bertie. A bitch Kelly. Montague Druitt. James Stephen. 9th November. HRH crown."

He then makes the following anagram:–

"To Charles Warren: 1.) A Annie Chapman did not hold Bertie's 2 souvenirs. 2.) I work at it – I lie in wait; ie. the 9th November, Montague Druitt and I gag a bitch. I rip open Kelly. I save HRH crown on a 12th stroke. James Stephen."

The second Liverpool letter is read as:–

"I kill. can the police trap me? I live in a Watling Street harem with people who love to fight fire. Come here. Yours, James Stephen. V.R."

He believes that Druitt became involved because Kelly approached him for legal help as a barrister – probably because she had heard of him or met him through her social network. Druitt, Wilding believes, knew J. K. and was then drawn into the plot. Wilding's belief that Druitt and J. K. were friends is based upon generalities. They were of a similar social background, and both were lawyers and keen sportsmen. He feels that Druitt made contact with J. K. to access the Royals by finding him at the family home (De Vere Gardens) or at the offices of the Reflector, J. K.'s short lived newspaper. A fantastical account follows of their use of a horse and cart, concealing the women under a taupaulin.

Wilding is perhaps on firmer ground than Sickert. A Kelly/Bertie link is entirely plausible given the known facts. Some of the way he sketches in the detail is fanciful and highly questionable. Would Kelly have approached the authorities if she was pregnant by Bertie? Would she have heard of Druitt, who was a minor lawyer (though admittedly he worked on poorer clients' cases) and mainly worked as a schoolmaster? The anagrams are interesting but it is difficult to know if they prove anything except the inventiveness of Wilding's mind – is it a case of seeing things in coals in the fire? J. K. and Druitt are certainly possible, if not likely suspects for the killings, but more evidence needs to be turned up to (a) link them as associates and (b) give them the necessary motive. More evidence is required if such a plot is to be sketched out with any degree of credibility.

The Penny Drops?

Drawing the Threads Together

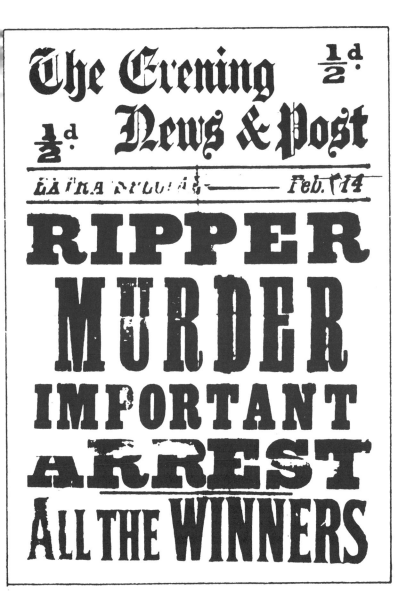

After presenting a row of suspects and the fascinating, though wild theories of Joseph Sickert, it is time to reveal some new insights that will re-open the conspiracy theory. We do not claim to have proof of a conspiracy, and we certainly do not have proof of the killer's identity, but we can make a new case, using various pieces of information. This is not the same theory as Sickert's. We hope to open up the case for a cover up after the sceptism and dismissive responses to the Sickert/Knight/Fairclough/Wilding material. It is time to begin to pull the strands of our case together.

Folk tradition surrounding Sir William Gull

William Withey Gull was born at St. Osyth Mill, on his father's barge "The Dove', on 31 December 1816, the youngest of eight children born to John and Elizabeth (nee Chilver) Gull. The earliest records of Gulls in Essex is in Fyfield in 1587. They were later to move from this small village on the River Roding, to Braintree, and then Colchester. John Gull was a bargemaster, and the family had settled in the Hythe area on the River Colne as this was ideal for mooring and loading/unloading goods. This was an exceptionally busy port at the time, dealing in building materials, livestock and produce grown by the local farmers. William Gull was baptised at St.Leonard's Church, Hythe on February 9 1817. William's second name came from his godfather, Captain Withey, a friend and employer of his father and a local barge owner. Shipping registers record that John Gull commanded 'The Dove' and Captain Withey 'The Amity' regularly at this time.

The family moved to Landermere Quay, Thorpe-le-Soken, after John acquired his own barge. William attended Mr. Seaman's local village school at Ivy House, Abbey Street, later furthering his education at Colchester, Lewes, Sussex and at Guy's Hospital. His time at Thorpe-le-Soken aroused his keen interest in natural history and botany in the fertile estuary. When William was ten, his father John Gull died, being buried in St. Michael's Churchyard, Thorpe-le-Soken. William's education at Colchester was at Shadrach Seaman's school and he acted as an assistant schoolmaster there in his late teens. When eighteen, he moved to Lewes to work as a schoolmaster for Benjamin Abbot, who was greatly interested in botany and natural history. His knowledge gained him the appointment to Guy's Hospital when only 21 as a cataloguer at the museum. Land at Thorpe-le-Soken belonged to Guy's, and hence the

Childhood home of Sir William Gull.

ink. Legend has it that a surgeon from the hospital was shoot-ng on this land and he became impressed with William's knowledge and promised to help his advancement. A definite sponsor can be found in Rev. Harrison, rector of the nearby parish of Beaumont, who took a kindly interest in the family after the death of John. Harrison's uncle was the Treasurer at Guy's.

William gained a BA in Medicine from the University of London in 1841 with honours in Physiology and Comparitive Anatomy and Surgery. He continued with placements at the hospital, being appointed Lecturer on Natural Philosophy in 1843 (as well as the Resident Superintendent of a small asylum for twenty insane women, which was part of the hospital). He became a Fellow of the College of Physicians in 1848. One year later, he was appointed to deliver the Goulstonian Lectures on paralysis. He was a fourth assistant physician through the 40's and 50s, developing an interest in insanity and illnesses of the mind. He married Susan Anne Dacre Lacy in 1848, and kept an early practice in Finsbury Square, before moving to 74, Brook Street in 1861. He came to the Queen's attention when he was in attendance upon the Prince of Wales with Sir William Jenner in 1871. The prince was critically ill with typhoid fever, and

171

St Michael's Church,
Thorpe-le-Soken.
(Photo: Andy Parlour)

Victoria honoured him with a baronetcy early in 1872, and appointed him as her Physician Extraordinary and Physician in Ordinary to the Prince of Wales.

He became known for fair mindedness at a time when relations between the nursing staff at Guy's and the professional staff were strained. On one occasion he gave exonerating evidence in the case of a nurse who was charged (unfairly) with homicidal negligence. In his own practice, he vowed that no patient should suffer in order to cover a professional miske, which did not always win him popularity with his fellows. He was a man of firm and outspoken views, condemning the use of alcohol, saying that he would rather eat raisins than drink wine! He did not suffer fools gladly, and could be blunt to the point of rudeness. This was highlighted in the case of his honesty with dying patients. He did not beat about the bush! To one he said, when asked if there was any hope, "There is very little life left in you. In fact you are heart-dead now." One peculiar tale about him is that he wanted to perform a post-mortem on a man who had died of heart disease. The relatives would only consent on the proviso that nothing was taken away from him, and they insisted on having a witness, the sister of the deceased. Gull cut out the heart before her eyes and stuffed it into his pocket. He declared., "I trust to your honour not to betray me.' and then he left with the organ!

William died in January 1890 after a severe stroke which made him lapse into unconsciousness. He was attended by three doctors, his son-in-law Theodore Dyke Acland, Dr. Hermann Weber and Dr. Charles Hood. He was then buried in the churchyard at Thorpe-le-Soken. The event was crowded, with a special train laid on from London, the village shops were closed, and blinds and shutters were drawn in the houses. The villagers thronged the Church and churchyard. The Gazette for 3 February 1890 reported,

Guy's hospital.

173

Sir William Withey Gull's grave.
(Photo: Andy Parlour)

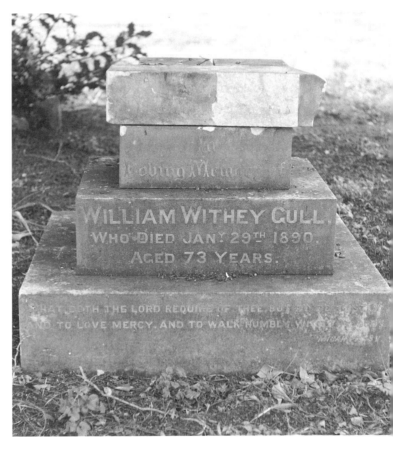

WILLIAM WITHEY GULL.
WHO DIED JAN.Y 29TH 1890.
AGED 73 YEARS.

"Sir William Gull's remains were interred 'far from th
madding crowd' in the quiet little village where he was brough
up, the funeral was a deeply impressive one, and althoug
unaccompanied by special pomp or circumstance, was
ceremony worthy of a great man who had died full of years an
honours...."

The earliest hint of Gull's involvement with the White
chapel murders and a cover up surrounding his death, came i
the two stories in the Chicago Sunday Times Herald of Apr
1895. The former was the revelation from a Dr. Howard tha
the Ripper was an eminent physician from the West End wh
was judged to be insane by a panel of twelve fellow doctors an
incarcerated in an Islington asylum under the assumed nam
of Thomas Mason, alias inmate 124. The report states that
"sham death and burial were gone through" to cover up th

sudden disappearance of the doctor. There are strong hints that this was Gull – a resident of the West End, and he had been a student at Guy's, and was an "enthusiastic vivisectionist". No one else but Gull fits this profile. (Gull had presented evidence in favour of vivisection before the Royal Commission for Vivisection in 1875, and had written a sixteen page article in its favour in 'The Nineteenth Century' in 1882.)

The second story in the paper was the Lees tale where he led the police to the house of a West End physician who later was sent to an asylum. Stephen Knight reported that Lees' great-niece, Mrs Emily Porter, related a version of the story she had heard through her family which contained the tradition of a fake burial, the coffin being filled with stones, and the whole affair was quite an event.

The items in the Chicago newspaper, and the Lees material, are fraught with difficulties, but whatever truth lies behind them, they are a very early testimony to a tradition about an eminent doctor being involved with the murders, and this doctor was most probably Sir William Gull. (There was an asylum, St Mary's, in Islington though no records survive, and a pauper named Thomas Mason died in 1896 at exactly the age Gull would have been had he lived on. This is all that can be said with certainty.) Another early tradition is attested by Michael Harrison, as reported earlier in our section on Dr. Stanley, when he heard a tale, when a child, of a royal doctor being involved early this century. This was a version of the 'doctor avenging his venereally infected son' variety. Dr Stowell was the first to name Gull as the doctor in the Lees story in his 'Criminologist' article in 1970. Interestingly, he took this as obvious knowledge and did not defend the association. He related Caroline Acland's account of the medium's visit to her father's house – and despite discrepancies in his overall story, he was a family friend of the Aclands, being one of the trustees of Acland's will. It is hard to imagine that Stowell would have wanted to slander Gull's memory on purpose. Knight, in fact, argued that Stowell was indirectly blaming Gull for the murders, using his cryptic 'S' as a foil to also protect the doctor. This is speculative, but possible. Indeed, Stowell asserts that there was a fantasy current at the time of the murders that the killer was a medical man, and "it was not unnatural for the rumour mongers to pick on a most illustrious member of my profession of the time – perhaps of all time – Sir William Gull…" It was not, actually, the most natural thing at the time. Why should someone as high up as Gull have been suspected?

The point is that Stowell, here, is naming Gull as the eminent or royal doctor of the much earlier tales and legends.

There might be more to Gull's involvement than has been allowed by many Ripperologists, quick to dismiss the Knight/ Sickert traditions as fantasy.

The Parlours have unearthed more early oral traditions surrounding Gull or an unnamed 'royal physician'. Andy Parlour has known an old East End emigre since his teens, when he worked with him on various scams and jobs like a Trotter partnership. This old friend, 'Charles' is a longstanding Mason of the 6th degree and now, late in life, and in poor health, has been relating various pieces of information to Andy and Sue.

'Charles' claims that at the higher levels of Masonry, there are various oral traditions which are told at meetings. These comprise chunks of Masonic history. The Parlours are sure that they were told that one such tradition relates that the Whitechapel murders were linked with a royal physician and the Brotherhood were ordered to close ranks and say nothing about the murders. (This is somewhat reminiscent of Dr Howard's claim in the Chicago report, that the panel of twelve doctors involved in sending the doctor to the asylum were all sworn to secrecy. They closed ranks.) When I spoke with 'Charles' later on, he appeared to backtrack, and said that he had only meant that there was a widespread rumour about a 'royal doctor' being involved in his youth ("Everybody knew that!") and that if the Masons had been involved, then they would have closed ranks. He went on to justify this by telling the tale of a time when he was stopped for a motoring offence. He did not give any Masonic signals and he later saw the same policeman at a Lodge meeting. The policeman was exasperated, and said that if only he had known, he would have helped him out. There are many tales of such low level corruption among the secret brotherhood, though such stories are always officially denied. 'Charles' told me that he is convinced that the Masons would have watched each other's backs at the time. I honestly did not know what to make of the man – was he telling the Parlours a fuller truth, or had they inadvertently misrepresented him? They are convinced that he claimed that there was a Masonic tradition.

We are on firmer ground with local traditions in Thorpe that the Parlours have unearthed. A mystery surrounds Gull's grave in Thorpe-le-Soken. Knight recounts how he was shown the grave by a verger, Mr Wally Downes. He had no idea why Knight wanted to see the grave. Wally commented, "This is a large grave, about twelve feet by nine, too large for two people. Some say more than two are buried there. It's big enough for three, that grave." (It is, in fact, 12 'by 9'.) When the Parlours took me to see the grave, we traced the outline of the plot. It is larger than an adjacent plot that holds five bodies!

He then went quiet and Knight presumed that this was out of deference to Gull. The silence might have concealed far more. Frank Gardiner, another emigre East Ender, tried to find out more about Gull after reading Knight's book in 1976. He walked into a local pub and asked some of the old men. They went silent and walked out on him. One even left a full pint of beer standing on the table!

L. Pearl Lonsdale, village history recorder, Thorpe-le-Soken.

The Parlours were once residents of the village and now live in the vicinity. The years have passed and many of the older generation have passed away. Thus they are trusted and have managed to find a wealth of oral traditions about the grave from their own generation of locals.

Pearl Lonsdale is the village history recorder and the author of the locally produced book, 'Changes in a Rural English Village – A Pictorial View of Thorpe-le-Soken & Landermere 1880-1990'. She was born in 1922 at Barkers Hall, and her father, Thomas, was born at 'Bradley Hall Farm' in 1885, in the village. She has lived in the village all her life and she heard a story about Gull from her childhood. He was not the murderer, but was linked to the murders. Gull was helping to cover up the misdeeds of the Prince of Wales, (Bertie, note, and not Eddy!). Bertie had "interfered" with one of the women.

Gull was sent to an asylum after he was supposed to have died and the grand funeral at Thorpe-le-Soken in 1890 was a fake. She was told about the 1890 funeral by a friend, Mr Ken Lines, a teacher. His grandfather remembered the grand funeral in 1890 and the crowds lining the ¾ mile funeral route from the station, where the coffin arrived by train from London, and was then taken to the Church by horse drawn funeral bier.

She recalls the village rumour that the coffin contained bags of sand. When Gull really died, several years later, the grave was opened up and another coffin was placed inside, in the middle of the night.

Another tradition comes from Mr John Otto, now living in Spain. This was related to the Parlours, firstly by his son, Eddie Otto, who still lives in Thorpe-le-Soken, and then by John himself. Again, the funeral was a sham, the coffin being rumoured to contain bags of sand. The later, middle of the night burial, involved grave diggers from outside the area and the local diggers were placed on the gates to stop anyone from entering. He spoke with the grandson of one of these men in the 1970s who confirmed the story. He was fascinated by the story that there were three coffins in the grave – a sand filled one, Gull's and his wife's. John also heard that there was a clue on the grave. He had no idea what this might be, and the inscriptions seem to give nothing away. Beneath Gull's name, there is a verse from Micah 6:8, a favourite of his, "What doth the Lord require of thee but to do justly and to love mercy and to walk humbly with thy God." This is the only item that could be a connection with Whitechapel, for the verse is also displayed at the Whitechapel Working Lad's Institute, where the inquests on Mary Ann Nichols and Annie Chapman were held. Read into that what you will. On top of the plot are three steps of stone with a cross on top (which is now in ruins on the floor because of vandals). Are the three stones a hint?

A third source for this fascinating oral tradition is Mr Stephen Unger, a member of the Essex County Fire Brigade. He was born in the village nearly 50 years ago. His grandfather was a farm labourer at Landermere, and his mother, Nell Turner, lived as a young girl in the 1920s at Landermere Cottages, near to Gull cottages. Nell told him the story that her father, Ernest, had told her, concerning Gull. Gull was rumoured to be linked with the murders, and they involved a member of the royal family. Gossip began after the grave was reopened one night, some years after 1890.

A final source is from Harold Salmon. He moved to the village just before the war to live with his grandmother at Railway Cottages. His grandmother, Mrs Waters, was born in 1877 and she lived to be 100. She would have been 13 at the time of Gull's funeral. He remembered, as a young man, being told by the locals that Gull's grave contained three coffins, and that one was full of rocks.

What can be made of these long-standing folk traditions? These rumours have been circulating around Thorpe-le-Soken right through this century. They pre-date any material published in Stephen Knights book in 1976, and any theories held by Joseph Sickert, or, indeed, Dr Stowell. They are consistent with the Howard/Lees material from 1895. They deserve serious attention, but short of exhuming the bodies from the grave, nothing can be conclusively proven by them. These, alone, though, should reopen the case connecting Gull in some way with the murders.

Fireman Stephen Unger wearing his 20-year Service and Good Conduct medal.

Knight relates the unusual nature of the death certificate. This was signed by Theodore Acland, even though other doctors were also in attendance upon Gull. It was unethical for a relative to witness the death, for they might gain from it, especially if other doctors were treating the patient. It was not illegal, merely bad form. The death certificate also states that he only had two attacks – one on Oct 10 1887, and the second on Jan 27 1890, although other accounts relate a third attack.

The Parlours have noted a peculiar detail surrounding Gull's will. This was probated in 1890, and the exact same details were re-entered in the registers in 1897 with 'double probate' entered, in red, in the margin.

The text of the second, 1897 entry is as follows:

"Sir William Withey Gull of 74, Brook Street, Baronet M.D. died 29 January 1890.

Probate LONDON 8 January to Edmund Hobhouse Esquire.

Effects £344,022 19s 7d   Former Grant March 1890."

(The words "Double Probate Jan 1897" are written in the margin of the entry).

The figures are exactly the same as in 1890. Why was this? Had the inheritance remained untouched all that time? Double probate happens when there are not the required number of executors to handle the will, though there is usually a short time between the sessions. Seven years seems inordinately long and would co-incide with the real time of Gull's death in the folklore! The will itself, was drawn up on 27 November 1888, shortly after Kelly's murder. He had his first seizure a year earlier. Some have wondered why he should have drawn up the will at this point. Could he have begun to plunge himself into remorse and guilt over his part in the crimes, and sensed that the end was not far off, if only of his sanity? Again, this could be pure co-incidence.

One final detail remains about Gull, to be added for completion. Gladstone said that Gull left £34,000 which sounds about right for a man of his station. "Do you observe Gull's very large fortune – £34,000 besides land. The Doctors are looking up." However, a copy of the will at Somerset House records that he left £344,000 – confirming the probate entry above – which would be worth nearly 15 million pounds today! This as an outstanding fortune for his day, and Sir Edward Muir, Sergeant

Surgeon to the Queen and President of the Royal College o
Surgeons, who died in 1973, left only £87,000. Could Gull'
large fortune have been swelled by funds for his secret service
to the Crown?

Gull and Goulston Street

The possible Masonic connections with the 'Juwes' of the graf
fito have already been suggested in Chapter 'The Plo
Thickens'. No one has ever answered the question why thi
enigmatic piece of writing should have been left in Goulstor
Street. A possible answer links the place name with Sir Willian
Gull. Gull delivered a series of lectures called the Goulstoniar
Lectures in 1849. Theodore Goulston (c1578-1632) was a
fellow of Merton College, Oxford, and a Fellow of the Roya
College of Physicians. He founded the lectures.

Gull delivered the lectures the year after he was appointec
Fellow of the Royal College of Physicians. His lectures were
about paralysis. This was a great honour and a help to hi
career and reputation. He went on to develop theories or

Goulston Street. Wentworth Buildings (left), site of cryptic message.

nsanity and illnesses of the mind afterwards. Close associates
of Gull would have known such details.

It might be significant that the doorway to Wentworth
Buildings could represent the gate of Solomon's Temple, a
Masonic symbol, with two pillars and a lintel. It looks strikingly
similar to pictures of the gate of the Temple in Masonic lore.
This was pointed out by 'Charles'. Could this have suggested
the exact point to leave the message? The original doorway was
built with engineering bricks – rounded, hardened black fire-
bricks which formed the pillars. The lintel was of a light
coloured sandstone with a lattice type design. The hallway was
about 6'-8' in depth and the stairs went up on the right hand
side. The section where the graffito was written was on smooth,
red brick. This information is provided by a few extant
witnesses, including Frank Gardiner of Walton-on-the-Naze,
mentioned above. He remembers seeing the doorway before it
was demolished in the early 1960s. He worked as a law writer for
the bank note printer's Waterlows at London Wall, City of
London.

A pattern emerges?

The Parlours believe that they have found a pattern to the
murder sites, when these are joined up in a certain manner.
This, if true, would implicate Parliament, and adds fuel to the
cause of the conspiracy theorists.

It is essential to determine how many victims there were of
the Whitechapel Murderer before trying to delineate any pattern to the killings. While it is generally reckoned that he had
five victims, four other women have been suggested as possible
victims, too. Two of these women were hurt or killed before the
five recognised killings, and two took place afterwards.

(a) Emma Elizabeth Smith – Easter Monday, 3 April 1888
Smith was a 45 year old widow with two children who
found work as a prostitute. She was attacked by four men and
staggered into her lodgings in the afternoon, covered in cuts
and bruises. She was urged to go to the London Hospital.
There, it was discovered that she had severe internal bleeding
owing to injuries to the vagina. An instrument, but not a knife,
had been inserted violently. She died the following day from
peritonitis. She is generally rejected as a Ripper victim for the
modus operandum was clearly different and she was not
directly killed in the attack.

(b) Martha Tabram – Bank Holiday Monday, 6 August 1888

Martha Tabram, also known as Martha Turner, was married and a prostitute. She spent the evening drinking in the Angel and Crown, near Whitechapel Church, and left at closing time, shortly after 1.30am. At 3.30am, a cab driver returning home, Albert Crow, saw her huddled up on the first floor of 35 George Yard Buildings. He passed by, assuming she was a drunk. At 5.00am, a market worker, John Reeves, set out to work. He saw her lying in a pool of blood and raised the alarm. She had been stabbed in the chest thirty nine times, and two weapons had been used. One might have been a long knife, or bayonet, and one a surgical instrument. Some surgical knowledge was assumed. The doctor examining the body declared, "Whoever it was, he knew how and where to cut."

She was known to solicit regularly in the Tower Hamlets and Dockland area, but she was a loner with few friends. A soldier was last seen in her company, but he had good alibis after 1.30am.

Tabram's case is closer to the Ripper murders, and might possibly be included, but the method of killing was still different. The Ripper used one weapon, sliced the throat clean across and mutilated deliberately rather than stabbing in a frenzied manner.

(c) Alice McKenzie, 17 July 1889

At about 1.00am, PC Walter Andrew found a woman in Castle Alley near Whitechapel High Street.

Her skirts were bunched up, suggesting a sexual motive, and a pool of blood was by her head. A clay pipe found next to her identified her as 'Claypipe Alice'. Her throat had been stabbed twice, but not cut. This had been done from above as she was held down. There were two cuts in the abdomen on the right side from the chest to the navel. These were a series of cuts, and they were not deep enough to open the abdominal cavity. Dr Phillips, attending the body, felt that the cuts were made by a smaller instrument than that used by the Ripper. This could have been a copy cat killing, but was clearly not the work of the Ripper's hands.

(d) Frances Coles – 13 February 1891

Coles, known as 'Carroty Nell', was found by PC Benjamin Leeson in Swallow Gardens. She was still breathing, but her throat was cut. He heard footsteps running off. He had been wearing rubber soled boots, and thus had surprised the murderer. Dr Phillips examined the body once she was dead. Her throat had been cut. A man had been seen with her earlier, who had returned to her lodgings twice, both times covered in blood, claiming that he had been mugged. The second time was at 3.30am and the landlord had refused him lodging. The man was James Sadler, a fireman on the SS Fez. The City police felt that they might have captured the Ripper at last and they were determined to press a conviction. Sadler enlisted the help of the Stokers' Union who provided excellent character references from previous captains, and he was eventually cleared.

There is simply not enough evidence to link this murder with the Ripper and it could be another example of a copycat crime.

The number of victims thus is held at five by most researchers.

A bizarre theory surrounding the dating of the murders was suggested by Michael Harrison. He took in two other women, Amelia Farmer and someone called Mallet. These two have not been considered as Ripper victims by anyone else, and Farmer was not actually killed; she was only injured and gave a full description of her assailant to the police. He counts the 'Double Event' as one killing, and thus he had the special number of ten. He argued that each one took place on a religious festival (pagan or Christian) or a date linked with the Royals. His chart appears like this:

Smith (3 April 1888) – Feast of Cybele

Tabram (6 August 1888) – Birthday of Duke of Edinburgh

Nichols (31 August 1888) – Birthday of Princess Wilhemina of the Netherlands

Chapman (8 September 1888) –

Stride and Eddowes (30 September 1888) –

Kelly (9 November 1888) – Birthday of Prince of Wales

Farmer (21 November 1888) – Birthday of the Empress Frederick

Mallet (28 December 1888) – Feast of the Holy Innocents

McKenzie (16 July 1889) – Anniversary of Eddy's nomination as a Freeman of London

Coles (13 February 1891) – The Ides of February

Opposite page: *Sites of the five canonical victims of Jack the Ripper.*
1. Mary Ann Nichols.
2. Annie Chapman.
3. Liz Stride.
4. Catherine Eddowes (aka Jane or Mary Ann Kelly).
5. Mary Jane Kelly.

This is really forcing the idea to fit the facts! There is not even a known festival or connection for the 'Double Event'. Colin Wilson has pointed out that a really obvious date was missed out, that of Queen Victoria's birthday on 24 May. A murder on that date would have been noticed.

Most Ripperologists fix the number of Ripper murders at five. Many have wondered if there is any pattern to the placing of the victim's bodies. No sensible pattern has been discerned, though there have been two ideas in the past. Stewart Evans, co-author of 'The Lodger', has seen some letters written to G. R. Sims. One, dated 1907, is from an Ernest Crawford of Bath. He relates the theory held by his friend, a 'Mr. S.'. This suggests that the Jesuits were behind the murders, having infiltrated the detectives in the London service. Right in the centre of the Whitechapel area was a Jesuit college. Crawford's friend suggested that if the murder sites are joined up, then they make a "fairly regular cross." This is true of the first four sites, though it is a slightly lopsided cross, but Crawford himself confesses that it is "wild speculation."

Another theory involved psychic interest. Students of the occult claimed that the Ripper practised the black arts, and that he had been ordered by the Master of his Lodge to kill seven women and to place their bodies about the area so that the positions would form a seven pointed star, with the head of the cross to the west. One occultist believed that the points, when joined up, would form the outline of a dagger. A member of the Crimes Club, Arthur Diosy, argued that the five bodies would mark out a pentagram, and that the killer was trying to draw an 'elixir of life' from the women.

No seven pointed star or dagger, and only the most lopsided pentagram can be defined from the pattern.

The Parlours believe, along with the Sickert tradition, that the fifth murder, of Mary Jane Kelly, was an afterthought. The Ripper would have believed that his task was complete with that of Eddowes. She was a case of mistaken identity, often calling herself 'Jane Kelly' as she lived with a John Kelly at the time of the murders.

The fourth murder victim was at Mitre Square. This, in itself, can have various symbols read into it.

Firstly, Masonic references can be inferred. 'Mitre' and 'Square' are tools of Freemasonry, tools of stonemasons, and given to Entered Apprentices in their initiation ceremony. Mitre Square was named after the Mitre Tavern that was on the spot. This was a meeting place for Masons at the time.

Opposite page: *Map showing the arrow formed by the first four murder sites pointing directly to the Houses of Parliament.*

Secondly, Mitre Square is on the site of the old Priory of the Holy Trinity. A woman was praying at the High Altar in 1530 when she was attacked by a mad monk. He killed her, and then himself, plunging the knife into his own heart. This murder is similar to the story of Hiram Abiff (see Chapter 'The Plot Thickens') who was in Solomon's Temple before his murder. The fact that this area became a centre of Masonic activity, with the presence of the Lodge of Hiram and other important lodges nearby, might suggest that a link was made between this ancient killing and that of Hiram in their folklore.

On a more mundane level, a mitre is an apex at the end of a structure, joining pieces together. This gave the clue that has cracked the code. Andy Parlour joined up the four murder sites, with Mitre Square as the apex. This reveals an arrow shape. If there is an intentional arrow, then where does it point? This points straight to the Houses of Parliament as can be seen on a map. Each point is exactly half a mile from the next.

We can only assume that this was a clue left to show that higher powers were implicated in the crimes. This was left to cover the killer's back, just as the Masonic references were scattered around to suggest a connection with certain dignitaries. This suggests a conspiracy and a playful, witty operator who was subtly turning the tables upon his masters.

'Charles' – the Masonic friend – saw the pattern of the arrow and immediately felt that this was also a Masonic symbol. It appeared to be a closed set of compasses on the square, which has sometimes been a tradition in some lodges to show that business is finished. The compasses are opened at the start of the meetings. The stem of the arrow is the right proportion, and the tips of the arrow head are the same proportion as the square is to the compasses. Was the killer telling his paymasters that 'business is finished', believing that he had killed Kelly?

Some might object that we can make any pattern up that we want. Try it. We challenge the reader. Very little can be made sensibly from the positioning of the bodies. An arrow is formed pointing in one direction only. It might point to many buildings along the line reaching Parliament, but they are of absolutely no significance. The straight line hits Parliament, unwaveringly. A witty genius such as J. K. Stephen would have thought up some sort of clue like this. The bare truth is that it might be *so* obvious that everyone has missed it until now! Such is life, after all.

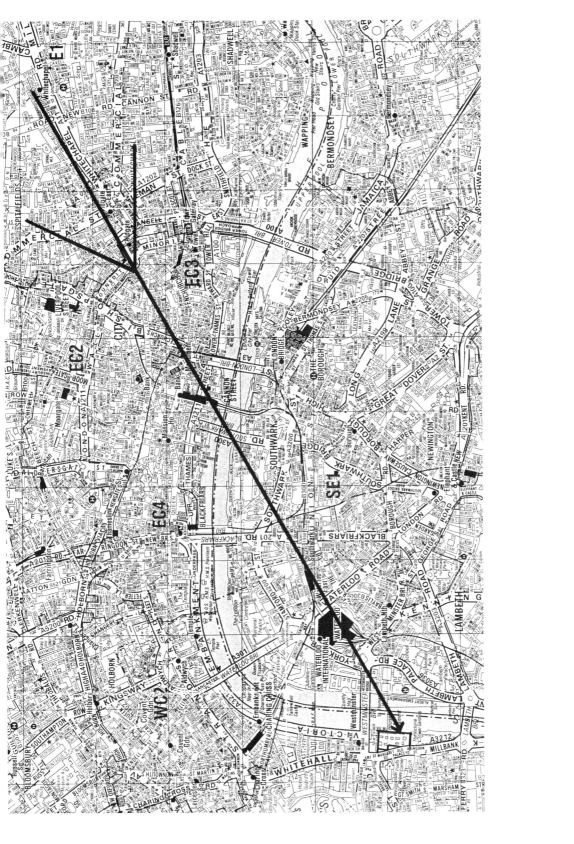

The Marny Hallam letter

A Mrs Marny Hallam wrote a letter to the Sunday Times on 16 February 1975. This reads as follows:

> "My grandmother was a young married woman with a family in the 1880s. She had a fierce, not to say morbid, interest in criminology, and Jack the Ripper was one of her favourite subjects for discussion.
>
> Her father was a barrister, and she always maintained that he had told her that the identity of the Ripper was known to the authorities. He was one J. K. Stephen, a tutor at Cambridge, one of whose students was the Duke of Clarence, eldest son of King Edward VII, who died prematurely.
>
> I believe that Stephen was ultimately confined in what was then properly called an asylum.
>
> Mrs Marny Hallam, Newbury."

This is the only definite external claim that J. K. Stephen was the Ripper. This letter has been paid scant attention, and has been dismissed as the typical flotsam encountered in Ripperology with hearsay stories and hoaxes abounding. There might be intriguing connections through Marny's husband's lineage. The Hallam family, at the time, were barristers, acquainted with the Stephen family. Henry Fitzmaurice Hallam was a contemporary of Sir James Fitzjames Stephen. The story points to Marny's family, though.

More was to emerge when the Parlours managed to contact Marny, not knowing if she were still alive or not. Marny was very tired, old and frail, but agreed to see the Parlours. She was bright and alert at times, and then tired and confused. She is in her eighties. She said that she had had a number of visitors after writing the letter, but none for years until now. When the Whitechapel Murderer was mentioned, she quipped, "You mean murderers!" but then lapsed into confusion and could not remember any more. The ramblings of an old lady, or dimly remembered stories passed down through her family? Her family name was Weaver, apparently. The Parlours set about tracing her family tree.

Marny's two great-grandfathers on her mother's side were Thomas Thornthwaite and William Tiffen, both farmers from Cockermouth, Cumberland. There is no evidence that either were barristers or that they had relations who were.

On her father's side, were Loraine Weaver, a surgeon from Friern Barnet, and Thomas Reynold Bartrum, a merchant.

Thomas' father, Charles, was one half of Bartrum and Prety-man who in 1827 were wholesale ironmongers at Upper Thames St. E.C. He lived at 1, Little Bush Lane. Thomas Bartrum was listed as a solicitor in this year in 9, Mildred's Court, Poultry, which was not far from Little Bush Lane. In 1837, Bartrum and Pretyman are at the same address, but only Thomas is mentioned at 1, Little Bush Lane, and he remains linked with the company through to 1892, when they moved to Leadenhall St. E.C., not far from Mitre Square. Presumably, Thomas had given up his legal practice after Charles' death when he took over the family firm. Thomas would have been Marny's grandmother's father, and her grandmother, Edith Emily, would have been a young married woman in the 1880s. No mention of a barrister, but we do have a solicitor.

On the Weaver side, her great grandfather was Loraine Weaver, a surgeon, and her grandfather, Thomas, was a regis-trar at the Anglo-American Cable Company. Her great-grand-father's nephew was Harold Baillie Weaver, a barrister. Harold's chambers were at 6, New Square and then at 14, Old Square Buildings, Lincoln's Inn. (J. K. Stephen's were at 3, Stone Buildings which were part of Old Square.) Harold's private address was 5, Melcombe Place, Dorset Square, across the road from J. K. Stephen's brother, Harry.

The executor for Harold Baillie's will was the Countess Muriel de la Warr , a member of the Sackville family. A relation of hers, Vita Sackville West, was the good friend and confidant of Virginia Woolf, daughter of Leslie Stephen, first cousin to J. K. Stephen.

Perhaps the tradition about Stephen had come from Harold Baillie Weaver rather than Thomas Bartrum. We do not know. There was a barrister in her family line who worked in proximity to J. K. Stephen, and who probably moved in some of the same social circles. (Harold Baillie Weaver, J. K. Stephen and Montague John Druitt, all worked as equity draughtsmen and conveyancers.) This makes it hard to dismiss Marny Hallam's family tradition as spurious and empty.

J. K. Stephen is as likely a candidate as any for involvement in a Royal conspiracy, through his connections with Prince Eddy as his former Cambridge tutor, and with Sir William Gull as his patient. He was a fiercely loyal monarchist and staunch Conservative. Whether he had the character to actually kill is a moot point. He might have employed an assistant to do the dirty work, being the brains behind the 'hit squad' on the streets.

189

'Charles' speculates that Stephen might have been rejected for membership of a Lodge on the grounds of his unsound mind – this is a specific reason for barring someone – as Stephen would have been drawn to such membership by his position as a barrister, and with his influential connections. (Oscar Browning was a Freemason for years, and was present at Eddy's passing the initiation to the level of Master Mason. When Browning first joined himself, he commented, "I joined it because I always like anything which forms a link between the transient undergraduate and myself." Might Browning have been an influence in J. K. trying to become a Mason?) J. K. also loved clubs and societies, having been a member of the Cambridge Apostles and the TAF (Twice a Fortnight) club, a name that he had coined. His bitterness over the rejection might go some way to explaining his various Masonic clues linked with the killings. 'Charles' also wondered if Stephen had then become a member of the Knights Templar, an order affiliated with the Masons, but not an actual branch of Masonry. They are independent, and do not have Craft degrees (though many Templars are also Masons in their own right.) This is not the old heretical group of the Middle Ages, though they claim some kind of continuity with them. Charles' claims that the Templars could have been the assassins, the 'hit-men' in the late 19th century, and they would work in pairs, one acting as an apprentice. They were fiercely independent, often unethical at the time, and more secret than the Masons. They would undertake tasks that the Masons would not get involved in. They are pledged to defend their secrecy and certain truths, and he found one meeting he was invited to be rather sinister, with drawn swords brandished at the doorway until he gave the password. It was also obvious to him that some Templars were using the meeting to further business links, quite openly. Whether this picture of the Templars is based upon his prejudice and limited experience, or upon fact, we simply cannot tell.

There is usually one lodge in each county with more in London. Their headquarters is in France, and if they keep old records of membership, they will probably be found there.

The Templar order see themselves as being descended, not only from the Medieval Knights Templars, but from orders within Solomon's Temple (according to "the Revelation of Sacred History and Ancient Mystery"). Their lodges are known as Encampments, and their ritual is explicitly Christian in content. A meeting opens with the members drawing their swords and placing them on their right hands, as various levels

THE CLOISTERS, THE TEMPLE

declare their readiness to guard certain secrets – the holy sepulchre and the faith that is proclaimed by the resurrection. The meeting closes with the swords drawn again and readings from the Passion of Christ. An initiate is robed as a pilgrim with staff, and he carries a burden on his back. At a certain point in the ceremony, the pilgrim's staff and robe are removed and the burden is loosed upon seeing the cross. Then the initiate is clothed with a mantle, apron, sash and jewel. Finally, the sword and shield are presented.

Headquarters of the Knights Templars from 1184.

The pass words and signs are disclosed – 'A-montra' as the hailing word, and 'Mahershalahashbaz' as the pass word. The sign is to seize a man by the thigh, as though he is to be thrown. The penal signs are made, of drawing the forefinger or thumb across the forehead, showing that the skull is to be sawn asunder, and the grand sign is to stand as one crucified, arms out, head drooping on the right shoulder, and right foot over left. Other sacred words are 'Emmanuel' and 'Adonai'. The badge is white with a red cross.

The Templars are made to pledge their readiness to fight for the Gospel, swords at the ready:

191

"I do furthermore swear, that with this, the sword of my faith, I will guard and defend the sepulchre of our Lord Jesus Christ against all Jews, Turks, infidels, heathens, or other opposers, of the Gospel."

'Charles' noted that the Temple area of London was originally the headquarters of the Medieval templars before they were declared heretics by Philip IV of France in the fourteenth century. It is thus feasible that young barristers might have joined this order.

While this is possible and interesting, the Parlours and I are reticent for there seems to have been something amateurish about the Masonic mutilations. It is more likely that the killer was playing a game with his masters and leaving clues to implicate them. 'Charles' rejoined that they were quite capable of implicating the Masons when they wanted to, and a Templar would not necessarily know Masonic rituals intimately. Let the reader make of this what she or he will. It is colourful, but maybe nothing more.

Druitt and J. K. Stephen

Montague John Druitt would be a possible candidate as the accomplice, suspected of sexual insanity by at least some of the police at the time of his suicide. There is circumstantial evidence that Druitt and Stephen must have been acquainted. This was pointed out by Martin Howells and Keith Skinner in 'The Ripper Legacy' but has been usually ignored. J. K. Stephen kept chambers at 3, Stone Buildings, Lincolns Inn. His father and brothers had chambers just around the corner – Sir James at 1, Paper Buildings; Herbert at 4, Paper Buildings; and Harry at 3, Kings Bench Walk. Druitt kept chambers at 9, Kings Bench Walk in the same block as Harry Stephen. J. K. and Druitt must at least have known of each other from this close proximity.

We can speculate that the fact that both were keen sportsmen would have made them converse, and Druitt bore an uncanny resemblance to Eddy, according to a few photographs that we possess. This was when he sported his moustache, but we do not know the dates of these. Would he have appeared similar to Eddy in the late 1880s? If so, a livewire and wit such as J. K. would have been drawn to the young barrister for this reason alone!

The choice of Chiswick as the place for Druitt's suicide has confused many. There might be a link with the boat race, for this ends at Chiswick. In 1880, J. K. would have been present as

3, Stone Buildings. J. K. Stephen had chambers here. (Photo: Andy Parlour)

incoming President of the Cambridge Union. Druitt probably would have been with his sporting interests. They might have met there, but it is more likely that they reminisced about this race years later when they met as barristers. It was a year to remember – it was so foggy that the race was postponed until

*9, Kings Bench Walk.
Montague Druitt had
chambers here.
(Photo: Andy Parlour)*

Opposite page: *James
Kenneth Stephen, painted
in 1891.(Published for the
first time by kind
permission of King's
College, Cambridge)*

the Monday for the first time in memory. The day of Druitt's
death was also extremely foggy. If there is a boat race connection, it cannot make much sense without a link with someone
like J. K. Did they arrange to meet there as it was so pregnant
with memory?

194

The poems of J. K. Stephen

J. K. published two collections of his poems in 1890 and 1891, 'Lapsus Calami', and 'Quo Musa Tendis?'.

These are made up of poems written over the years and published in various magazines and newspapers. Some date back to his Cambridge days from editions of 'Granta', and others were printed in his short-lived 'The Reflector' or in newspapers such as 'The Pall Mall Gazette'.Thus, many were written before the murders. Only certain of these have been highlighted before, claiming various things are revealed about J. K.'s character, such as his attitude to women mentioned earlier (see Chapter 'Rogues Gallery'). The poems reveal a lively and erudite mind, fond of word play and human observation. He can be very witty and amusing. Perhaps some show black moods and a temper, but we cannot read too much into them. Any violent reference is seized upon, such as the lines:

"They brought the Times:
A list of crimes:
A deadly fight
'Twixt black and white:…"

These are from 'The Splinter' and some see a reference to the murders. Other lines might refer to Bertie and Gull:

"A note from "B"
On Mr. G.,
And other things
From cats to Kings,
Known to that grand Inquisitor:-….."

Harrison quoted a section of another poem in 'Clarence' without giving the source, and we have, so far, not been able to trace this in the J. K. corpus:

"I have no time to tell you how
I came to be a killer
But you should know, as time will show,
That I'm society's pillar."

Curious, but we need to see the whole context of the poem before reading too much into this.

However, the very titles of the two collections are perhaps the biggest clue to J. K.'s involvement in the Whitechapel Murders as far as his poetry is concerned. They are staring us in the face, if we have decoded an earlier clue left by him. Given the arrow design of the placing of the bodies, the titles, 'Lapsus

'Calami' and 'Quo Musa Tendis?', translated as 'Flight of the Arrow' and 'Where the Muse Aims' are possibly oblique references to the murders. True, the Latin is capable of several layers of meaning, and we can see mere points about the direction of the pen, and the poet's inspiration striking. The titles are tantalising, though, given the arrow pattern.

There is one other poem which is worthy of mention. This is about J. K.'s pipe, 'The Grand Old Pipe' in which he rejoices, "My pipe was my one consolation…" We can see him smoking this in photographs, and he was known to pull on this when relaxed or troubled. This fits with the witness of Israel Schwartz before Stride was murdered. Schwartz saw a man step out of the shadows, smoking a pipe. The only time a witness reported two men involved, one of them had a pipe. Could this have been J. K.?

J.K. and the colour red

A portrait of J. K. hangs in the Conversation Room at King's College, Cambridge. J.K. is seated, alert, possibly lecturing his students. He wears a red flower – a carnation or a rose – in his lapel. The colour red recurs in the witness reports of the murderer. Chapman was wearing a red scarf; Stride wore a red flower, and Kelly was offered a red handkerchief.

J. K.'s flamboyant style would suit the flashy colour red as an affectation, and this could be a link with the murders.

'Charles' speculates that the red was from the acacia blossom that was used in Masonic lore as a symbol of Hiram Abiff's immortality. The Ark of the Covenant, in the Temple, was made of acacia wood, and the acacia is a special kind of mistletoe which bears a red and white flower. Red and white are the colours of the Knights Templar. Interestingly, some descriptions of Stride's flower said it was red and white. All of this is pure speculation, and possibly no more than a series of co-incidences.

Sickert and the Stephen family

The Parlours have traced references to Sickert as a friend of the Stephen family. Virginia Woolf writes that he was a frequent visitor to their family home when it moved to Gordon Square, Bloomsbury, after the death of her father, Leslie Stephen, in 1904. Sickert also travelled to St. Ives to paint, and this might form another link with the Stephens. Leslie Stephen dis-

"Talland House", St. Ives, Cornwall. Summer home of Sir Leslie Stephen, J. K.'s uncle. (Photo: Andy Parlour)

covered St. Ives in 1881 and he leased Talland House as a summer retreat. It was not far from the station, and many friends and visitors were encouraged during the summer. J. K. often stayed, and it was in St. Ives that he discovered his love of painting. (It is not impossible that Sickert helped him to get started.) It should also be noted that Sickert's sister, Mrs Swanick, wrote in her biography that she knew the Stephens at St. Ives. Given the story that Sickert used to claim that he lived in the same house as the Ripper – a jest, or an apocryphal tale? – the link with Talland House is extremely interesting.

The arrow pattern is intriguing and suggestive; the early oral tradtions about Gull's fake death re-open the case of the conspiracy theorists, and Marny hallam's descendents were barristers in association with the Stephens. The other details presented here are smaller fry and more speculative, but all together, a plausible and convincing picture starts to emerge. The next chapter will attempt to sketch that out.

Royal Blood?

Weaving a Web

H.R.H. Edward, Prince of Wales (Bertie).

The cast have been introduced, theories and counter theories have been assembled, and the bare facts displayed. The last chapter presented intriguing pieces of new information, and we would now like to try to pull those pieces together and present a possible situation that would explain the Whitechapel murders. We stress this is only a theory, a working hypothesis. We begin with the premise that it is likely that we are dealing with a conspiracy and not a random serial killer. The reasons for thinking that there was a conspiracy are as follows:

(a) The fact that five women who lived so close to each other, and who had similar backgrounds, were picked out and murdered.
(b) The position of the bodies suggests an arrow pointing towards the Houses of Parliament.
(c) Some of the mutilations suggest a link with the Masons.
(d) Clues such as the coins left face up, showing the monarch.
(e) The Goulston Street graffito might implicate Sir William Gull, and others.
(f) It is striking that the rambling reminiscences of Joseph Sickert have pointed out certain places and characters that had not been thought of before – the link with the Providence Row Refuge, the premises on Cleveland Street, the mention of John Netley. There might a kernel of truth in his stories.
(g) Local traditions in Thorpe-le-Soken suggest that Gull did not die in 1890, but a sham funeral was held.
(h) Marny Hallam's family tree reveals barrister links with the Temple and the Stephen family, and therefore cannot be dismissed out of hand.

The core problem that needed to be solved might have involved an illegitimate pregnancy, but we feel it is more likely that Bertie was involved than Eddy. His rakish behaviour, and the strong rumours of his Watling Street flat, highly probable as this was near to the fire stations he attended, probably brought him into contact with the likes of Mary Kelly. She might have been introduced to such high class brothel circles through Walter Sickert, if indeed, he did keep a studio in Cleveland Street. From Joseph Barnett's testimony, we know that Kelly had worked in a high class brothel in the West End when she first came to London. She was young, attractive and fiery spirited, the sort of girl that would attract a character such as Bertie.

She might have become pregnant by accident, or by design, seeing the child as a royal passport out of misery and whoredom. Bertie was known to have looked after the interests of Lady Susan Pelham-Clinton when it was rumoured that she was pregnant with his child. Or, alternatively, Kelly's pregnancy might have been a ruse to blackmail Bertie to give her financial aid.

Joseph Barnett who lived with Mary Jane Kelly at Miller's Court until two weeks before her death.

Kelly descended into the slums of Whitechapel after her West End adventures, taking up with various men. It is possible that she was sought out later by Bertie or his friends. A suitable occasion might have been the silver wedding anniversary of Bertie and Alix in March 1888. Apparently, Alix accompanied Victoria in a coach around the City after the dinner, and it can be reasonably assumed that Bertie and his friends celebrated in a more promiscuous manner. One can imagine his roguish companions plotting some little treat. Tracking down Kelly might have fitted the bill, and it was after this renewed tryst that she might have become pregnant, offering a way out of her poverty trap.

The reason for her original departure from the West End might have been a breakdown in her relationship with Walter Sickert. Joseph Sickert claims that Walter took Kelly to Dieppe with him, and Barnett claims that Kelly had told him that she had been to France with a gentleman and visited Paris, but did not like it and returned. As she spurned Sickert, she might have found herself excluded from the more fashionable circles she was frequenting. The France/Dieppe connection is fascinating in the light of the knowledge from the 1891 census that John McCarthy was born in Dieppe, and the Irish records suggest that Kelly's mother might have been a relation of McCarthy's. What was the connection with Dieppe? According to Barnett, Kelly said she had a sister who was living with her aunt and who followed "a respectable calling". Were the aunt and sister also in Dieppe? Annie Chapman was also reckoned by some to have sent a daughter to France. Why, and where? Was this through links with Kelly? A final French connection comes through the organiser of the Cleveland Street brothel, Charles Hammond, and he was allowed to leave for France. Did Hammond travel to Dieppe? More research is needed to try to track this information down, but we mention it as an intriguing possibility. This is harried by the almost total destruction of French records in the war years. Some original and lateral thinking here might put a new perspective on the case.

News of Kelly's pregnancy might have reached Bertie as a

plea for help, a blackmail attempt, or might have done so by accident. For Bertie to have sired a child by a Catholic prostitute would have been a terrible scandal and they would have feared for the future of the monarchy given the state that Britain was in at that time. A meeting would have been called to discuss the matter, and the likes of Lord Salisbury, the PM, and Sir Charles Warren, as Chief of Police, would have been involved. Sir William Gull might have been drawn in as the Royal Physician, as well as any number of highly placed personages and associates of Bertie, such as Randolph Churchill who had been recently reconciled with the Prince. There would have been a tight-lipped attempt to keep this from the Queen, for her temper would have burst all bounds. Most of these men, if not all, would have been Masons. It is interesting that the figure of John Netley could have linked Gull, Churchill and the Stephen family if he acted as their driver, though this is only supposition.

Another interesting link might be through 'Fingers Freddy'. Melvyn Fairclough, in 'The Ripper and the Royals', made a connection between the East End crook, 'Fingers Freddy' who entertained crowds by juggling while boys picked pockets for him, with one Frederick Albericci, an Italian American footman who worked for Gull in the early 1880s. For some reason he descended to a life of crime. Was Freddy used as a runner or spy on the ground to help track the women?

The high ranking Cabal of conspirators would not have risked bloodying their own hands. They would have agonised over the task ahead, with the likes of Warren as an evangelical Christian and custodian of the law fearing for his conscience. The throne must be preserved and this was their duty under God, and an uncritical reading of Scripture passages such as Romans 13:1-2 might suggest this:

> "Let every soul be subject unto the higher powers. For there is no power but of God: the powers that be are ordained of God. Whosoever therefore resisteth the power, resisteth the ordinance of God: and they that resist shall receive to themselves damnation...."

This subservient attitude to the rulers was not so easily claimed by the early Christians a little later when the Emperors demanded that the Christians worship them as gods and offer sacrifices to them. Church theology then developed the idea that only moral laws were to be kept as binding, though such sentiments tended to be lost on Victorian gentry. The religious attitude of these men must have been like that expressed in the film 'Chariots of Fire' when Eric Liddell says he will not run on the sabbath because he has to put God first. One man responds that the King must be first and God second!

The conspirators would have sought loyal and trustworthy agents to oversee the killing for them. J. K. Stephen would have been a very likely candidate, well placed with the Royals, the patient of Gull, of a strong physique, and a passionate loyalty to the throne. Perhaps Gull was well placed to assess him as a candidate, seeing him as impressionable and malleable in his illness, and perhaps also J. K. was in a more lucid and trust-worthy period, having just worked on 'The Reflector'.

J. K. could then have drawn in Montague John Druitt as an associate, with equally fierce loyalty to the throne, some surgical skill, and perhaps a known downer on prostitutes, which might be inferred from his deteriorating state of mind and Macnaghten's reference to him being "sexually insane".

J. K. Stephen (from a pencil drawing by F. Miller in 1887).

Netley and Freddy could have scouted out the territory, and set up meetings with the women. Polly Ann Nichols' new bonnet, that she so proudly showed off, might have been a gift that served to mark her out, as Annie Chapman's red scarf might have been, as well as Stride's carnation. The cab would have been on hand either to transport the victim's bodies to various spots, or to hurry the team out of the area. Hansoms clattered back and forth at all hours of the night, and another one would not arouse any undue suspicion. Perhaps the two men were taken back to their Temple chambers, or to De Vere Gardens. It is also possible that they stayed in a respectable lodging house near the area. The Parlours have suggested that Mrs Seyler's house at Stepney Causeway ("for respectable gentlemen") might have been the base, for this was near Stepney Green where Benson's stables were located. These would probably have been used by Netley.

M. J. Druitt.

The killings would have begun to turn the minds of the two men. Druitt became more fevered and violent, and J. K. began to scatter clues to cover their backs should they be caught, or just because he had a teasing sense of humour. If neither of the two were Masons, information on Masonic ritual could be accessed fairly easily, such as in 'Freemasonry Exposed' by William Morgan, or in Carlile's 'Manual of Masonry'. The Masonic links were a pointer to their pay-masters, and not a Masonic warning to others.

It might be objected that if the five women were very much a little gang of friends, then they would have realised that they

New College, Oxford, where Druitt was a scholar from 1876–80. (Photo: Andy Parlour)

were being picked off and would have done something about it – going to the police, the press or leaving the area for a time. They might have been too frightened to go to the police, whom they would not have trusted. Would the press listen to unfortunates, and would they have had the funds and connections to travel any distance for a lengthy period of time? They were living a hand-to-mouth existence.

The women were probably not an exclusive group, being associated with many others in the area, and they might not, ironically, have shared Kelly's secret. They would thus have been nonplussed about their friends being killed. If Eddowes was a case of mistaken identity, then it is possible that she was an outsider to the group, and nothing to do with the friends who were suspected of carrying the scandalous secret. There are two indications that some of the women might have had an inkling that something was very wrong, though. Michael Kidney told the police that he knew something that might have stopped Liz Stride being killed, though he subsequently refused to give any information. Also, when Eddowes returned from Kent, she declared that she was going to claim the reward for informing on the Ripper. Her tone did not seem to be a jest, but a boast. What did she know, or guess? Also, Barnett's testimony claimed that "He did not think the deceased feared any one in particular, but she asked witness to read to her about the murders." Fascination or fear?

The Parlours believe that Kelly survived, and that another was killed in her place. Perhaps Bertie heard of the plot and acted to save his former lover and his child. Perhaps J. K. turned the tables with a twist of black humour. He could not take royal blood, after all; that was sacred! Perhaps he had tired of the mayhem and his conscience would not let him carry on. Druitt was on the verge of cracking, and J. K. told him to disfigure the substituted woman while Kelly was spirited away – first to Liverpool, and then to Canada, the route taken by many poor Irish emigrants? Druitt's frenzy made him crack, building upon the tension caused by his mother's illness. His erratic behaviour lost him his teaching job.

Perhaps the meeting at Chiswick was with J. K., meeting on old, nostalgic ground, remembering the foggy boat race of 1880. There Druitt demanded more money as he had lost his

King's College Chapel, Cambridge. J. K.'s rooms were in the building on the right from 1879–83. (Photo: Andy Parlour)

205

St. Andrew's Hospital, Northampton. The asylum where J. K. Stephen died February 1892. (Photo: Andy Parlour)

job, or perhaps he threatened to reveal all to appease his conscience. Maybe he was pushed into the Thames. Or, severely disturbed, perhaps he jumped, after all.

J. K. tried to get on with life by relocating to Cambridge, the scene of happier days. Slowly, his conscience weighed upon him and something snapped in 1891 when he was found naked and ranting. Interestingly, he was yelling that there was a warrant out for his arrest. He would have been referring to his guilty secret. J. K. was committed very quickly to an asylum a long way from London. He was safely out of the way.

One Ripper accomplice died; one was sent to an asylum. Thus we have the dual tradition that seems to have circulated early on among the police. The Ripper had died soon after the last murder, or had been incarcerated as a lunatic. The truth behind the Ripper's identity would have been closely guarded and only the most senior figures would have known. Only rumours, snatches of gossip and guesses would have abounded at lower levels. Perhaps Druitt's death was a useful scapegoat. The Ripper had died and escaped justice and that was that.

It is possible that news of J. K.'s possible involvement with

he murders began Sir James Fitzjames Stephen's rapid decline
which forced his retirement.

Gull felt the toll of conscience, too. His condition
worsened and epileptic attacks or one or two further strokes
ither finished him or he lost his mind, being secreted away in
n asylum. Perhaps there is some substance to the tale of Lees

J. K. Stephen's final resting place.
(Photo: Andy Parlour)

207

The Houses of Parliament
c 1890. (By kind
permission of Frank
Gardiner from his original
painting.)
"Quo Musa Tendis?"

trailing the Ripper to his house. Lees would have been dismissed as a madman for taking the police to such an eminent person as Gull, but this might have caused the beginning of the end for the man within his own mind and bodily health. The tale of the bloodstained shirt and memory lapses might be pure fiction, but a germ of truth might reside in this Lees tradition. One can imagine Lees elaborating the story to cover up his rejection and disillusionment when he had led the police to Gull's house. (The Ripper material has a number of tales that might have been twisted and exaggerated with the telling, such as the Pizer/Kosminski/Cohen mix up as an example, from Anderson and Swanson's reminiscences.)

It is tempting to claim that the Scotland Yard File on the case was officially closed in 1892, after J. K.'s death. This is not quite clear. The files were moved to the Public Record Office in the 1950s, and it was then decided that these should remain closed until 1992 (although they were opened to the public earlier). This would have been determined by the last entry of an active investigation, being 1891. That the investigation wound down is certainly true after J. K.'s death, though.

If there had been a cover-up, a man well-placed to influence police investigations would have been Godfrey Lushington, Permanent Under Secretary at the Home Office.

It was his duty to mediate between Sir Henry Matthews, Home Secretary, and Sir Charles Warren, Metropolitan Police Commissioner. Godfrey's twin brother, Judge Vernon Lushington, was a close friend of Sir James Fitzjames Stephen and godfather to J. K.'s younger brother, Harry Lushington Stephen!

Finally, Abberline might have been brought into the conspiracy by Henry Matthews, and assigned to the Cleveland Street brothel scandal, where the police behaviour seems lax and extraordinary, as though they wanted certain people to make good their escape to protect Eddy.

All of this is speculation. We are being deliberately playful and spinning a yarn. But we have weaved an intriguing web. As soon as we try to flesh out the details of a conspiracy we are in the land of the imagination. There are too few cast iron facts to build upon, but the scene outlined above is plausible and possible. There is a wealth of circumstantial evidence to support it. Research must go on, and our assessment will alter and shift with any new results.

An arrow pointing to the Houses of Parliament – what was going on? Who was implicated, and why?

So much is now lost to the ravages of time. Perhaps we might find J. K.'s hidden diary under the floorboards of the Blue Boar Inn one day. Now, that would be something!

Amos Simpson and Catharine Eddowes' Shawl

Bill Waddell wrote in his book, 'The Black Museum', "Recently I acquired a silk screen printed shawl. It had been in the donor's family for years and a large section had been cut out, reputedly by his mother, because she did not like the blood stains on it. I am told that it was the shawl worn by Catharine Eddowes when she was killed. Who knows what will come to light, next?" These words were written in 1993. Bill Waddell is no longer the Curator of the Black Museum at New Scotland Yard. John Ross has taken his place.

Residents of the Clacton area, in Essex, have known about two framed cuttings from a silk cloth that were claimed to be pieces of the silk shawl worn by Catharine Eddowes, for some time. These were in a video shop until about 1996 when they were sold to an antique dealer in Thetford, Norfolk. The owners of the video shop in St.Osyth Road, John and Janice Dowler, had been told about the shawl by a friend who knew an antique dealer. They saw the entire shawl but did not feel easy with it in their property in case it really was genuine – it would then have grisly connections! Their friend returned with two cuttings, which were framed, and they eventually accepted these which they agreed to display, but remained somewhat sceptical about their authenticity. (They exchanged a rare copy of the first edition of the 'Radio Times' for these!) They had noticed that some fabric had been removed from the shawl when they had viewed it earlier. These were obviously the cuttings that had been taken from it. On the rear of the frame is the inscription:

'Two silk samples taken from Catherine Eddowes' shawl at the time of the discovery of her body by Constable Amos Simpson in 1888 (end of September) victim of Jack the Ripper.

Arabella Vincent (Fine Art)
Hand-made   Illustrated Mounts
UK. Studio, Tel. Clacton _____
Surface printed silk
Circa 1886.
Framed 100 years to the day.
(A.Vincent)'

Opposite page: *Acting Sergeant, Amos Simpson, Metropolitan Police, wearing the 1887 Golden Jubilee Medal. (First time published, from family collection)*

No records of an Amos Simpson exist in the City Police, in whose territory the body was found, and the first reported police officer at the murder site was Edward Watkins.

The existence of these cuttings, and the shawl, was first made public in Paul Harrison's 'Jack the Ripper: the mystery solved' (1991). He spoke with the Dowlers and saw the framed pieces. He asserted that though there was no mention of a shawl in the police inventory of her belongings, contemporary press reports of her dress match the style of the cloth cuttings:

> "...tiny flowered patterns, containing the colours blue, pink, green, yellow, and maroon. It is an almost identical description..."

(The police list merely states that she had "Chintz skirt, 3 flounces, brown button on waistband.") Regrettably, Harrison does not give any exact references, and Stewart Evans has pointed out (Ripperana 20 April 1997) that the reference in the Times of Monday, October 1 1888 describes the dress thus:

> "her dress is of dark green print the pattern consisting of Michaelmas daisies and golden lillies."

The actual cloth of the shawl is a dark green with brown edges, with a colourful pattern of small, rather non-descript flowers as in Harrison's description.

Evans contacted the antiques dealer, Malcolm, in Thetford, and photographed the cuttings. He did not see the full shawl, which is kept at the Black Museum at New Scotland Yard. John Ross of the Museum had arranged for Sotheby's to inspect this. They were unsure of when it should be dated to, admitting that it was very difficult to be accurate, but guessed the early 1900s.

I went to see the shawl, in the company of the Parlours, and Keith Skinner. John Ross is an amiable, seasoned policeman with a wealth of stories. The shawl is large enough to cover a person's shoulders, and has brown edges. Pieces have been removed, and one brown section has become detached. He is lightly sceptical, thinking that the shawl is from a murder at the time, but not an actual Ripper murder. Possibly, it has been associated and the story has been garbled in the telling. Failing that, he laughs it off as any old shawl which a policeman dipped in animal's blood to pass off as the genuine object! He has seen and heard too many things to make him innocent of police trickery. Yet, he is prepared to give it the benefit of the doubt. The shawl has never been forensically tested for the presence of human blood, for this would be costly and is of no current police interest. (We noticed, in fact, some small markings, like bleach stains, that were small splashes, and we wondered if these might be the remnants of blood splattering.)

Evans wonders if some item of Eddowes' clothes might have been kept for police evidence or the use of the Coroner, as Eddowes was initially identified by Joseph Lawende by her clothes. The police list describes "1 piece of red guaze silk... found on neck". Could this be the shawl in question, or the origin of the idea that a silk item was taken from her belongings at some time? (It is not red, but there are prominently red flowers in the design.)

We are now in a position to open out the story much more. The antiques dealer who first passed the shawl to the Dowlers, and thence to the Black Museum (for safe keeping) was one David Melville Hayes of Arabella Vincent Fine Art. He met Andy and Sue Parlour early in 1997 at an Antiques Fayre. They asked David if he had any prints relating to the Whitechapel murders. David specialises in the colouring of rare prints from the 18th and 19th centuries. As fellow locals with a London background they struck up a friendship, and David related the full tale of the shawl.

David Melville Hayes, great-great-nephew of Amos Simpson. (Photo Andy Parlour)

This is the oral tradition that has passed down his family. Amos Simpson was the great-great-uncle of David Melville Hayes. He was a police constable who was the first person to find the body in Mitre Square. He had picked the shawl up that night and had kept it. Amos was on some kind of special duty, which he assumed to mean that he was in plain clothes on surveillance duty with two or three other officers. He remembers seeing the shawl for the first time when he was 8 or 9 years old, when it was kept in an old sea-chest with waxed rope handles at his grandmother's house. The chest was about 18" x 15" x 4'. His mother also recalls it being kept in this chest, which is now in David's possession. She recalls how her mother kept their Sunday best clothes in the same chest, with the shawl! One corner of the shawl was tattered and some material had been cut away. David has always assumed that this had been bloodstained and his grandmother had cut this off and thrown it away, also dabbing out one or two more stains with bleach (David himself had cut out the two sections which were later framed.).

Amos' niece, Eliza, (David's grandmother) had been nannying in London in Plaistow, near to where Amos lived when he was in police service (This was in Queen Street,

Camden Town). He had obviously kept up a close contact with Eliza, being protective of her, and he had passed the shawl into her keeping. David presumed that this was because Eliza was a dressmaker and the piece of silk might have come in useful.

Keith Skinner and I held an interview with David and his mother, Elsie Hayes. Elsie is 95 and very frail, though alert

The wedding of David Melville Hayes' parents. Elsie's mother, Eliza, seated to her left, with Amos' sister, Mary, directly behind the happy couple (1924). (From family collection)

214

mentally. She was keen to talk to us, but struggled to make herself understood. She remembers pieces of the story, but not all of it. She recalls that her mother (Eliza) claimed that Amos had told her to look after the shawl as it might be valuable one day. She kept it in the chest, and never bothered with it again. She might have used it for dressmaking, but she was too busy looking after all the children! She had seen the shawl in her youth, when Amos was still alive, but was told very little about it. It was something to do with the Ripper, and Eddowes. When asked if she knew how he got it, she replied, "No one knows. He was on duty then. He must have taken it off her. It got into his hands, anyway!"

Elsie left home when she was 15, just before Amos died (in 1917). She went to nanny in Newmarket, Suffolk, before moving to Plaistow, East London, where she worked for a Dr. Kennedy and his wife, sister of Robert Falcon Scott of the Antarctic fame. Their father was rector of Lavenham and it was he who recommended Elsie for the position.

In 1919, Elsie became housekeeper to Frank Reynolds, cartoonist to Punch magazine, a position she held for five years. Frank Reynolds' wife, whose stage name was Winifred Milne, was an acquaintance of Emily Pankhurst, the suffragette leader, who often stayed with the Reynolds in Ealing. David's mother, more than once, related the tale of how, on occasion, she would take Emily breakfast or an early cup of tea and was once left half a crown by her!

She remembers Amos as being "very kind, very nice" and something of a "favourite" with the family. He came to Sunday dinner regularly, though not with his wife who was tiny, a "poor little thing". She also remembers being taken out in her pram to Barrow Hill, Acton, to the cottage where Amos lived in his retirement. Amos often spoke fondly of his time in the police, but when asked if he ever talked about the Ripper she replied, "What he didn't tell us, mother did." which amounted to the fact that it was thought dangerous to go out at night. David was slightly confused as to how much of the story had come from his mother and how much from his grandmother as this was a long time ago when he was a youth. Clearly, as the interview progressed, Elsie knew very little about the shawl's history. Eliza was the main source.

The Parlours started to try to trace this elusive Amos Simpson with the help of researcher Keith Skinner. The lead they needed was provided by the birth certificate of Amos' son, Henry Simpson, which confirmed that the occupation of Amos was 'police constable'. Henry was born in 1877 and the family were then at 35, Queen Street, Camden Town. Amos was traced in Metropolitan Police records as an acting sergeant in 'N' division (Islington), which at its most southern point, brings it near the City boundary near Mitre Square. Amos had been born and raised in Acton, near Sudbury in Suffolk. He joined the Metropolitan Police in 1868 aged 21, being posted to 'Y' Division (Kentish Town) and hence to 'N' Division in 1886. He was promoted to acting sergeant in 1881. Amos was probably one of many men from agricultural areas that were drafted into the Metropolitan Police on the grounds of their usually superior physique, and their lack of knowledge of the locals. They were deemed more trustworthy and pliant. This practice was regular until the 1890 Police Act, which made the grant of pensions compulsory in every force.

There is the curious floating tradition (see chapter, Ghastly Crimes By a Maniac) of Sergeant White being on surveillance duty with two unnamed officers – a tradition impossible to locate as it describes an alley off the Whitechapel Road that could only be entered at one point. This does not fit the facts of the area, and many have wondered if it is a garbled account of activities near Mitre Square. If so, White and his companions would have been on City Police territory and would have not wanted to draw attention to that. (Were they involved in Fenian surveillance, or were they watching Jewish anarchists who could have been meeting in a room of the Great Synagogue that was just by Mitre Square? Radical Jewish groups were sometimes allowed to meet in rooms in synagogues so long as they did not hold their business in the worship area.) We might have a Metropolitan Police sergeant supposedly on surveillance in Mitre Square with two others – hence the oral tradition stemming from David Melville Hayes' family. Was Amos one of the other two men in the White story? It is interesting that such sensitive surveillance work was usually handed out to sergeants. If so, this adds credibility to the idea that Amos might have found the victim first, and the shawl, and would not have dared report this as he was on an undercover mission. We can only speculate as to why he took the shawl. Did he pick this up to take a closer look at the body and then realising that other men were arriving, flee the scene with his two colleagues, shawl still in hand?

Keith pointed out that the term 'special duties' that was in the family tradition would not usually mean plain clothes work. It simply meant being drafted in from another area to help with a case. This happened frequently in the Whitechapel area to reinforce the police on the streets. If Amos had been in uniform, what would he have been doing on City territory? When we thought through the known facts of the scene on 30 September, we realised that there must have been a great deal of confusion, a melee of running policemen between the Square and nearby Goulston Street. Goulston Street was in Metropolitan territory, and yet Detective Constable Halse of the City Police was present, arguing that the graffito should be photographed. Here we have City police on Met territory, and so the reverse was probably true that night. Indeed, Amos might have been patrolling near to the boundary, when he would have heard the police whistle blown by Watkins. He might have been the *first* Metropolitan policeman on the scene! Thus it is possible that a uniformed Amos was present in the Square soon after the body had been found, though how and why he took the shawl we cannot know.

If Amos had been in plain clothes that night, a police order listing his name should be in the Scotland Yard files. Keith is searching for such an order, but nothing has come to light as we go to print.

Then again, it could be argued that Amos might have found the shawl on just about anybody and claimed it as a 'genuine Ripper souvenir' as the police at the time delighted in such trophies and tall tales. We cannot authenticate the shawl, but we can authenticate the part of the oral family tradition that Amos Simpson was a serving Metropolitan Police Sergeant whose definite existence no one has discovered until now. That adds a degree of credibility to the shawl's provenance.

We might strengthen the case in favour in two, small ways. Firstly, concerning the description of Eddowes' dress, the Parlours found another contemporary description in the East London Observer, 10 October 1888:

> "Her dress was made of green chintz, the pattern consisting of Michaelmas daises."

This exact description is also found in the Illustrated Police News of 6 October, 1888.

We do not have any colours of the daisies, and no mention of chrysanthemums or lillies! Press reports of the actual patterns varied, but the green background with some sort of floral pattern does fit that of the shawl. This should be noted as significant and quite remarkable. It is also interesting that the Spitalfields area was still the main centre for silk weaving in the

The silk shawl claimed by Amos Simpson to have come from the body of Catharine Eddowes (measures 8' x 2'). (Photo Keith Skinner)

The two cuttings from the shawl. Framed by David Melville Hayes in 1988. (Photo: Andy Parlour)

1880s, with many small looms at work in private houses, producing very colourful and varied patterns, as has been confirmed to us by the Curator of the Whitechapel Library. This could explain why an 'unfortunate' such as Eddowes came to possess such an item.

Secondly, Amos was remembered as a very upright and moral man by the family – remember the description of Amos given by Elsie. The report of his death in the 'Suffolk and Essex Free Press' for 18 April 1917 recounts:

> "The parishioners mourn the death of an old and highly respected parishioner in Mr Amos Simpson (late of the Metropolitan Police) of Barrow Hill, Acton, who passed away on April 10th at the age of 70 years. Mr. Simpson served for 25 years in the police, for 13 years at St. Pancras, London and 12 years at Cheshunt, Herts. From there he retired to his birthplace to end his days.
>
> His wife died 5 years ago and since then he has been attended to by his devoted daughter who lost her husband (killed in action) on September 13th 1916 leaving 5 young children. His son and daughter-in-law came to spend the Easter with him and they had a pleasant time. Mr Simpson was very cheerful on the Monday morning and sang, 'The Last Rose of Summer' to the

*Unidentified police office.
Could this be Amos
Simpson?*

monophone. He was taken suddenly ill in the evening and died on Tuesday morning at 8 o'clock leaving 1 son, a widowed daughter, a daughter-in-law, 5 grandchildren and many relatives and old friends to mourn their loss.

He will be greatly missed by all, being a devoted husband, loving father and a warm friend."

Granted the flowery language of obituary, he was greatly loved and respected. This inclines one to feel that he was not an old rogue who would have deliberately taken any old shawl dipped in anyone (or anything's) blood, and passed it off as that of a Ripper victim. Still, we cannot be sure.

A final point about Amos, though irrelevant to discussions about the shawl, touches on the police number on his collar in the photograph of him. It is difficult to make this out. It is either 'Z 89' , 'L89' or ' 2 89'. 'Z' division (Croydon) was not in existence until the 1920s. Amos should have been in 'N division. Maybe the two 'N's had slipped? It was then thought that 'Z' might have been used as a temporary division when he returned to service for the Diamond Jubilee along with other retired officers. Yet, his records show that he was classified as 'CO' division for this. It must be pointed out that the photograph has been authenticated by his family, and bears his name and address on the back. The photographer's was local to where he lived. It is him. Further details on the uniform suggest it was a policeman of the right period.

Keith drew our attention to the drawing of an unidentified policeman in the 'Illustrated Police News' that covered the story of Kelly's death. He appears on the front page but is not mentioned in the interior copy, which is unusual as the artists picked their illustrations from the copy. He is listed as what looks like 'L 63' though the 'L' is rather truncated. He is quoted as saying, "I was on duty all night and never heard a sound." He looks *very* similar to the photograph of Amos! The designation 'L63' cannot be traced to any listed policeman, yet, if the picture is turned upside down, 'L 63' turns into a similar image to what we see on Amos' collar – 'something 89'! Did the artist have access to journalist's notes that did not make the number clear, and he has turned this around until it made sense? Could this be Amos staring out at us?

The Essex and Suffolk Connection

Researcher Andy Parlour.

Andy Parlour moved to Essex from the East End of London in 1964. Sue has lived in the Clacton-on-Sea area most of her life. After their marriage in 1968, they lived in Brightlingsea until 1983 when they moved to Thorpe-le-Soken, where they spent the next ten years. Their ongoing interest in the Ripper found some surprising local connections through Sir William Gull and the Stephen family.

Gull was born at St. Osyth, Essex, on 31 December 1816, the youngest of eight children born to John and Elizabeth. John was a bargemaster so the family had settled in the Hythe area of Colchester on the River Colne. This was ideal for mooring barges as it was a tidal river. The record of William's baptism is at St. Leonard's Parish Church on Hythe Hill, for 9 February 1817. When William was about six years old, John acquired his own barge and moved his family to the New Wharf, later to be known as Landermere Quay, Thorpe-le-Soken. William then attended Mr. Seaman's local village school at Ivy House, Abbey Street. He had a long walk each day from the Quay across fields into the heart of the village. It is a peaceful, picturesque location that is often used for filming TV programmes, such as the children's series, 'Swallows and Amazons'.

St. Leonard's Church, Hythe, Colchester, where William Gull was baptised on 9th February 1817. (Photo: Andy Parlour)

221

Sir James Fitzjames Stephen.

When William was ten years old, John Gull died, and was buried in St. Michael's churchyard, Thorpe-le-Soken, where other family members were to be buried, including William himself.

Gull had developed his interest in botany and natural history when at Thorpe-le-Soken, as the estuary gave him plenty of specimens of wildlife.

There is another connection with Landermere Quay, this time through the Stephen family. J. K.'s first cousin, Adrian and his wife, Karin, purchased what had once been the 'King's Head' at Landermere Quay as a holiday home and later their daughter Judith Henderson and her family were to make it their home. The 'King's Head' had once been owned by William Gull's older brother, John, who was registered as a licensed victualler, brewer, lime burner and coal merchant. Coincidentally, in the sixties, Judith worked in the Clacton Youth Centre with Sue Parlour's mother, Eira Hargreaves.

Yet another Essex connection comes through J. K.'s father Sir James Fitzjames Stephen. In 1865, he endeavoured to enter politics when he stood for Parliament in the general election as the Prospective Parliamentary Candidate for the Harwich constituency, a division which took in the wards of Landermere and Thorpe-le-Soken. He failed to win the seat but was long remembered for the gallant way in which he fought his campaign.

The Suffolk connection is twofold. Sir James Fitzjames Stephen was in poor health in 1891 so he retired from the Bench and moved with his wife, Lady Mary Richenda Stephen to the village of Westerfield on the outskirts of Ipswich. He

The Red House, Westerfield.

St. Margaret's Church,
Westerfield Road, Ipswich.
(Photo: Andy Parlour)

rented part of the 'Red House' from William E. Maunde, a
South African diamond magnate who had recently retired and
leased the house and surrounding parkland from the owner,
Mr. Edgar, who had moved out on the death of his wife in 1890.
Sir James' first cousin, the Rev. Samuel Garratt, Canon of
Norwich and Rural Dean of Ipswich, had been vicar of St.
Margaret's Church, Westerfield Road, Ipswich, where the
Edgar family worshipped, since 1867. It would have been
Samuel who recommended the 'Red House' as a place of
retirement to his cousin. Sir James died there on 11th March
1894.

223

*Gull Court, Thorpe-le-Soken, built from the John & Sarah Gull Fund, for the senior citizens of the village. John was William's elder brother.
(Photo: Andy Parlour)*

J. K. Stephen had his accident at Felixstowe in 1886. He was probably staying at 'The Lodge', situated on the clifftop to the east of Felixstowe. It was owned by the wealthy banking and brewing family, the Cobbolds. John Dupuis Cobbold, the nephew of the owner, was at Cambridge with J. K.. The accident took place at Walton Mill, near to the Dock railway line.

*Mill Lane, Felixstowe. The railway crossing as it is today. Scene of J. K. Stephen's accident in 1886/7.
(Photo: Andy Parlour)*

224

APPENDIX THREE

The Providence Row Refuge

The only Catholic Church within the City of London in the middle of the 19th century was St. Mary Moorfields, Eldon Street, between Moorgate and Bishopsgate. This was before the days of Westminster Cathedral and it served as the pro-Cathedral for the Westminster diocese. In 1858, Fr Daniel Gilbert became the administrator, having served there as curate for five years. He was no stranger to poverty himself, having been reared in London as the only son of Irish immigrants from Wexford. Through the charity and support of the Christian Brothers, he received an education and trained for the priesthood. Late one night in 1857, he was returning home from a sick call when he was approached by a woman taking shelter in a doorway. He was so moved by her plight that he set about opening up a Refuge.

Five Sisters of Mercy arrived from Ireland on 23 September 1858. They had travelled from the order's second house in Wexford. The Sisters of Mercy had begun in Dublin in 1831, founded by Catherine McAuley. They were committed to relief work with the poor, famous for their 'Walking Nuns' who were like the precursers to 'Meals on Wheels'!

The London Sisters lived in Broad Street, near to the present Liverpool Street Station. The house was over-run with rats and food had to be kept in baskets hanging from the ceiling. They ran a school for 400-500 infants which crowded the place out. The Sisters were soon housed in better conditions in Finsbury Square. As Fr Gilbert said, "I brought the Sisters to work the mission, not to kill them."

At the rear of the new house, in Providence Row, were stables and a coach house. This was converted into Refuge accommodation with 14 beds, which opened in 1860. This enlarged, gradually, to accommodate 40 women and children. Getting women and children off the streets was the priority, but men needed help too.

The move to Crispin Street, building on the old plot that the local Jewish population had used for fairs and games, allowed for a much larger building. This was in 1867, and the cost of the plot and the new building was £19,000. The Sisters moved into an adjoining building and formed a convent. When the Providence Row Night Refuge opened on 8 December 1868, there was accomodation for 140 women and 60 men. This was enlarged, later, to allow for 140 men and 100 women. The men and women had separate wings each with its own dormitory and sitting/dining room. The sanitary conditions were first rate, and it was remarked that a decent bath could be had for free, whereas it would cost a shilling anywhere else in London! Clean towels and soap were provided free of charge. Long before opening time at 5.00pm, long queues would have formed with pushing and shoving. Supper was served at 6.45pm, of either a large bowl of gruel or cocoa and bread. On Sundays, soup and bread was also served at 1.30pm.

Fr Gilbert died in 1895, and the Refuge continued to develop. Various other buildings have been acquired in the area at various times. The present work of the Refuge covers the following properties:

The Refuge – still at 50, Crispin Street – is a radical and unusual 'wet shelter' for crisis care. People on the streets with alcohol problems can be cleanly and safely housed. They are allowed to bring drink onto the premises. The average length of stay seems to be 125 days. They can cope with 28 residents. The target clients are long term street drinkers who find that they are excluded from most hostels. There are single rooms, breakfast and evening meals, laundry facilities, help with support agencies, TVs and a pool table. The average ages of the residents are higher than usual, reflecting the seasoned rough sleepers who use the premises.

The Dellow Centre – in Wentworth Street – has a hostel for 30 men and a drop in centre that is visited by between 100 and 150 homeless men and women each day. There is a famously nutritional soup, a place to wash and shave and to find a change of clothes. Doctors and chiropodists lend their services, too. There is help on hand for housing or employment retraining. Each resident has a keyworker to befriend them and to help then define their future goals.

Bartlett House – adjoining the Dellow Centre – is a women only hostel for eight. There are single en-suite rooms, and five two-person flats. There are shared kitchens and living rooms.

Daniel Gilbert House – in Code Street – houses 82 single people. This includes 37 single rooms, 26 self-catering bedsits and 19 self-contained flats. Since it opened in 1993, it has housed 337 people, 244 men and 93 women, ranging in age from 21 to 65. There are at least two staff on the premises, day and night, to provide support. Most residents only stay for a few months

There are also premises that are part of a Supported Housing Unit. These comprise Fidelis House with 22 single rooms for women; Club Row, with 12 single flats; and Middle Street, with 20 single flats.

If you have been moved by the story of the Whitechapel women and their horrific deaths, then a practical response might be to make a donation to the ongoing work of the Refuge, where it seems that Mary Kelly started out when she first came to London.

Above left: *Sister Winefride at the old women's refuge.*

Left: *Serving the famously nutritional soup.*

Above: *The Dellow Centre.*

For contributions to The Refuge, The Dellow Centre and Daniel Gilbert House, contact Sister Winefride at The Providence Row Refuge, 50 Crispin Street, London E1 6HQ, England.

Bibliography

Books concerning Jack the Ripper

'Jack the Ripper reavealed' by John Wilding (Constable/Volcano Bks 1993) 0-09-472960-3

'The Mystery of Jack the Ripper' by Leonard Matters (Hutchinson 1928)

'Jack the Ripper: Summing Up and Verdict' by Colin Wilson and Robin Odell (Corgi 1987) 0-552-12858-9

'Jack the Ripper' by Mark Daniel (Penguin Books 1988) 0-14-011423-8

'Jack the Ripper: The Final Solution' by Stephen Knight (Harper Collins 1976) 0-586-04652-6

'Murder and Madness – The Secret Life of Jack the Ripper' by Dr. David Abrahamson (Robson Books 1994) 0-86051-909-0

'The Complete Jack the Ripper' by Donald Rumbelow (W. H. Allen 1975) 0-49-10346-7

'The Complete History of Jack the Ripper' by Philip Sugden (Robinson 1994) 1-85487-416-0

'The Crimes and Times of Jack the Ripper' by Tom Cullen (Fontana 1966) 0-00-613403-3

'The Diary of Jack the Ripper – The Chilling Confessions of James Maybrick' by Shirley Harrison (Smith Gryphon 1994) 1-85685-074-9

'The Jack the Ripper A–Z' by Paul Begg, Martin Fido and Keith Skinner (Headline 1991) 0-7472-4445-6

'The Lodger – the Arrest and Escape of Jack the Ripper' by Stewart Evans and Paul Gainey (Century 1995) 0-7126-7625-2

'The Ripper and the Royals' by Melvyn Fairclough (Duckworth 1992) 0-7156-2444-X

'The Ripper Legacy' by Martin Howells and Keith Skinner (Warner Books 1987) 07221 48712

'The True Face of Jack the Ripper' by Melvin Harris (Michael O'Mara Books Ltd 1995) 1-85479 726-3

'The Black Museum' by Bill Waddell (Warner Books 1993) 0751510335

Books concerning the social background

'London Characters and Crooks' by Henry Mayhew (Folio Society 1996)

'Sex in History' by Raey Tannahill (Abacus 1989) 0-349-104-86-7

'Oscar Browning' by H. E. Wortham (Constable 1927)

'The Victorian Underworld' by Kellow Chesney (P.B.S. 1970)

'Bernard Shaw His Life and Personality', by Hesketh Pearson (The Reprint Society 1942)

'The Leaves of the Tree' by A. C. Benson (Smith, Elder & Co 1911)

'Virginia Woolf' by Hermione Lee (Chatto & Windus 1996) 0701165073

'King Edward the Seventh' by Philip Magnus (Dutton 1964)

'King Edward and His Times' by André Mavros (Cassell) 1933

'Victoria's Reign by A. Cammiade (Methuen's Outlines)

'Clarence' by Michael Harrison (W. H. Allen 1972) 0491007221

'Lapsus Calami' by J. K. Stephen (Macmillan and Bowes 1892)

'Quo Musa Tendis' by J. K. Stephen (Macmillan and Bowes 1891)

'Lapsus Calami and Other Verses' by J. K. Stephen (Macmillan & Bowes 1898)

'Changes in a Rural English Village' by L. P. Lonsdale (Lavenham Press Ltd 1994) ISBN 0952497506

'The Face of London' by Harold Clunn (Simpkin Marshall 1935)

'Dictionary of Crime' by Jay Robert nash (Headline 1993) ISBN 0747206252

'Recollections of the Cambridge Union 1815–1939' by Percy Craddock (Bowes and Bowes 1953)

Books concerning Freemasonry

'Manual of Freemasonry' by Richard Carlile (Reeves and Turner, 19th century)

'The Brotherhood' by Stephen Knight (Harper Collins 1985) 0-586-05983-0

'The Hiram Key' by Christopher Knight and Robert Lomas (Arrow 1997) 0-09-969941-9

Index